The Way of Abundance and Joy

"In this era of ecological crisis, the human spirit cries out for teachings and practices that can restore balance between our species and the rest of God's creation. Drawing from a range of genres—interviews, personal reflection, and stories—Shirley Blancke conveys the wisdom of don Alberto Taxo, a revered shaman and spiritual teacher from Ecuador, whose insights can awaken humanity to the interconnection of all beings and our responsibility to live more gently on Earth. His heart-centered perspectives will resonate with people of all faith traditions who seek healing for our planet."

MARGARET BULLITT-JONAS, EPISCOPAL PRIEST, CLIMATE ACTIVIST, AND COEDITOR OF *ROOTED AND RISING: VOICES OF COURAGE IN A TIME OF CLIMATE CRISIS*

The Way of
Abundance and Joy

The Shamanic Teachings
of don Alberto Taxo

Shirley Blancke

Destiny Books
Rochester, Vermont

Destiny Books
One Park Street
Rochester, Vermont 05767
www.DestinyBooks.com

Text stock is SFI certified

Destiny Books is a division of Inner Traditions International

Cataloging-in-Publication Data for this title is available from the Library of Congress

ISBN 978-1-64411-216-8 (print)
ISBN 978-1-64411-217-5 (ebook)

Printed and bound in the United States by Lake Book Manufacturing, Inc. The text stock is SFI certified. The Sustainable Forestry Initiative® program promotes sustainable forest management.

10   9   8   7   6   5   4   3   2   1

Text design and layout by Virginia Scott Bowman
This book was typeset in Garamond Premier Pro, Futura, and Optima with NixRift used as the display typeface
Photographs by the author unless otherwise indicated

To send correspondence to the author of this book, mail a first-class letter to the author c/o Inner Traditions • Bear & Company, One Park Street, Rochester, VT 05767, and we will forward the communication.

Contents

PART I

Upbringing

Foreword

Many years ago I was leading a travel group in Peru where I met a Qechua man in Cuzco, a man from the Andes who was a pharmacist by trade . . . and who was also a shaman. However, he insisted that he *wasn't* a shaman, for as many of you know, no authentic shaman ever claims the title. But when we—as a group under his direction—had created a *despacho* offering with coca leaves, cookies, candy, and other things as well, he engaged in ceremony with a sacred fire he had created. And when he offered the collective assemblage of all our offerings to the fire, I watched entranced as the flames actually reached toward his hands to receive them.

In a private moment with this shaman, he informed me that in response to Westernization, his peoples on the altiplano of the Andes were less inclined to live up there in the cold and grow potatoes. He smiled knowingly at me and revealed that his people wished to move down to Lima and Cuzco and engage with the Western world: living in apartments, getting jobs in banks and offices, wearing suits and ties and dresses, and having cars and computers. For them, he said, the shaman's path was sometimes like old-fashion hocus-pocus; the practice of shamanism was beginning to fade among the traditional peoples.

Then he brightened visibly and informed me that as the shaman's path dimmed among the traditionals, something wonderful was happening. Shamanism was taking root once more in the Western world and we Westerners could very well be the next carriers of the tradition.

When I lamented that we had no long-lived tradition of the shaman's path, he swept my reservations aside.

"It is important to understand," he proclaimed, "that if we go far enough back, we are all descended from indigenous ancestors and they all had powerful shamans. Their ability to vision and access the hidden worlds for power, protection, and healing is one of our birthrights, no matter what our cultural origins may be. In addition, each new generation has the responsibility to restore and refresh a continuously re-created tradition, even adding to and changing the accumulating treasure of wisdom and technique. For it was always in this way that the ancient spiritual path of the shaman remained vital and meaningful to those who walked it.

"The path will change, it will evolve," he continued, "in response to who and what you choose to become during the time given to you here on our world. It's been like this forever; the path is immortal. It will change you as well." He grinned with the delight of it.

In response to his thoughts, I might observe that we live in a time in which the traditional spiritual wisdom of the indigenous people around the world is being rediscovered and reconsidered by increasing numbers of Western people who are involved in an expanding spiritual awakening that is happening among us. We discover that across time, through trial and error, the traditionals created families of techniques that could be called a technology of the sacred. In this technology are bright jewels of great interest to modern mystics and spiritual seekers alike—of many persuasions. These are spiritual methods, not organized religions, which we may practice with reverence and self-discipline to make contact with transpersonal forces that reside in the hidden worlds that we may explore with their assistance.

In response our life is capable of becoming an incredibly enriched adventure.

What a gift for anthropologist Shirley Blancke to have gotten to know shaman-priest don Alberto at a deep level. What a gift for don Alberto to have had such a friend as Shirley Blancke. And what a gift that the beautiful and powerful story of their friendship is now available for us to read and witness. Together they have created a wonderful book, giving us glimpses into a non-Western culture and way of life.

In doing so, they have created very good medicine indeed.

HANK WESSELMAN, PHD (1941–2021), was a paleoanthropologist who was introduced to a shamanic worldview while researching the environments of early human fossils in Africa. He subsequently explored shamanism in Hawaii and gave workshops with his wife, Jill Kuykendall. He was author of the Spiritwalker trilogy, *The Bowl of Light, The Re-Enchantment,* and the award-winning *Awakening to the Spirit World* (with Sandra Ingerman). For additional information, visit Sharedwisdom.com.

Acknowledgments

My deep thanks go to don Alberto Taxo for trusting me enough to undertake a presentation in English of his life, teaching, and influence, as related in the three sections of this book, and for inviting me to include accounts of my own experience with him. Patricia Noriega Rivera gave me permission to translate the interviews she conducted with don Alberto as well as some other material published in *El vuelo del águila y el cóndor: Historia de vida del tayta yachak Alberto Taxo*. This book would not have been possible without this and I owe her my deep gratitude. Similarly my thanks go to Patricio Guerrero Arias for granting me permission to summarize a long passage on the Medicine Wheel, from his book *La chakana del corazonar: Desde las espirituales y las sabidurías insurgentes de Abya Yala*, which constitutes my chapter 15.

Hank Wesselman, before his sudden and unexpected passing, gave me a real gift in his foreword for this book, which expresses so well his warm and generous spirit. He will be sorely missed by many.

The third part of this book was made possible by the work of don Alberto's students and associates, and I am most grateful for their participation. His students are Susan Cooper, Christiane Gottwald, Caty Laignel, Lucas K., Shari Parslow, Susan Martin, and Jeanne Dooley. His students Julie Bloomer and Martha W. Travers are also authors, and his associates are authors John Perkins and Itzhak Beery.

I also want to recognize the support I have received from Laszlo Slomovits during the gestation of this project. Laz and his late wife, Helen, expressed their appreciation of don Alberto by writing, illustrating, and self-publishing his previous books in English. These include *An Invitation from the Andes; Friendship with the Elements;* and *Reconnecting with Our Indigenous Heart,* which are listed in the bibliography under Taxo. As musicians, Laz and Helen also made a CD—*Friendship with the Elements*—of don Alberto's singing.

My heartfelt thanks go to Gabriela Ansari for drawing the Chakana diagrams and for helping me with Spanish interpretation; also to Susan Martin and Denis Jenssen who chased typos at different stages of the manuscript. The knowledge that my husband, Timothy, has about computers saved my bacon on untold occasions, and I doubt I could have done this without his support. William Sullivan's photograph at the Indigenous Women's Conference and Dori Smith's at the waterfall are great additions. I am also very grateful to all the staff members at Inner Traditions who have helped me through the publication process, and particularly to Jamaica Burns Griffin for her advice in clarifying the text. Artist Iza Paez's lovely photograph graces the cover.

My Trail Winds to Shamanism

Don Alberto Taxo is a much revered and beloved senior medicine man, or shaman, a Hatun Tayta Yachak* from the Andes Mountains of Ecuador. A hereditary teacher and healer of the pre-Inca Atik people of the Mt. Cotopaxi region, his influence extends far beyond the local area. He was awarded the high honor of master *yachak* by the Shamanic Council of South America. He was in attendance in 1992 when the Dalai Lama visited with Andean shamans of Ecuador and Peru to pass on to them spiritual responsibility for the planet because of the Tibetan understanding that this Dalai Lama would be the last. Don Alberto has traveled to the United States since 1998 to further the Andean indigenous prophecy that the Eagle and Condor will fly together in the same sky.

This is understood to be a reciprocal relationship between North and South America through which both may benefit from the respective expertise of each other's regions. For him it requires teaching his

---

Hatun Tayta means a high-ranking shamanic spiritual leader. *Don* is an informal Spanish title of respect, like *Sir*. Don Alberto does not like the word *shaman* because it is foreign to his culture and there are differences between yachak practice and shamanic practice as usually understood in the West. It is used here because it is a term familiar to Westerners, to indicate someone who regularly accesses other levels of reality to obtain information. In Kichwa, the indigenous Ecuadorian dialect of Quechua, *ay* is pronounced like *eye*, not *way*. This is true of all words with an *ay* spelling in this book, and the *y* spelling that is typical in Ecuador is used instead of the alternate *ai* for *ay* or *ia* for *yachak*.

tradition of connecting with nature to receive its help. This is a gift he extends to Westerners—many of whom have lost their connection to nature. He has also taught and been associated with some renowned shamanic practitioners in the United States such as John Perkins and Itzhak Beery, and his teachings are the subject of three books in English.

I first met don Alberto seven years ago when he gave a talk near my home. I give an elaboration of this and further events later in this book. I believe it's important to include mention of those events here by way of an explanation as to how I came to know him initially, and then later as well in order to give the reader a more definitive account of how our relationship developed. When we first met, he seemed interested in me, showing me a poster of Mt. Cotapaxi and telling me that was where he lived. I learned from perusing his literature set out on a table that he was a shaman of the elements. By the end of the session I felt I should tell him that a dance group I belonged to was about to dance at the Old North Bridge in Concord, Massachusetts, to promote the health of water. From that moment on an association developed that seemed quickly to get onto a fast track.

I never set out to write a book about don Alberto—it happened as the result of a dream. I usually set little store by my dreams because on the rare occasions that I remember them they seem to be about anxiety. This one was different, though. Toward the end of an unusually trying New England winter five years ago I went on a family vacation with my husband and two adult children and twin grandsons to the "Mayan Riviera" on the east coast of Mexico. Swimming in a warm ocean and breathing in the balmy air provided the relaxation I needed at that time.

One day toward daybreak I experienced a vivid dream that startled me.

I found myself at the entrance to a large cave looking out on a sunlit green landscape. As I watched, a dark shadow arose from the far horizon, getting bigger and bigger until I saw it was the wings of a huge eagle shutting out the sunlight as it rose to fill the whole sky. It flew in my direction, finally landing just in front of me at the mouth of the cave. Although the light was dim, I saw that the eagle had the face of a Native American lady I knew. Then my attention was drawn to a ball-point pen that had grown small wings and fluttered between us, drawing lines in the air. The eagle smiled and said what I took to be a jest, "Now we know why what you write is so good—you have a magic pen!" I looked more carefully at the pen and saw it was light blue with a black design by which I could identify it as mine although I was not conscious of what the design represented.

At that point I woke up. It occurred to me that the pen was one I had received unbidden in the mail. It too was light blue. Having it with me, I looked at its design. It was covered with different feathers of varying size, in black. It then came to me that the word for both *feather* and *pen* in Spanish is *pluma,* which I took to be a suggestion that I tell don Alberto about the dream. The upshot was that he invited me to write a book for him.

I told don Alberto I felt I had not known him long enough to write a book for him. (It had only been two years!) In addition, I had only ever written academic papers. I suggested to him that perhaps his long-time students might be persuaded to write something about how he had impacted their lives. He liked the idea and gave me a list of their names and email addresses. He also said that a book had been written about him in Spanish in Ecuador and asked if I would be interested in translating it as well as writing about my own experiences with him in Ecuador. Because of this, my approach to *this* book has several facets.

The main text of the first two parts consists of my translation of interviews of don Alberto conducted by the anthropologist Patricia Noriega Rivera, published in her book *El vuelo del águila y el cóndor: Historia de vida del tayta yachak Alberto Taxo.* Rather than placing these interviews in a context of anthropological theory as Noriega Rivera does, I am presenting their material in a different sequence in order to tell a story about don Alberto's upbringing and teaching. Where I wished to expand on a particular topic, I recorded further interviews with him. Don Alberto's text is set in a different font for clarity and ease of reading.

The third part of the book consists of contributions by don Alberto's students and associates, or my interviews of them.

In terms of content, the first part of the book deals with how don Alberto was brought up by parents and grandparents who were themselves medicine people, yachaks. His father clearly expected his son would have to interact with the West in furthering the prophecy of the Eagle and the Condor, and sent him to learn from groups practicing various Western religions and philosophies. After his father's death and his own initiation as yachak, don Alberto learned valuable lessons from a Colombian medicine man. Difficulties of don Alberto's related to the political context at the time are outlined as well as his great belief in the value of sharing his ancestral wisdom with foreigners.

The second part of this book comprises don Alberto's teachings: how all life is energy and how to relate to and receive help from the elements. Also discussed are some ethical ramifications following from a very different view of the nature of the cosmos than that of the West. (A description of the Andean cosmos is found in chapter 16.) In both part 1 and part 2, interwoven around his story, I relay a few of my own experiences. These are drawn from the years I have known him; I feel they help to illustrate the points don Alberto is making in the narrative.

The book's third part is comprised of accounts by a few of his students, longtime and recent, as to how he has influenced their lives and/or the impressions he has made on them. They include an interview of one young American man who lived with don Alberto for two years while he was training to be a yachak. My own story is given there, pertaining to how my relationship with him developed over my first two weeks in Ecuador, and how he influenced me. An important life principle for him is a willingness to experiment, or fly higher like the condor or Jonathan Livingston Seagull. This is an example he gave me without telling me why he wanted me to read that book by Richard Bach. (I hadn't read it when it was popular in the seventies.)

Some description of my background follows here by way of an introduction to who I am and what transpired that set the groundwork to my meeting don Alberto late in life. I am an archaeologist with training in both anthropology and shamanism. I had never thought myself to be a shaman, not least because it is not something I consider that one can determine for oneself but rather is a status conferred by others. It implies that there is a community that one serves, and this is still a work in progress for me. My journey into a shamanic way of being has been slow and gradual with occasional stunning experiences. Not the least of these was my experience with the Oglala Lakota medicine man Sidney Has No Horses, whose *yuwipi* ceremony led me to believe our Western view of the nature of reality is inadequate. My encounter with shamanism has been one of deepening and informing what I was already doing in my life rather than catapulting me into a new kind of life as has been the experience of many who have published stories of their sudden transformation through shamanic experiences.

My first introduction to shamanism came by reading for a degree in archaeology and anthropology at Cambridge University. On looking back on my childhood though, I see that I was close to nature in a way that I am now trying to recapture. I grew up on a farm in England, roaming through the fields, learning about animals pointed out to me in the hedgerows, and picking primroses and bluebells in the woods. But what stays most vividly in my mind is looking out my bedroom window at the moon, especially the huge golden hunter's moon that was close to the horizon in the fall that I recently experienced again in Massachusetts. The moon is liable to wake me in the early morning hours in winter, shining through my bedroom window as it does.

The academic study of shamanism fascinated me and continued to be an interest, but my early adult years were focused on archaeology. Marrying an American, I settled in the New York area and worked for several years on new exhibits for the American Museum of Natural History. On moving to Massachusetts and obtaining a doctorate, I had the great good fortune in the 1980s to get to know a senior Wampanoag medicine man by the name of John Peters Slow Turtle. He occasionally invited me to give public presentations with him. I became acquainted with him because I asked for his assistance with respect to a lecture I was asked to give on Native history in a series on the experiences of minorities in Concord, Massachusetts.

I also reconstructed the Native American history of the area as demonstrated by archaeology, for eventual new exhibits at the local museum. The residents of this town typically thought of its history as beginning with the English settlers of the seventeenth century. However, its artifacts extended back to the Ice Age. In collaboration with a Wampanoag artist, I recently created a turtle out of artifacts that represent a time line of that history; it is now on permanent display at the museum.

It was through my friendship with Slow Turtle that I gradually got drawn into a shamanic view of life without realizing that was happening. Slow Turtle explained to me that he was sponsoring powwows as a means of building community among Native Americans. In attending some of these I realized the importance of dance as a means to that end. I had been raised in a family that did not practice a religion, although I experimented briefly with church attendance as a young adult. By this time of my life, when I was in my middle age, I began again to feel a need for some kind of spiritual expression.

I joined a sacred dance group that gave programs in churches, nursing homes, and even prisons and whenever possible involved the audience in the movement. The group's inspiration, "Then weave for us a garment of brightness," came from a Tewa Pueblo prayer poem "The Song of the Skyloom." It describes a weaving together of various aspects of nature—the morning and evening light, the rain, and the grass—and offers gratitude to the Creator for the joys of life, which is a deep, shamanic perspective.

Eventually I joined the Episcopal Church, whose liberal expression of Christianity appealed to me. As well, its music reminded me of my grandfather, a man I knew well, who served as the organist in an Anglican Church without belonging to it. At this time I experimented with shamanism by attending a weekend retreat given by the well-known American shaman and anthropologist Michael Harner. I didn't think shamanism was for me, but looking back on the experience I realized that I was afraid. In my view there need be no separation between formal religious expression and a shamanic perspective if one understands the mythic aspect of religion. I see these as different but related facets of spirituality. Joining a hands-on healing group in my church offered me a means of following a shamanic path by giving back to a community. It is also of course a Christian path.

It took dance to launch me further into shamanism. In 2001 I attended a Sacred Dance Guild Festival in Hawaii. The drumming associated with four days of training in traditional male-style hula taught by a kahuna put me into an altered state wherein my emotions swung up and down like a roller coaster. This was a deeply unsettling experience for me, accustomed as I was to controlling my emotions in true British fashion. The dancing produced a high but I also found myself grieving the loss of a cherished friend in a way I had not done before. Slow Turtle had died in 1997.

After the festival, for the two weeks that I remained in Hawaii I heard blissful and relaxing Hawaiian guitar music, only to discover— when I returned to Hawaii another time and heard none—it had been in my head. On recounting this to a friend, she gave me a shamanic book entitled *Spiritwalker* by Hank Wesselman, another American shaman-anthropologist; the book was set in Hawaii. Although I had not been searching for a shamanic teacher, after reading the book, I felt that I had finally encountered someone who could be the right teacher for me. He graciously responded to my email and I took his classes in shamanic practice for ten years. At the end he urged me to try to write about the wisdom of an indigenous leader to preserve this knowledge.

It was my first encounter with don Alberto that again shook my confidence in my Western culture's understanding of the nature of existence. He was to give a talk that was only fifteen minutes from my home, which I had learned about from a friend who thought I might be interested. I had not heard a South American indigenous medicine man speak in a long time, but I almost didn't go as it was a very hot June evening. My decision to attend was casual to the point of being offhand. But on my way there I felt strangely excited and wondered why.

What I eventually learned from don Alberto catapulted me into an image of myself that was new and that continues to evolve over time. His aim is to help people live more abundantly. The title of this book is based on the name of one of his workshops entitled Abundant Life: An Introduction to the Rituals of Andean Spirituality. The principle of Sumak Kausay, "Abundant Life," is basic to the spirituality of the Andes. I have become drawn into don Alberto's life in a way I would not have thought possible, a way that brings continued magic and excitement into my experiences through my exploration into the mysteries of the Great Spirit of Life, or God.

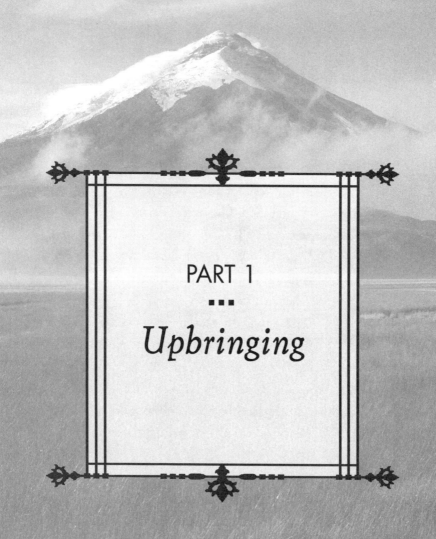

PART 1

...

Upbringing

1

A Walk in Quito

"Do you want to come for a walk?"

Don Alberto's baritone penetrated my slumber sufficiently that I cocked an eye open to look at the clock. It was 7:00 a.m. *No way!* my inner night owl screeched, but in a moment I was awake enough to think, *You fool, how could you pass up a chance to walk with such a remarkable man? The opportunity might never come again.*

"Give me five minutes!" I called out.

It was a sun-drenched morning in Quito, the capital of Ecuador. At nine thousand feet, it is an Andean mountain city with spectacular views of distant volcanoes. We passed through the vine-covered outer gate of the hotel where we were staying, and the sun lit up don Alberto's bright orange T-shirt and bronze shaven head. I happened to have put on an orange shirt myself that morning, and we both wore beige pants, so we appeared to be twins except that my light skin felt merely a pale shadow next to his.

A FOR SALE sign was attached to the hotel. Don Alberto pointed to it. "This building will probably be torn down and replaced by a faceless concrete structure as has happened to all these blocks around here," he told me.

The hotel was a charming, small, Spanish-style building constructed in the 1930s. We were a couple of blocks from a big city park where the large national cultural museum was located. This was an area that, before all the new building, had been an indigenous area of town. Don

Alberto knew it well because he'd been born a few blocks away and had grown up here. At that time the residents were all indigenous and people wore distinctive clothes—but not anymore. "Now they look like me," he said, indicating his T-shirt.

A September nip was in the air as we headed downhill toward the park. At our feet the roots of stunted and severely pollarded trees had extended under the concrete, beyond the small open circles left for the base of their trunks, creating big fissures in the sidewalk as the roots heaved upward to find moisture. "Look at the power of nature," he said, gesturing to the trees, "to break out of obstacles and create new leaves on those stunted trunks."

This led naturally to discussing the new *pachakuti,* a "turning over" to a new age already in motion. "It will bring women to the fore and, like the trees, they will be breaking away from the obstacles that constrict them. Men are afraid of women because when they really come into their power, men will have to take an inferior position. All the beings in our cosmology are female," don Alberto added.

Just before reaching the park we came to the patio of a gloomy concrete building, the former American embassy, on a side street. "My mother used to have a space inside there where she set out textiles for sale," don Alberto said, and mimed being weighed down by a heavy load on his back.

"Did she make them?"

"Yes, we all did in the family. There was a loom set up in our house so that whenever anyone had a moment they would weave."

Going on to the park we reached a grassy area with shade trees where children's swings and play furniture were set up. It was deserted at that time in the morning. "I like to bring Waira here when she is with me," he said, referring to his eleven-year-old daughter.

We moved on past the Casa de Cultura, a huge edifice taking up the space of a city block. Casa de Cultura houses both the national archaeological museum and a large government department overseeing all aspects of culture in the Ecuadorian nation. Patty Noriega Rivera, who is an apprentice of don Alberto's, works there.

We passed the museum and walked for some time in the city until I lost my sense of direction; eventually we stopped at a small park. There were four life-size bronze statues of poets in the middle of the grassy expanse.

"I knew two of them," he said gesturing casually. "This is very close to where I went to school. After class I used to come here with my classmates and we would fight."

"Why was that?"

"They used to pick on me because I was indigenous. In the beginning, I didn't want to go to school but my father insisted, and I got good enough at fighting that I could beat them all in the end. They left me alone after that."

A look of pride and a slow smile spread over his handsome face as he remembered the small boy who overcame fear to become victorious in a hostile environment.

"Why didn't the teachers step in to stop it?"

"They were just as bad; they would hit me too."

As we made our way back to the hotel and breakfast, we saw a gorgeous pink laburnum tree weighed down with blossoms leaning over a garden wall to the street. I had never seen pink laburnum before but had fond memories of the yellow kind that had graced my childhood in England. "I want one of those for La Loma," don Alberto said, referring to his home in Quilajaló, a village close to the town of Salcedo two hours south of Quito by bus.

My official name is Luis Alberto Taco Chicaiza, and I was born on March 20, 1954.[1] About my parents: My mother's name is Tránsito Chicaiza Mallinquinga, and my father was José Taco Conterón. Both came from communities in the Salcedo area, my mother from Quilajaló, and my father from Salache. I was given my name, Taxo, in 1989, as a practitioner of Andean traditional medicine. It refers to the plant we are familiar with here and its fruit of the same name. I was known publicly by the name Taxo in the indigenous uprising of 1991.

According to the *taytas* and *mamas* [elders or mentors, literally "fathers" and "mothers" in Kichwa] who gave me this name, it was bestowed on me because I have the qualities of this plant. They say that all this plant needs is a foothold, a spot such as a tree or some such place, which will allow it to grow up and establish itself. Almost all year it produces flowers and fruit, but keeps on expanding while putting out flowers and fruit. I've had a large number of taytas and mamas. I call tayta or mama not only my biological parents and grandparents, but all those who have been in my life from whom I have learned or with whom I have shared wisdom. I've had very many from all regions of Ecuador—the coast, the sierra, and the east—as well as from Colombia, Peru, Bolivia, and Teotihuacan in Mexico.

My mother came to Quito because my parents were practitioners of our traditions; my father as much as my mother. At that time there was persecution, especially by a certain current in the Catholic Church that believed that they were witches, or practitioners of bad things. And so my grandfather was persecuted, my father too, and during one of these persecutions my mother was pregnant. Quito was a center within whose boundaries there were many indigenous communities, and I was born in the community of Pambachupa. It is on the northeast side of Quito where the Avenida La Gasca continues toward the east.

These persecutions lasted only a short time, I think three to six months, and shortly thereafter we were able to be with my grandparents. At first we would leave at night and arrive at dawn, but later we stayed until my father was no longer persecuted.

My maternal grandfather, and more insistently my father, determined that I was to go to school when I was nine years old. After a few months my courage failed me, and crying I told my father that I wasn't going to learn anything there, what were they going to teach me? But my father told me I would learn to read there, so I then went to my grandfather to tell him I didn't want to go. He hugged me very gently and said, *"Pacha chayangi chaipimi kikinya rikungui imagu alli kanka yachaykuna"** (The time will come when you will see this is useful, necessary, and good). After that I didn't protest anymore and finished school.

To the questions I was asked in exams or in class I deliberately answered what the truth was for me, even though I knew they were going to say this was wrong and would give me a zero. For example, they would say that minerals are not alive or water is not alive, and I would say, but they *are* alive. And they would say too that water has no smell, or color, or taste, and I would say, no, each spring has a different taste. And so they got annoyed a lot, and at times ordered me out of the classroom, but I put up with it.

I thought that the kind of indigenous education I had received was typical of the whole world, but when I got to know city people, I realized this wasn't so. They don't feel the water or the earth. They think that water, earth, wind, and fire aren't alive, and so it's impossible for them to be able to communicate with these elements. This was when I understood that I had been blessed to receive such an education.

As I remember, my grandfather told me that his grandfather had the responsibility of being a *yachak*, and as I came to know when I reached the age of reason, my grandfather was a *tayta yachak,* as was my father also. My father, before leaving his body, told me I needed to continue this responsibility.

None of us ate meat—neither my grandparents, parents, nor I—because all of us had a mission as tayta yachaks, and we could not eat meat because of our vision of nature and being in communion with it. It is also necessary for everyone to recover how to be in harmony with plants, animals, the elements, and stones. I want us to know the

---

*This is Kichwa language from the Salcedo-Cotapaxi area. Formal teaching of Kichwa in school is relatively recent; don Alberto was a consultant for the book by Enrique Cañar, *Kichwa unificado: Sistema de escritura de fácil aprendizaje* (Kichwa unified: Easy-to-learn writing system). This book unifies different Kichwa dialects.

practices of daily living, the exercises or *kuyuris* that our ancestors engaged in every day at daybreak. For them it was basic to welcome the day in the open, as a form of thanks. They bathed with plants and engaged in *limpiezas,* or cleansings and natural purges; they sunbathed, took steam baths, and fasted.

This we know as Sumak Kausay, which means "Living Well" or "Well-Being." We are in an important period, a special *pacha* (time-space moment), talking of something my grandparents talked of but now the elders speak about it extremely openly: Sumak Kausay. Our governments may not know what that is perhaps, but it is very important that this ancient term be spread around on all sides and is in everyone's mouth. This is what we need to recover from our ancestors: a healthy diet without so many chemicals and without meat, too. In the past, while the eating of meat was not nonexistent, it was limited, and only took place during important fiestas. It was not consumed on a daily basis and as indiscriminately as it is now. The relationship with the animals that our ancestors ate—the guinea pig, small hen, llama, and deer—was direct. Some they raised and fed, but also before going on a hunt they prepared themselves by conversing with the animal and making a ritual of thanksgiving to them for offering their meat. Cattle and pigs did not exist here; they were brought from Europe.

There will be people who feel drawn to eating chicken, who long to eat it, and when they stop in front of a store window, they really desire to eat it. If you are one of these people, then do so. Thank the Great Spirit, and feel happy to be eating what you like. I don't eat my little animal friends, but for the person who feels deprived, or suffers, or dreams of eating chicken, I say do it, so that you experience it and enjoy what you like and are happy.

Each person has his or her walk and we walk in different ways. No path is the same, not even in the physical sphere. We all have feet but we don't walk the same way. We can all have similarity of movement in certain parts of our bodies, but no one can walk in exactly the same way. The path of power on which we walk, the Qhapaq Ñan, is the same—no one is behind or ahead. We are all exactly where we are meant to be in the present moment, although there are times when people feel they are behind because they are paying attention to someone who is ahead. If you feel you are behind, then move forward and hurry up to arrive at where you feel you are meant to be.

I once asked don Alberto why it was worse to eat meat than plants given that both plants and animals are alive and part of nature. He replied that plants exist to be eaten while that is not necessarily the case with animals. While this rationale might be debated, balance in what we eat is certainly a desirable goal for one's health, an idea that Americans are increasingly coming to appreciate.

2

Grandparent Wisdom

I teach the way of Qhapaq Ñan, the path of power, of feeling, the path of opening our awareness all the time. This is the Andean path.[1] This is my *ñan*, my road, one I have traveled my whole life, and I feel I shall persevere on it up to my last drop of blood. I have handed my whole life over to this dream and until I leave my body, I will struggle for the dream of Qhapaq Ñan.

We, the people of North and South, belong together as Eagle and Condor. We have been together before and it is no accident that we should be together again now. Being together validates the prophecy of my ancestors: "The time will come when the Eagle of the North and the Condor of the South fly together in the same sky."

In this life it is important to combine the Eagle's gift with that of the Condor. We need both powers, the Eagle's, which is the power of the mind and which includes the gift of science and technology, and the Condor's, which is the power of the heart and which includes the gift of sensing or feeling and of being able to connect with the elements of nature. These two powers, of mind and of heart, are within each one of us. We need to fly together and they need to fly together within us: the Eagle's power of thinking and planning, the Condor's of sensing and connecting.

The sky represents our daily life. To fly is to enjoy each moment of our daily life and, from this experience of life, continue to spontaneously express gratitude. This prophecy is saying that when the Condor and

Eagle are flying in the same sky, we will be in harmony. What I am bringing is the Condor's power, the power of having the ability to sense and feel everywhere at every moment. This is the power of the Condor of the Andes.

When I was young my grandmother said to me, "Nothing in life is negative. Some circumstance may be difficult, but when it has passed and we have left it behind, we need to recognize that we are coming out of it with more knowledge, and we are always learning something new. The great majority of people don't remember the good things when everything goes well. My advice to you is to remember the Great Spirit every moment of every day, and one way to do it is with gratitude."

Every moment and every place present us with great opportunities. Don't think that we have certain magical and unique places that allow us to be connected and enter into harmony; the whole world is special and each and every moment is special. In every action we pay attention to, each place we occupy, and in every moment of the day, we can fill ourselves up with thankfulness. In the same way when we go to sleep, we can appreciate and relive everything we did during the day. And our dreams will be lessons about our lives, our walk.

When we leave our bodies in bed, we can do things we can't do when we have a body in this reality, and we can understand things we don't otherwise understand on Earth. We are one with Mother Nature and receive her benefits. Life's problems are natural, but Mother Earth helps us understand these things and be happy.

When we eat we have an opportunity to increase our intimacy with our Mother Earth; in breathing we are handed an opportunity for intimate relationship with air; when we feel heat in our bodies, or feel friendship, this is a channel of communication with sacred fire. Drinking water and washing ourselves are great opportunities for cleansing our physical parts as well as other aspects of us that need to be cleansed. In this way our lives become transparent and fluid. Birds don't struggle against the wind, they use it to rise up, and trees make a sound when the wind is strong. Many possibilities exist for transforming moments when one is blocked or in situations that are difficult. These problems can help us walk more carefully in life and with more knowledge and awareness.

We need to give thanks not only when the sun is shining but also when the clouds are dark and rain falls. We may give thanks for all of our moments of regret. I know the mind will say we are crazy. How can we give thanks for difficult moments? I can assure you that when we do it, as my grandmother taught me, we will have more power to resolve adverse circumstances, and I know, I have lived this. It is wonderful to feel this. When the wind blows very strongly against us, when the difficulty is very great, we can fly higher; this is what I learned from the condor. The condor waits until there is a strong wind against it because it is the largest bird in the world,* so that when a strong, contrary wind comes up, it hurls itself in the direction of the abyss and flies higher. When difficulties come to us, we have great opportunities for discovering wisdom inside of ourselves.

I don't call difficulties problems because difficulties come on our behalf, and I remember what my grandfather said, "When you begin to give thanks with your whole heart and fully throw yourself into it, you will have flown higher. I can feel and give thanks for these gifts everywhere, at every moment, and after it one will be in harmony with life so that a problem becomes less and less insoluble. Many times difficulties are our teachers. It's very simple; we should never close ourselves to receiving life's gifts, but we have to be open in mind and heart to receive them. Every element—everything—exists in this reality to help us receive the gifts we need to receive. Because of this, every moment is an opportunity.

"Reaching this connection with the elements is the moment when respect and gratitude emerge. One doesn't need to think about being grateful because it comes naturally; we become aware that we depend

---

*The condor is the largest bird in the Americas.

on the elements, and that we are a part of the great energy force of life, and that great force of life is a part of us."

You know that, historically, indigenous people have not been treated well, and even now fair treatment doesn't exist. In spite of all this, we express gratitude to Earth. We help plants grow and then we harvest, and at every moment we express gratitude either with words or mentally, showing our intentions. At the time of harvest we have a celebration and prepare all the kinds of grain that Mother Earth gifts us.

In summary, I want to emphasize that in life every activity is an opportunity to express gratitude in a natural way. We give thanks for things spontaneously because we feel love for the earth, not feeling it as a duty that we *ought* to be grateful. We are thankful for everything we receive, even if we don't like or understand it. As far as I am concerned punishment doesn't exist in Creation.

There are many things that we don't like and repudiate, but in time we recognize they are necessary for us. We only want and ask for the things we like, and when the opposite comes we believe the Creator has not heard us. However, it may be that when we ask for what we want and life doesn't give it to us, it's because what we want is not appropriate for us at that moment in our lives. My elders taught me to give thanks both for what I receive and what I don't receive. In giving thanks for a difficult moment, being grateful for it, this difficulty will disappear and grow lighter. It's possible it may be a lesson, but never a punishment.

There are many people who are not conscious of what they receive every morning when they wake. They think they need more things and ask for them. I consider that we should give thanks for all the marvelous gifts we receive every day with our whole heart and in a way that is sincere and spontaneous. Give thanks for what we are able to see—that we can walk, breathe, feel distinct textures—and give a huge amount of thanks for what we can smell. We offer thanks through our songs, and through pleasure and joy. But people have forgotten how to be joyful; they are serious growing up.

We don't allow our children to be serious. Happiness is a way of giving thanks to life, and kids perhaps don't say thank you, thank you, but through their happiness and their games they express gratitude to life. In my tradition we are always having fiestas with the whole community. Everyone takes part. The house is open and everyone comes in, eats, dances, and participates. No one is invited, but everyone comes. In this way we give thanks at every moment with our whole heart. Our way of life is threaded with gratitude.

Allpa Mama, Mother Earth, is like our own mother. When our physical mother gives us food, when we eat with gratitude and happiness and eat everything she gives us, Mother offers us a little more because she sees we are eating with delight and joy and gratitude, and that we are eating everything and might like more. Our Allpa Mama is the same way. If she sees we receive the food she gives us with love, and that we take pleasure in and feel the eating and connect ourselves with her, she always offers more. We eat with gratitude to continue to receive Mother Earth's gifts and aim not to leave even a single grain of quinoa on the plate.

The chroniclers said we were savages because we went about laughing and happy all the time. That was because before the Spanish arrival we knew nothing of the concept of sin that the church imposed. For us, to be with God was, and is, to be happy, but for Catholics, their approach to life is marked by original sin and sorrow. Our way of living has to be happiness; we need to wake up happy. If the day before was bad, something sad happened, we shouldn't go on being sorrowful or negative the following day because this will mean we'll spend the whole day in the same state.

What do we hope for in life? Happiness, of course, and tranquility and peace. To provide an example, if we are hungry, where do we go if not the kitchen? Or do we go to the bathroom or living room? No, we go to where we need to go to acquire food and be able to eat. And so if we want to go in the direction of happiness, what does our approach to life need to be? Should we be negative, sad, and bitter perhaps? No, we need to be joyful and content. We need to smile and have a positive mental attitude. We need to be with God, and this is being with God.

This is a time in which we must go beyond good and evil. All this is relative because all moral systems have been put in place by human morality. Who can decide whether this or that thing is good or bad? By what parameters do we judge, by what mandates? If what we call "good" were not to exist, neither would what we call "bad." In my way of seeing things, they are complementary and necessary for equilibrium to exist.

When we succeed in finding harmony on our path, when we are happy with the energetic frequency we desire, and when we are successful in developing our two cerebral hemispheres, the concept of good and bad becomes moot. The left hemisphere controls logic and the right intuition, and when we allow Western knowledge and Andean wisdom to sprout and fly in the same sky of every human being's life, we find the equilibrium we need. The Chakana, the indigenous cross, like everything, is marked off and divided into four parts that shape the whole. These are the Hanan Pacha or upper and superior realm; the Kay Pacha, the middle and terrestrial realm; the Uku Pacha, the lower and subhuman realm; and the Sumak Pacha, all of it the union of the other three. One can observe this plan in macrocosmic and microcosmic terms, including in the human body as a whole. And so the Chakana has these parts that are constitutive of the whole, and it can reflect that realm in which a human being can grow.*

What I mean to say is that if a human being encounters harmony in the development of the two brain hemispheres, he or she can be located at any point in the Chakana, in the upper, middle, or lower plane, and wherever it is, the concept of good and bad is void. Human morality would say that a man is good if he is placed in the Hanan Pacha because that is where celestial beings develop, and he would be bad if he is found in the Uku Pacha. However, this is so only in

*The Chakana is described more fully in chapter 16.

human conception. The presence of good and bad is necessary for harmony to exist in the development of life. If this were not so, what would happen to the Western concept? What would have happened if Judas [his betrayal of Jesus] had not existed? The prophecy of salvation simply would not have been realized. We can't say just because of this that Judas was bad; his actions were necessary in that time and space. I am not justifying by any concept actions that can do harm to other people. I am just saying that their presence and effects are necessary in this aspect of the Chakana.

The lady who hosted don Alberto for the talk where I first met him wanted to go to Ecuador to receive healing from him for a fall she had suffered and asked me to accompany her. On that trip I eventually found myself alone with him. Given this, I asked him about something I'd been curious about ever since our initial meeting in Concord, Massachusetts, wherein I had experienced a very strange phenomenon, the likes of which I had never experienced before.

After his fascinating talk, don Alberto and I were standing about fifteen feet away from each other. As I asked the interpreter to tell him about my dance group's dance to honor water, don Alberto was turned away from me. On hearing the translation, he suddenly wheeled around to face me, and as he did so, a ray of light, laser-like in its focus, shot out from his eyes and curled its way into mine. It lasted only a few seconds but it was definitely real: it dazzled me. I did not at that moment have a chance to ask him what it meant, but I was amazed.

Later in Ecuador when I found myself alone with him, I had the opportunity to ask him about this very strange thing that had happened between us. At first he seemed unsure of what to say, perhaps evaluating whether I could accept what he was about to tell me. He then knocked me backward by saying it was a signal we had known each other in previous lives. Never having given any serious thought to the possibility of other lives, this presented me with a challenge to my whole understanding of life. It was something that was to happen time and again in my association with don Alberto.

Before going to Ecuador I was working with a small group of people to explore shamanic journeying. On two occasions I had the same shamanic waking dream: I found myself to be an eagle flying with a condor around the snowcapped peak of Mt. Cotopaxi. I understood the condor to be don Alberto and I was the eagle. I was quite sure my ego was intruding on my ability to vision properly, as I simply did not think this could be a reflection of reality. He was a senior medicine man but who was I?

During my first trip to Ecuador, don Alberto took my traveling companion and me to participate in sweat lodge ceremonies he was conducting for an extended family and their friends. At the outset, when fifteen people were gathered, he made some introductory remarks and then introduced me as the Eagle of the North, handing me his drum and asking me to sing a song. I froze. Could my shamanic vision be a reality?

Don Alberto came up to me and whispered, *"En inglés, en inglés,"* and I thought *There's no way I can sing in Spanish but what am I going to sing in English?* Mercifully, what came to me was a song I knew from an Irish folk singer's album that I sang or hummed while he spoke further to the participants. The song goes like this:

> *There is a ship that sails the sea that is as deep as*
> *deep may be, but not as deep as the love I'm in, I*
> *know not if I sink or swim.**

I know full well there is not just one Eagle of the North, but this brought my shamanic journeys home to me and I realized I could not simply dismiss them as dreams that had no reflection in reality.

---

*Paraphrase of the first verse of lyrics by Peter, Paul, and Mary, sung by Maura O'Connell. The tune is an old British folk song, well-known as "The Water is Wide," with many different word settings.

3

The Power of Water

At first I didn't think I'd find myself one day following the path of tayta yachak.[1] I merely did things I saw my grandfather do, and when a bit older, as a youth, what my father did. Both my grandfather and my father liked to take me along, and I was happy they would take me on the paths they trod. A favorite spot of my grandfather's was a sacred spring that is in the community of Quilajaló, near the river Catuche. He used to take me regularly to this place. My father as well made a very special contribution to my path by taking me to places outside the community, to Otavalo [an indigenous town north of Quito], to the Amazon district, to the coast. All of my grandparents as well as my parents were yachaks. My mother, who is still living, is a mama yachak.

And so as I said, I wasn't thinking about this being a path of Andean wisdom. I was just copying what I was seeing my grandparents do, my father and mother as well. And then while still very young I found myself being an assistant. I didn't ask to do this, but would stop eating or playing when I was a small child to be with them while they tended to their patients or when they were in their meetings. I would say to my grandpa or my papa, "I am bringing you the plants," and I would run to bring plants or eggs for the limpieza.

One of my favorite memories, primarily because water is one of the elements with which I connect and intermingle the most, is of a visit I made with my grandfather to a sacred spring in Quilajaló; a beautiful spot. He used to take me in his poncho on his lap. I must have been seven or eight years old for sure. I remember that he used to stroke my hair from the forehead back, and it was so delicious. I was lulled, that is to say, I was neither asleep nor awake. I loved to feel this because I used to see other children that appeared around me and I would play with them in the spring. This made me one of them, because I would ask my grandfather to take me to the spring because I wanted to play with these children who were my only friends. They were the only boys I connected with. Some days he took me and on others he would say, "tomorrow or another day."

On one occasion I asked for the same thing, but already I was playing. I felt as if a part of my body was asleep on my grandfather's lap and another part was playing with the children. It was a lovely feeling. After this, what happened was we went into the water and were not only plunging in, but went completely underwater, going toward the hole where the water goes out. I didn't think anything about it because nothing happened to us; we didn't drown in spite of spending so much time submerged. I only thought about it years later. On that occasion I simply enjoyed a lot of time in the water.

Don Alberto allayed his childhood loneliness through his imaginative and intuitive abilities, which were the basis of his later powers as a yachak. In early youth he connected with the power of water, or as we might be more inclined to say, its spirit or energy. His visionary account of playing with children underwater took me back to book illustrations I had pored over as a child. These were pictures of children living and playing underwater in Charles Kingsley's *The Water Babies*. Might these be trace memories of the comfort of the amniotic sac? I was totally unaware of Kingsley's underlying polemic against child employment and abuse in mid-nineteenth-century England, although my heart registered a threatening witch-like character, a Mrs. Be-done-by-as-you-did. Her image stayed with me but I unwittingly attached to it the less threatening name of the motherly Mrs. Do-as-you-would-be-done-by.

Living underwater never seemed unreal to me until I was a little older. I pored over a brightly colored German picture book of children floating in multiple streams that looked delightful until I saw the streams led to waterfalls whose threat of pushing me under frightened me. I loved real water as long as I stayed on top of it, whether swimming in a pond on my grandparents' farm, rowing boats, or yachting on the ocean. I've learned to swim underwater, if uneasily, without snorkeling gear. Don Alberto's teachings have become a continuing source of opening my understanding to the power of water.

Early on during my first two weeks in Ecuador, don Alberto took me and my traveling companion, together with his partner and their young son, to a sacred lake south of his home. This was Lake Colta, in the shadow of Mt. Chimborazo. Around noon on an overcast and rather dull day, we walked out into the lake on a man-made grassy promontory where don Alberto and family settled down for a picnic. He gave my friend and me pieces of bread, directing us to walk around leaving our bread as offerings in different places, then make our prayers to the lake, and return for some lunch. I left my bread in various spots along the water's edge and then found a place behind a bank that gave me privacy from the others. I stared out at the lake and then . . .

I feel self-conscious and wonder what I am doing there praying to a lake. After all, I am supposed to be Christian, aren't I? Ultimately deciding that my scruples don't have to prevent me from giving thanks for the opportunity to be in such a beautiful spot, I manage to offer up a prayer. A moment later I catch a glimpse out of the corner of my left eye of don Alberto. He has come around the bank and is carrying a condor feather. He dips it in the lake and flicks the droplets in my direction. I feel a splat of water on my chest. He dips the feather again and flicks it again. The water hits me so hard in the face that I half-close my eyes and recoil slightly. When I look straight in his direction, I find he is gone. That's odd, I think. It seems like some kind of initiation ritual, but I am surprised he said nothing to me beforehand and reason that I'll have to ask him about it.

The rest of the day was spent very busily sightseeing and looking at goods set out for sale in stalls, so I didn't have a chance to think again about the experience at the water's edge until I was in bed that night. As I went through the events at the lake it suddenly hit me that *I did not get wet!* My shirt wasn't wet and I didn't have to wipe my face. I was in shock as I realized it must have been a visionary experience. I'd had plenty of experience previously with the practice of shamanic journeying, but always knew which reality I was in, the dreamworld or everyday life. Not this time, however. *Am I cracking up,* I wondered?

The next day I got a chance to speak to don Alberto alone. I described what I had seen, and relayed my realization that the water coming at me had not made me wet. Then I looked at him doubtfully and said hesitatingly, "Were you even there?"

"No, I wasn't there," he replied.

He became very animated, his black eyes flashing as he went on, "What you experienced was the *power* of water, not actual water. Water is an important element for you. Everything in nature has power. Most people have no idea about that, and it is very difficult to explain it. There are some people, though, like you, who catch on quickly."

I was thunderstruck. I didn't feel as if I was catching on quickly at all.

Toward the end of that first trip, don Alberto took me to a spring and a natural pool favored by his father; it was a long distance from his home. It has now been developed as a swimming pool, but is still lovely, with a flower garden and trees beside a stream. As we approached the entrance, the mood was set when he came up behind me and poked me in the ribs from both sides. I jumped in the air with a yell and, turning, almost fell down when I landed, but for his outstretched arm. We doubled up laughing.

I ventured slowly into the pool, which was chilly enough to remind me of swimming in fifty-four-degree Fahrenheit water in my youth. Don Alberto, who had previously dived in and quickly got out, gingerly remained on the steps at one end, clearly not wishing to enter the water again. I saw my opportunity for revenge for the rib-poking and advanced on him menacingly. He braced for what he knew was coming and yelled as an icy wave propelled by my arm hit him full in the chest. We both collapsed with laughter yet again and then ensconced ourselves on swings in the garden, a favorite activity of mine as a child.

While on the swings don Alberto asks me if I would like to do a plant cleansing then and there. I have learned the basics from him previously through observation, so of course I say yes. "Well, there are five rules," he begins. "Connect with yourself, connect with the plant, ask permission to pick it, give thanks to the Great Spirit, and then thank the plant and pick it. All of this shouldn't be a solemn practice but done as a child's game." He directs me to a small garden to find the plants to do a cleansing on a young woman who is accompanying us; she is due to give birth very soon. I spend some time walking around the garden, trying to put his directions into practice. I begin to see flowers I recognize from my grandparents' garden in England that I'd roamed as a child. The first ones I really notice are orange trumpet-shaped flowers whose name I can't immediately recall: nasturtium.

There's a large black stone in the middle of them so I rest a hand on it for balance while I massage a cramp in one ankle. As I do this I connect with two of the flowers below me in my line of sight. They appear to glow. I ask their permission, give thanks, and pick them. I repeat this process on the other side of the flower bed with white-and-purple alyssum, purple phlox, and other flowers. Finally I visit a shrub that don Alberto pointed out as sacred. It has flowers that are similar to and smell like a giant meadowsweet, and I pick one of them.

Finally I am ready and don Alberto takes me over to the pregnant young woman. I sweep the flowers in a serpentine path across her forehead and put them under her nose for a few seconds so she can smell the meadowsweet. Then I continue sweeping over her face and down her body. I take each hand of hers and sweep the flowers back and forth, then over the bare patch of skin at her throat. I sweep her legs and her feet and then work up and down the backs of her legs. Lifting her ponytail from the back of her neck, I sweep there too, then finally come back to her hands and put the flowers between them, closing my hands over hers. I step back a few steps and stand, waiting for her to open her eyes. When she does, don Alberto comes up and asks her how it was. I don't understand her reply, but as she turns away he gives me a big smile and a thumbs-up with both hands, saying "Muy bonito" (Very lovely).

The most important lesson I learned from this experience was, as don Alberto said, that all of this shouldn't be a solemn practice but be done joyfully as a child would play a game.

4

Initiation

Don Alberto grew up learning how to be a yachak from watching his father and grandfather, and he became their assistant in many rituals. In 1977, at a time when they had passed into another reality as he puts it, he attended a large gathering of elders in Colombia where a number of indigenous people were to be initiated as yachak. It is possible to experience many different kinds of initiation or new beginnings in life. What follows is his account of how he underwent one that formally made him a yachak, something that implies a greater level of responsibility in serving others.

It was very interesting for me because I wasn't among those to be chosen that day; I was just there at this *hatun tandanakuy,* a great gathering of elders where they were initiating various people as yachak and making important decisions for our culture.[1] It was in the Sierra Nevada of Cocuy, Colombia, a private gathering where elders met with candidates in circles representing different places in the Andes. So I was there as an assistant; I had already taken part in meetings like this, but just as an assistant. I was fascinated by this great ritual that lasted for a month. There were more than a hundred candidates from Peru, Bolivia, Ecuador, Colombia, and Central America—and there were more women than men. And so, after days and weeks passed, many took on the responsibility [of being a yachak] and many did not take it on. Since I wasn't a candidate I was happy and relaxed; I didn't want that responsibility.

Then the Hatun Tayta Yachak (Great Wise Father) who was directing the *ruray* (the ritual) suddenly took me by the hair and led me to the center of the circle where they were doing rituals. At that moment I wanted to say to him respectfully, "Tayta, you are mistaken, I am not a candidate," but he didn't give me time because while dragging me to the center by my hair he began singing and the rest accompanied him in the ritual. I just kept quiet, and I began to feel something beautiful. At first it was a sensation like heat in my body that started in the crown, then moved to the belly button, then the chest, then the soles of my feet, then behind the knees. And then a very wonderful feeling spread throughout my whole body as if I was going to come apart slowly, but I allowed myself to maintain this very special experience. I believe my legs gave way as two people supported me so that I didn't fall to the ground. And yes, a whole day was spent before I was rational again, but I wasn't conscious of this.

Later I embraced the Hatun Tayta and cried a lot. I embraced him for all I was feeling. Everyone congratulated me, and then I spoke and thanked them and said that I had not been a candidate, that I just wanted to remain an assistant, and did not want to become a public yachak. There are tayta and mama yachaks who live beneficially without being in public, living as ordinary people in communities or cities, and many are urban mestizo people who live there. I knew these taytas and mamas [at the ritual], and since they made the ritual for me, I said I accepted it but wanted to choose the option of being anonymous. I wanted to be a yachak who was not known as such but who had within himself all that richness. Then a younger yachak hugged me and took me outside the circle where we walked and opened up to our feelings. He said to me, "How is it that you don't want to take on public responsibility?"

Then I remembered that there was a tayta who years ago also took me out of the circle. He took me out of the house because as a small boy I behaved very badly. I was doing this while the elders were meeting to make decisions about our culture and knowledge.

They were saying that the time is already here when we will not have to hide ourselves, nor our voice; our wisdom and tradition will be accepted by the whites and mestizos. At that I reacted terribly badly. I started to yell and stamp my feet and cry saying, "Why didn't they say this to the whole community?" They should make known what they were talking about: that we indigenous people suffered repression because we hid ourselves to do our healings and our rituals, that they should talk about how we were to live, and that they were egoists.

The yachak who took me out that first time told me that it was not yet time for that, that the right *pacha* (time-space era) had not yet arrived. So then, this second time I was taken out, this man said, "How is it that at that time you wanted something, were demanding, were crying because we were egoists, because we were not open to the public? And yet now that you are chosen, and now is the time when all is to be made public and hidden no more, now you say you don't want it?"

I admitted it, embraced him, and said that at the time I wasn't aware of the magnitude of what I was saying. I apologized, and said that I accepted being yachak, but not yet a public one. And so I got started.

"What is a yachak?"

Don Alberto and I were seated comfortably in my living room in Massachusetts. Besides the answer being of general interest, I also had a personal reason for asking the question. The first two weeks I spent in Ecuador traveling with don Alberto had been filled with all kinds of marvels, not the least of which was what he said to me at the end, which was, "You are a mama yachak."

I was stunned.

"How can you say that? I don't know anything about your traditions."

"I am not making you anything; we recognize people from other traditions. I'm just recognizing what you already are because you need it. You have everything, the inner tranquility, and just need a few technical things that I can easily teach you."

I was amazed and honored, but it created a tension in me so it never occurred to me to thank him. When I first went to Ecuador, I thought I knew that a yachak was a medicine person or healer, and assumed that if one put *mama* in front of it, it meant a medicine woman. I was too chicken to ask why he thought I needed this title. That may have been just as well, because two years later he took me to an indigenous women's conference led by mama yachaks who were mainly from Ecuador, but also other South American countries such as Bolivia. It was held at Cochasqui, north of Quito, an impressive thousand-year-old site with fifteen pyramid mounds, minimally excavated, which I had never heard of.

Wandering over the grassy mounds was a herd of llamas. The women had made a beautiful circular sacred arrangement of flowers and fruit with a central fire, and I was invited into the circle for the ritual. Here we sat around the edge, inside a rope separating us from the onlookers. Afterward everyone—about a hundred people—gathered in a large tent for a morning of speeches followed by lunch.

After the meal, don Alberto notified me that he had signed me up to give a talk. This gave me an hour's notice to give a fifteen-minute talk in Spanish. My Spanish isn't fluent but there was no one there to translate for me so I knew I had to focus intently rather than panic. For the next hour I walked alone to an excavated astronomical monument on top of one of the mounds while thinking about what to say and how to say it.

When the time came, don Alberto stood behind me to give me support. I talked of my work over the past thirty years identifying and cataloging thousands of stone tools from collections given to the history museum in Concord, Massachusetts, over the past one hundred years. I expect to create new exhibits with these collections. And with the help that scientific excavations give, I'm in the process of reconstructing the indigenous history of the area back to the Ice Age. I spoke too of my experiences with the Massachusetts Wampanoag supreme medicine

Cochasqui: mama yachaks' ceremony
Photo by William Sullivan

man, John Peters Slow Turtle, when he invited me to give public presentations with him. I would give a historical introduction before his talk when he often spoke about the genocide of Native Americans in the United States. I commented how this was really hard for his audience to hear.

Much to my relief the talk that don Alberto had assigned me to give went over well, and I was even complimented on my Spanish.

Later I realized don Alberto had thrown me into that situation trusting I could handle it. Because he had sponsored me, his reputation was at stake, but also I felt it was my initiation into being a mama yachak. By the time I left the conference I had learned that *mama* and *tayta yachaks,* "mothers and fathers of wisdom," were respected elders and mentors. I have also learned that *yachak,* while indicating someone with wisdom, literally means "birdperson," or someone who can fly to other dimensions of reality.

Now in my own home, I had a chance to learn from a master yachak how he perceived the yachak role, and to record his answers:[2] "A yachak is someone who has walked the walk, has made their perception come alive, and has experimented with living, flowing, perceiving, intuiting, and respecting all manifestations of life. Yachaks, while they are experiencing, keep tabs on whether their whole way of life sustains what they are doing, and they benefit from respecting and greatly loving all existence.

"And then too, a yachak is a man or woman who has accepted his or her responsibility to make this knowledge of the ancestral peoples of Ecuador, the original peoples of antiquity, known through sharing. A yachak is a person who holds responsibility for maintaining, looking after, preserving, spreading, and sharing their experience with everyone who wants it."

"You have apprentices," I said. "How does one learn to become a yachak?"

"Yes, I have many women and men who walk with me, who learn those things that I learned from my elders, men and women of wisdom. All the women I have trained have remained private; they are not public yachaks.

"I receive everyone with pleasure and without regard to language, social or economic condition, or what their country may be, because the physical appearance of our bodies is immaterial. What is necessary is that all their senses come alive, that they become open to their other power, the power of perception. I have many students who walk with me, and I am open to all who have felt so inclined to come, and for them to come walk the mountains together, to make alive the wisdom that is within each.

"It is not that I give them wisdom, rather the ability to perceive is (or exists) everywhere in everything: in the person themselves, in the trees, the mountains; it is in the rivers, lakes, and in everything alive. What one needs, the only thing necessary, is to feel strongly in your heart and mind that you want to explore, to know, to practice; you want to have the kind of life that is in harmony with nature.

"So, yes, I have students, and a yachak is someone who has returned to the kind of life I lead, or has learned from my life how I am, and who takes responsibility for sharing."

On another occasion years later when don Alberto and I were standing in the yard outside his home, I had an opportunity to ask him about different levels or grades of being a yachak, whether there was a hierarchy or not. He described three yachak grades and made it plain that trying to understand these in terms of a vertical Western pyramidal model is a misconception. His description may be visualized as three horizontal concentric or nested circles.

The outer circle represents beginners on the yachak path. By beginners I mean those starting out with a single competency or gift. This might include individuals such as a visionary or one who has speaking ability, which confers whatever responsibility that gift may entail. Or they may be just setting out to walk the path. The second circle (tayta or mama yachak) indicates more competencies and responsibilities. And the third inner circle (Hatun Tayta Yachak or Hatun Mama Yachak) represents those with the most of both, but a willingness to take on more responsibility is the important key aspect. This "top" level or rather central level, it should be understood, is not at the top of a pyramid that grants special privileges that those lower down do not have. It is on the same horizontal level as the "bottom," so the progression is one of taking on more responsibility in service to others, and those who do so are given greater respect.

5

An Encounter with Francis

Don Alberto has had ample opportunity in his life to emulate the condor, to access its strength by, in his words, hurling oneself toward the abyss and flying higher. When he was nineteen years of age his father, to whom he was greatly attached and who was an important mentor to him, was killed in front of him, deliberately run over by a car in the street. He has mentioned previously the persecution that his family suffered as indigenous people, an animosity that later ended in murder. Don Alberto was distraught and sequestered himself in an isolated cabin where he did not eat for days. During that time, however, his father came to him in vision, telling him it was not his path to follow in his father's exact footsteps, that their ways had now diverged, and that don Alberto needed to continue his life as he had important work to do. This was sufficient for him to pull himself together and gain the courage to go on without his father's direct support.[1]

His formal initiation as a yachak, just described, happened three to four years after this tragedy, but a year or two later he reached a point of dissatisfaction. This was a dark night of the soul that caused him to doubt his path. His encounter with Francis of Assisi sowed a seed that led him eventually to build anew on his ancestral teachings.

In my youth, a moment arrived in my walk with the taytas and mamas when I found their teaching fulfilling enough, but I began to feel I was missing something more.[2] I didn't feel happy with all the gifts life was giving me—I wanted more. I had so much already [social position as the son of a known yachak family, property, a comfortable life] that certain people felt envious and actually said to me, "Who wouldn't want to be at the place you have arrived at in life?"

But no, I wasn't happy; I didn't feel complete. In this state I started doing what I often did, which is to put my forehead on the ground and say, "Good Pachakamak, what is going on with me? Why am I like this, so sad when I have so much? When I even have people who are envious of me, why am I not satisfied?"

After I had cycled through some convents where I was looking for certain answers, I arrived in this sorry condition at the Monastery of St. Clare (Monasterio Santa Clara) in the historical center of Quito, to talk to the nuns there. The Monastery of St. Clare is a closed convent, that is, the nuns don't even leave when dead because once they enter they are buried there too.

For reasons unclear to me, I entered the convent as a visitor—not, of course, as a postulant since it was for women only. I was shown to a cell that once inside caught my attention. It had within it an alcove with a grille secured by ancient padlocks. I got close enough to look into the alcove and saw a mound of dusty books. I then spoke to the Mother Superior to see if she would allow me to see these books. Her reply was, "No. They are in Latin, which is why they're stowed there: to be out of the way."

But I persisted. I even begged for a while, and eventually she let me inside the grille.

I began to examine these books with leather covers and one in particular caught my attention. Its title was *The Principles of Francis,* and it was about some guy called Francis of Assisi. It was written in Old Castilian but I could understand it. So then I asked her if I could take it out of the convent when I left. She agreed, but told me that was the only precious book of their Father Francis I could take, and to please return it. So I left and read some of his advice. It was his diary, and somehow what I read calmed me down and made me think a lot about Francis.

There was a Catholic library in front of the plaza of St. Francis so I went in and saw a book, the title of which was *Biography of Francis*. I bought the book, and it told me he wasn't a mystic or anything but an ordinary man of his time, an Italian citizen in the town of his birth, Assisi. He was bohemian, that is, the guitar, wine, and women were his life. He had a girlfriend, Clare, and was happy. Later he joined the military and afterward, well, his life was very interesting and intense. At a certain point, when he returned from a military expedition and was ill, he saw a bird through the window and experienced something wonderful. His parents maintained that his illness was responsible for the unusual things he saw.

Then he went to the woods and mountains and walked and walked and he came across a ruined church, an abandoned chapel in one of the fields. He went into the church and felt a strange need that would not allow him to be satisfied. What was he doing; what was the purpose of his life? His parents were in a very favorable economic position, they were businesspeople. His father wanted to hand the whole business on to him and pointed to the riches that he as his only son would one day receive.

And so I identified with him, this guy who had everything but wasn't satisfied, and I saw that the same thing was happening to me. Then they say that there, in that chapel, he heard the words "Francis, rebuild my church." He understood it to mean the ruined church right there that he had to restore.

Then he went to his father and acted wild and renounced him. He took money, cloth, and clothes and gave them to the poor. His father told him he was mad and lashed him with a whip. He then took his son to the bishop, and Francis complained that he wanted no part of any riches or any such thing, but he wanted to follow the path of Jesus. The bishop offered him the priesthood but also told him that those with riches are also on the path. And his father said to him, "I have given you everything." Francis handed everything over to his father in the plaza and left the plaza naked. They say that at that time there was a rule that anyone who became a beggar had to wear a long robe and hood the color of the earth, and so Francis changed his clothing to that of a beggar.

I changed my clothes into those of a beggar in the Santo Domingo area of Quito, near Rocafuerte Street. Up to that moment, at age twenty-five, I was doing well physically and economically in the path of being a yachak, but I wasn't satisfied. No one resonated with me. I didn't want any church, but I made myself a beggar. I decided then to read the book that had made me a beggar to see if I had missed anything. However, I also told myself that neither fear nor timidity existed in me and that I would find this very easy.

This is what I believed, but when I began to be seen in beggars' clothing and someone I knew appeared, my whole body would break out in a sweat and I felt publicly shamed. Many people learned I was a beggar, and it was very difficult because I had not gotten to the root of certain things. At first I thought of doing this in a city where no one would know me, but then I saw that Francis did it in his home territory, so I stayed on the streets of Quito for a year, sleeping in the entrance portal of the Santo Domingo Church. My first day there I became cold, so moved close to other beggars in the portal. It was freezing! Later they shifted themselves to one side and started to snore. When some drunkards walked by, I moved myself over as well. How on earth was I going to sleep? The first nights I didn't get a wink. I saw that other beggars asked people for food, so I did the same. I'd get close to people to ask them, but they'd see I was young and in good health, so they'd call me idle. They said I was shameful, told me I had to be a drunk, and to go and work, and wasn't I ashamed of myself? But there I remained with hand outstretched and head down. Of course, they were right.

At that time there were good restaurants and shops on Guayaquil, Bolivar, and Rocafuerte streets; it was Quito's economic center as well. No one was giving me anything. So when I went by restaurant windows and saw that people were leaving the table after having eaten just a little bit, I would enter the restaurant, grab as much of the food as I could, and leave to eat it. Of course it was disagreeable for most of the patrons when beggars did this, so I would be ordered to leave right away, but at least I already had a little bit of something to eat.

This experience taught me a great deal. I saw there were other worlds on the physical plane. I was owner of all, I had everything, and yet I had nothing. A beggar has nothing material, but he has something that many do not have. I am talking about liberty. Since then, beggars have been very valuable to me; their lives teach me a huge amount. A beggar is free, free, completely free, without doing anything. A beggar does what he wants, when he wants, out on the sidewalk. I spent my time out on the street, sleeping in broad daylight in the sun. It was a great lesson for me to see how loners would talk to each other, others would fight, others would laugh, and I could see everything ordinary people do and could understand their lives. What I was doing was observing with utter liberty.

It helped me understand myself and other people, and to understand the wisdom of my taytas with respect to not wasting a single grain of quinoa. I came to value food, home, bath, and the fact that there are wise beggars. I came to value everything, and when beggars converse, their analysis of things is extraordinary. I ascertained that a child of eight knows much more than a lawyer or a professor of psychology. It was one of the loveliest stages of my life. Physically the first weeks were very painful, but later I too lay down and snored on bare stone.

Dawn was the most dismal time as firemen arrived, typically at four in the morning, not because there was a fire but to clean the streets. They hosed down the portal with pressure hoses. They would wash everything and us too, beggars and drunks alike, if we didn't look out. One's body became numb with cold so one stayed there frozen and quiet. Later, when many of us heard the firemen coming, we moved, slowly crawling, crawling, to leave and not get wet, but other poor people got used to it.

I learned much, and for me ever since, a beggar has value. At times I feel I am on the street again and I give them food. Now, as always, there are great people who give food at dawn. There are times of plenty; at Christmas they left us food, blankets, and drink—there was everything. But some malicious drunk types, warm and well covered, would hold candles to our feet. Again, at times there were no blankets and the implacable cold in Quito made us get boxes or newspapers for cover to keep us from freezing, but even so some mean people went around holding candles to us.

Being at the equator but also in the mountains, the temperature in Quito can be in the forty-degree Fahrenheit range. After this time he spent living on the street, don Alberto set about trying to find shelter for youth living on the streets of Quito, and to find a way for them to earn a little money without selling themselves. He got a group of them together, and pooling their earnings, they rented a room in which they all slept. He also helped them figure out how to acquire small items they could sell on the street rather than having to prostitute themselves.[3]

6

The Formation of a Public Yachak

A public yachak is a yachak who works in the public sphere, which may include the political arena. This leads to public recognition in the broader society and by the media. It's a path that many yachaks do not think they want, preferring to work privately. Don Alberto at first wanted to be private, as he stated at his initiation, but he was led elsewhere by his destiny.

Don Alberto's father clearly foresaw that his son, in following the yachak path and the prophecy of the Eagle and the Condor, was going to be led to interact with people of Western religious culture and needed to be prepared for how to deal with that. This part of the story starts when his father was still alive, and shows that although resistant, he followed the direction given him while not being sure at the time that the yachak calling was even for him.

One day in St. Francis Square in Quito my father said to me, "You need to go to where there are evangelicals because you need to know what they think."[1]

So I replied, "Why, if these persons are already lost?"

But he told me I needed to go there and participate and afterward we would talk. So I went, and of course, I learned something about the life of Jesus that was fairly different from what I had learned about him previously from priests and monks in the Catholic way, but not the evangelical one. I learned there certain principles that distinguished the one religion from the others. Later on when my father and I were talking, he said, "Very well, now you need to go learn from the Jehovah's Witnesses everything they have to offer. Go there, take note, and learn about everything because this will serve you well one day."

After that I was told by a mama yachak in Agato near Otavalo, "You need to go to institutions of spiritual knowledge that are not open to the public to study there and learn."

I asked her why.

She merely replied, "Because it's necessary."

So I went first to the Universal Great Brotherhood of Dr. Raynaud de la Ferrière,* and thought it was great because I realized there were people who weren't just sticking with some Catholic or evangelical question. I said to myself, *How stupid can you be; these people know so much more than you.* I started to "tune in" to my own traditions because I came to understand that my elders knew much more too, perhaps not using the same terms or symbols, but really it is all the same. It was wonderful to discover that the wisdom of our elders was even beyond what I was learning from these folks. I liked it, especially how they understood the importance of good food for health and practiced what they preached.

After that, through a friend, I had a way to access gnosis and there I was even happier. At the same time I took a correspondence course at a Rosicrucian school. They sent me their pamphlets, which seemed to me to be interesting and good for my formation. As often as I paid attention to these other types of learning, the more I understood my

---

*Serge Raynaud de la Ferrière (1916–1962) was a French esoteric philosopher who was very interested in South America's ancient civilizations. In Venezuela in 1948 he founded the Universal Great Brotherhood whose purpose was to study all religions equally. With branches all over the world, the brotherhood exists mainly in South America.

own. Other terms and other symbols were used, but thanks to knowing that our wisdom is very rich and full and comprises all these other forms of wisdom, I arrived at wanting more of our own. I wanted to know it more clearly and with respect for my elders, because their wisdom is immense. Without having read in order to learn, and without having put themselves through so many schools and philosophies, they practiced these things in their daily lives. These schools would be observing one type of practice, say to do with food, for example; elsewhere the practice in question would involve mysticism instead. My parents and grandparents, without having these approaches, interwove all of this: food, mysticism, *and* spirituality. And so I said to myself, "Alright then, our wisdom we have here is the fullest; other streams have pieces, but by contrast, Andean wisdom is complete." And so I took personal satisfaction in my journey up to that point, and I thanked Pachakamak and my elders, male and female, for bringing me to the point of understanding this.

But what's really interesting is what happened after 1991 when I started acting on my responsibility as a public yachak.* From this time on I have been able to give even more thanks, given that the men and women who were my mentors have passed away. This is because now if there is a question about what I'm saying, I have the tools, words, concepts, and examples to be able to offer a counterargument: I am able to validate and talk about my own tradition.

Or say I give examples of how esoteric philosophical schools in India or Tibet see life. I am able to compare them with how our taytas, mamas, and elders used to live. Many people pay attention to these Oriental traditions, but they don't know about our Andean way of life. And so, using these examples and strands of knowledge, I can better fulfill my responsibility as a public yachak. And this is not just for the indigenous but also for mestizos and foreigners. As you will remember, my mission was to be a public yachak, and for

---

*In 1990 don Alberto became a leader in an indigenous insurrection, a story told in chapter 8.

this the minimum requirement is for me to be able to express myself correctly.* Since 1991, I've had the responsibility of giving conferences to defend Andean wisdom when everyone thought we didn't *have* any religion or philosophy. This was the case particularly in the 1990s when Indianists [people interested in indigenous culture] asserted that we had no philosophy or religion of our own. So with these strands that my elders told me to learn and absorb, I am able to defend our own traditions.

Also, this past year [2008] a group of mamas and taytas said to me, "Why don't you go to a university, and matriculate from there?" Inside I always had a desire for learning and dreamed of being a student. Because some time ago I had been a university professor but never a formal university student, I applied to [Quito's] St. Francis University and was accepted, but I was the eldest and withdrew. Last year, though, I decided again to go to university as a student.

I was in a health-food restaurant here in Quito when a gentleman came up to me and said, "You are Alberto Taxo, the yachak."

I said yes, and he went on. "Why aren't you helping us in a seminar at the University of the Andes? Come and lead a discussion one day, we want you to help us in our workshop."

I said, "No, I wish to be a student."

He replied, "Fine, then come as a student."

And so I completed my diploma.

Don Alberto reflects:

There have been steps in the human walk both necessary and natural that direct life toward unified action and understanding. A step is taken and an older one discarded, or something else is proposed—as in the Renaissance. Before the Renaissance, the Catholic religion provided the framework, but then other possibilities appeared in religion and

---

*Don Alberto's experiences with a Colombian yachak, described in the next chapter, helped him to develop his public speaking.

art. These processes of change provide wealth for humanity because they move us to another level of comprehension.

At this time we are living something very similar, something with very beautiful properties for this present moment. I believe we mustn't waste time or energy in defending one religion and attacking another, or in looking for the defects of one and valuing only the other. Rather what we should do is carry on with our way of life as harmoniously as possible, as happily as possible, as connected as possible to the dynamic life of nature. We should devote ourselves to what we see, and to whatever is set before us. This is the religion of this time, and it may be we are already leaving behind a time of attacking or defending one religion versus another.

Religion as practiced today is not primarily institutional; it is a life process that requires maturity because only maturity determines what is beneficial or prejudicial. Many practices can seem appropriate on our walk to become transcendent beings, but a moment can come when we realize they are not the most suitable, and we need to change our religious behavior. It takes much spiritual maturity to choose the appropriate path or religion. We don't all need the same path to reach our transcendence. For this reason it is unnecessary to say that this or that religion is mistaken. The way is not important, nor are the rituals or ceremonies by which the seeker reaches fulfillment. The important thing is to know how to walk with spiritual maturity.

As I've told you, I am acquainted with many philosophies and religions, but the one I identify with is that of my forbears. Certainly this is the case with other people; they are following a particular path. For me it is neither good nor bad, it is just their path, their essential means of receiving wisdom.

7

A Colombian Yachak

Don Alberto met Luis Gustavo Morales Sierra for the first time in 1982 when he was twenty-eight.[1] Don Gustavo, as he was known at the time, is a Colombian spiritual leader who for more than two years became a mentor to don Alberto at his home in the Cocuy area of the northern Andes of Colombia where he lived with his wife and son. Don Gustavo, a man of humble origins, not indigenous, grew up in the school of hard knocks. He had a small following in Quito at that time.

Don Alberto became impressed by the disciplined life don Gustavo led close to nature and saw it as building on what he himself had learned from his indigenous elders. Some of don Gustavo's daily practices he adopted. A man of impressive physique, don Gustavo reached a high level of competition in weight lifting and bodybuilding and could have represented his nation had he been willing to shave his long hair and beard. Considering hair sacred, he declined to do this. He had a charismatic personality that eventually drew many people to him who were of an esoteric bent.

Don Gustavo lost his father as a small child and in childhood had to work to help support his mother, many times working too many hours for little pay and inadequate food. His life experience was hard-won through many different kinds of work: he helped his mother process tobacco leaves to make cigarillos; he herded sheep and goats; he sold the Encyclopedia Britannica; he made and distributed bread by bicycle, and later drove a truck. An attempt to enter school in 1948 at age eight was foiled by revolutionaries who destroyed his school with a bomb, and he never acquired a formal education.

Don Gustavo describes his spiritual message as one of liberation to humanity. Toward the end of don Alberto's time with him, don Gustavo was persuaded to start a school of philosophy based on the interests of an associate who was drawn to the Chinese Tao, something that in fact triggered don Alberto's departure from living with him. Added to this over time were the esoteric interests of others, with the end result appearing to be a mix of different religious and philosophical ingredients that consisted, in addition to the Tao, of gnostic and Judaic beliefs as well as beliefs concerning the energy contained in the atom. Out of this came the name that don Gustavo is now known by, Kelium Zeus Iduceus, with some followers revering him as a god. The adherents of this school, but not Kelium Zeus himself, came to resent don Alberto's loyalty to his Andean spiritual roots.

At one point, while don Alberto was still residing with don Gustavo's community, don Gustavo was receiving death threats for speaking out against the pope and Opus Dei. Many in Ecuador consider Kelium Zeus to be the leader of a cult and don Alberto has been criticized for his association with him. And yet one can see from the following account that he had a beneficial effect on the young Alberto, who found in him a soul mate. Don Gustavo encouraged don Alberto to develop his own spiritual style of expressing his ancestral beliefs, and to express them through public speaking. This he did; he has been teaching for over twenty-five years.

Not least in importance with respect to the long-term influence of Kelium Zeus on don Alberto is the reference below to bees, given that don Alberto was recently licensed to use bees in healing.

A long time ago, when I was twenty-eight, I rendered my services in a cultural institution in this city [Quito].[2] One day, I was given an official check of the Central Bank for those services, and so, standing in line in the Central Bank of La Alameda, I saw two people ahead of me who were also going to cash a check. They were talking in low voices, worried that someone might hear them. One of them said, "This man is a master, the greatest." I pricked up my ears. Because of what I learned from my elders I always wanted to learn more about these things; everything one might learn about philosophy and wisdom, no matter the label. I don't care about the color, the language, or what country it comes from, wisdom for me is sustenance.

And so they were talking in such a way that I covertly listened harder, looking away of course, but my ears were taking in their words. Only two people were left in line before they cashed their check so I jumped in and said, "Excuse me, I know something of what you are talking about, and I would like for us to have a conversation, to be included in this."

One of them said to me very seriously, "Don't you know that to listen to other people's conversations is ill-bred?"

I replied, "Yes it is, and I am sorry, it is just that I am so interested in what you are talking about. I am really enthusiastic and fascinated."

And they replied, "No, forget everything you heard." And so they cut me off, cashed their check, and left.

I cashed mine as well and ran out, looked all around, and saw them two blocks away, more or less near San Blas. So I followed behind them, and they went into a restaurant. *Great,* I thought. Here was my opportunity, as it's a public place and they couldn't stop me from going in. I sat with my back to them at a table near theirs.

What I heard was, "Come again tomorrow at three in the afternoon to the second floor. A man is coming from there who is going to tell us the latest."

I said to myself, *That's it, I'm done here.* I'd learned where I had to go the next day and at what time. So I left.

The next day at a quarter to three I arrived at Oriente and Esmeralda streets. I went in the corridor and up to the second floor as they said, but all the doors on that floor were closed. I went up to one, then another and another, because I wanted to hear something that would let me know I was in the right place. And when I got close to yet another door, I heard, "Yes, yes, we said at three; that's when everyone will arrive."

I thought to myself, *I don't need to hear more, it's here.* I pushed the door open, went in, and saw two distracted fellows talking in a large room. I sat down, crossed my arms and legs, other people came in, and in the course of these entrances I saw the two people I had seen at the Central Bank.

They looked at me strangely, went up to the group, and came back. At this point everyone stopped and came close to me.

Someone said, "Why are you here?"

I replied, "I believe I am meant to be here; I am here for this."

He said, "Who invited you?"

And I said, "I can't tell you the name of the person who invited me, but I am here."

And then this person threatened me by saying, "Leave this minute!"

At that time I had recently completed practicing boxing, karate, judo, and kung fu, and physically I was in super shape.

I said to him, "Okay then, however many you are, throw me out." And no one touched me.

During this discussion, this fuss, a man in a kimono came in, perhaps a man who was a student of the martial arts, with a black belt and a *bo* [a long staff that wields authority]. Shoot, I was unnerved, but only a little.

Then the others said to him, "Vicente, here's this man who has come without being invited, doesn't want to leave, and on top of that is challenging us."

At that I said, "Yes, things are becoming serious." I found my spot, relaxed, and then continued. "Okay, at the first move, I take action." I took a breath and lowered my arms—putting myself on guard, in other words.

Eyeing me from head to toe, the man in the kimono let me be and said, "Welcome!"

It was that easy, and I bowed to him as one does in the martial arts, and he then bowed to me and said, "Sit down." Everyone was full of admiration, but one could also hear: "How is it that this unknown, arrogant, and rude man, who was challenging all of us, is allowed to sit down now that the presenter of the talk has arrived?"

While he gave his presentation I was ruminating about this special master who was not in the public sphere. Everything the speaker said filled me with enormous enthusiasm. They were talking about don Gustavo. I asked no questions up to the end of the meeting and they announced that the next meeting would be at the same time and place the following week. When I was on my way out the door, the man in the karate outfit came up to me and said, "I want to talk to you."

I said, "Yes, okay."

"Do you know that I need a guard?" he asked me.

I said, "And?"

Then he continued, "I would like it if you would work for me as my guard."

Then I said, "But I am not a part of your group."

He replied, "Yes, I have been looking among all those who were present at this meeting, and others who didn't come today, but no one meets my expectations. I have been looking at you, and I want you to be my guard."

I served as Vicente's guard as he traveled through Ecuador. He was Venezuelan but he had come to Ecuador from Colombia. I think at about that time was when there began to be antagonism and envy, because—just imagine—one day an ill-bred man, unknown to the group, won everyone's plum job. When we had made our way through Ecuador, Vicente said to me, "Why don't we go to Colombia, that's where don Gustavo is. You should get to know him."

Of course, I had been telling my boss things about my elders and what I practiced, things about the Andes, and this was why he said the maestro ought to know me and that, in fact, he would be happy to know me.

We went right away to Colombia and I arrived at kilometer 8 in Bucaramanga going via Pamplona. We arrived at a place in the country, an old adobe house with a tiled roof and a lovely view toward the valley, and a warm climate as well. It was similar to Santo Domingo de los Tsachilas [west of Quito]. Here don Gustavo devoted himself to the care of bees, to apiculture, and here he sold his honey along with goat cheese. He covered both products in grass sheaths that he dried and wrapped himself. And from time to time patients came to him and he attended them. They called him an herbalist, a *pegua,* which means "yachak" in that locale, a honeypot.

His way of life was interesting to me, and when I'd first arrived, he said, "Why did you take so long?" and afterward, just to me, he asked, "When did we two see each other before?" [thereby acknowledging a felt connection between us].

This is all well and good, I thought, and I stayed there.

Five workmen lived near him, people who helped him, and I was one of them, living there more than two years. At this time people began coming to him, and he hardly spoke publicly at all other than speaking through his life, his actions, and his family, because he was not in the public sphere. Yes, I recognized right away that he was a yachak, a sage; he didn't teach me verbally at all but through his life, his work, his exercises at dawn, and what he ate. He must have lived like this for forty years, and he was happy with his family. Consequently, many people started to arrive to see him, especially from Ecuador and Venezuela, and fewer from Colombia.

One day there was a gathering of radio and newspaper journalists and many other people who were interviewing him. I suddenly heard high-energy speech that was very powerful, [and only I among those gathered heard it] while don Gustavo was very quiet. [It seems he must have heard it too or received the message in some other way.] His silence indicated it was probably a rare occurrence for him.* I noted

___

*This was the equivalent of a vision but auditory. Not everyone receives spirit messages in the same way, and "visions" may come by means of any of the senses.

that at that moment he received something, some special force, a spirit. He was speaking, but he stopped being his usual self. Rather than arguing against the gnostics as he had been doing, he was questioning them in a friendly manner. [Because of the spiritual intervention he received, his approach to them was peaceful instead of confrontational.]

And so I just explored, learned much of his discipline, woke up at four in the morning to do exercises, to welcome the sun, and immediately afterward took a shower and then fasted. All of this is to say that at that place there was almost no talk of the spiritual, but rather the emphasis was put on living in a spiritual way, and respecting plants. Many of his habits coincided with much of the way we used to live, derived from our ancestral wisdom. Thus, I learned when I was with don Gustavo, because there is much discipline in these things.

About a year passed in this way. Then there was an influx of people, and those Colombians who were esoteric and somewhat intellectual suggested he start a school. At first he didn't want to but he agreed finally to open a Taoist school of wisdom, urged to do so by a Colombian student and assistant of his who knew a lot about martial arts and Chinese philosophy. This gentleman was the one who would speak the most in interviews and who, on the weekend, taught groups of youths in parks and on the street. In his teaching he said equilibrium is very important—not to go to one extreme or the other. The important thing is to seek harmony, happiness, and well-being, and for this one needs adequate nutrition, physical, mental, and emotional cleanliness, making a habit of regular activity. All this agreed with my manner of living and thinking.

Many of don Gustavo's followers say today and said then that he was a living god of the Taoists, but if we let that idea go, the reality is God is combined with existence, God is everything. And if we are part of the whole, then we are all gods. "I am a god, you are a god," he might say at a meeting or conference, and people kneeling in front of him felt something special being conferred upon them. I have seen some people do this because they felt the strong energy of this awakened being.

Don Gustavo recorded everything he said and I was the recording technician; I was his headman. And so I got to know very important things about his spiritual and material walk that became a part of what I teach [see part 2: Teachings]. We talked personally a lot, and at that time I said to him, "With all due respect to you, maestro, I don't connect much with the things in the Tao school."

And he replied, "Of course."

He used to call me *cacique,* "chief," with affection, because according to him, I had once been the *cacique* of Barranquilla [Colombia]. One time he took me there, put me in front of a monument to a *cacique* and said, "This was you. Chief, you need to teach not what you are thinking deeply about, but what you are practicing and living. If you want to talk about the things we are learning about here, talk in your own idiom, teach your own culture. I am doing what I have to do."

This was very motivational for me, because he never at any moment gave me offense or berated me, but of course, as always, there were people at the school who were resentful of me [because I was not interested in the Tao]. . . . At that time there were procedures that to me were not punishments but actions that helped one wake up, for example, prolonged fasting. If a tayta or mama tells me to fast, well, I leave off eating immediately. I don't see it as an order. Rather it is a suggestion, something they need to say to me that is good. The maestro paid no attention to the tittle-tattle about me and would say, "Chief, come on, let's go eat," and we would go.

And so I helped them for two years with the Tao school, not because of the institution but out of the gratitude I had to Kelium Zeus Iduceus. I met this being at that stage of my life when everyone wanted more and more answers from me, and I was looking for other answers; I was looking for someone who could address my questions. Out of gratitude I helped the foundation in Pichincha, Ambato, and Esmeraldas [which are all towns in Ecuador]. I went all over, and without shyness started to talk. At first, people certainly must have been saying I was turning into a crazy man, so they came to see what I would say. I started talking and talking, and it was being well received by people who would say to me, "What do you need?"

I would reply, "I need a place where I can talk, a hall." They gave it to me, and many people turned up from various towns and right away started forming schools.

But what I talked about agreed with what I feel now. I put great emphasis on feeling, on connecting with the elements of nature, and not simply by saying, "O Pachakamak, my dear God, I thank you, help me, I thank you for the food. . . ." I believe that what is most important is to feel Pachakamak's gift. Everywhere, every moment is adequate for experimenting with spirituality, which is not separated from material things: making love is totally sacred, eating is totally sacred, taking a bath is totally sacred, using the toilet is totally sacred; life within you is totally sacred.

For some, God's name is Jehovah, for others it's Krishna, for others Kelium Zeus, for others Pachakamak. They are all the same, but for me, I identify with the name of Pachakamak, nothing else. I see no problem with this. I believe this is the moment when the limitations of institutions, of regions, of religions are being broken down. If we each are sincere, we are going to realize that we have both everything and nothing. It is a big mistake, then, to judge others just because they have one name or another. We say this is the way things are, and we don't see the qualities or virtues, but don't put others right away in a bag. It is as if someone sees another dressed as an indigenous person and says, "Ah, this person is Indian, dirty, and idle." But if they see someone dressed as a city person who smells better, then people say that he's a fine gentleman. Everything is relative.

8

Contrary Winds and
the Value of Spirituality

There have been periods in don Alberto's life when the contrary winds have been strong. These are times that he rarely mentions, but which show how often his life has been difficult. They demonstrate how he has been able to overcome hatred and conflict in his personal life to the benefit of his teaching. His life also reveals how indigenous spiritual leaders may be political ones as well. They can play a very important role in confronting a country's dominant society when minorities are oppressed.

In the 1990s indigenous political organizing in Ecuador resulted in several *levantamientos,* or uprisings, starting with a big one in 1990 in which don Alberto became a leader. The first street demonstration in fact happened outside the Santo Domingo Church in Quito, where he had spent a year living outside in the covered portal.

Sitting in my living room he showed me a YouTube video of himself wearing an indigenous fedora while giving an impassioned speech to what looked to be a crowd of thousands. I would not have recognized him. As described in an American account of Ecuadorian indigenous political history:

> The 1990 levantamiento, a nationwide uprising of many thousands [of indigenous people] . . . organized by local, regional, and national indigenous organizations, was an unexpected occurrence

to Ecuador's whites and mestizos, who were shocked to see indigenous people being "uppity." [It] clearly demonstrated that, despite the efforts of Ecuador's white and mestizo leaders to encourage the disappearance of *el indio,* many of the country's indigenous people were proudly and boldly asserting their claims to their indigenous identities, cultural practices, and community rights and territory. Importantly, Ecuador's Indian population was demanding a central role in the country's politics, a role that would enfranchise them to participate in decision-making about how they live and how they are governed. In short, the levantamiento gave notice that Ecuador's Indians were not simply rebelling; they were insisting that the country live up to its claim to be a democracy that was truly attentive to their interests and needs.[1]

In a recent presentation don Alberto was asked how one might respond to leaders who make one angry, seeing that his past response was leading street demonstrations. He said that at that time force was necessary as the only thing understood by governmental leadership, but that now we are in a different pacha where Eagle and Condor are indeed flying together in the same sky of our lives. Thus we need to meet violence with loving action that provides a shock of surprise to those employing aggression. All the great religious leaders have said to turn the other cheek.[2]

One result of the indigenous efforts of the 1990s was that care for the natural world was written into the constitution. At that time this was the only constitution in the world for which this was true, but now a movement in that direction exists internationally. This achievement greatly increased the political stature of indigenous people in Ecuador, but since then the government has been backsliding and has allowed big oil interests to take over indigenous land in the Amazon region and exploit it.[3] Very recently [2019], after riots occurred when the government tried to remove gasoline subsidies, don Alberto once again was involved in indigenous politics.

Because of his involvement in the levantamiento, don Alberto became a marked man at that time and had to go into hiding for several weeks. Soldiers were searching for him and a number of assassinations had taken place. He tells of an incident where he hid in a sagebrush bush when his pursuers were nearby; he was not seen. It appeared that he had become invisible. I have read of other incidents of indigenous people avoiding danger by becoming invisible, so I asked him how it was done. He replied, "It's natural. You were invisible, yesterday sitting on the hillside. Our friend here asked me where you were. I knew, but he didn't."

I had spent the day sitting on the slope behind his house with its sparse trees and shrubs in a parched area, my lunch brought to me. This was something he suggested that I do as an exercise for getting close to nature. It is true that I moved very little, but I find it hard to believe that I was not seen because I was invisible. Maybe my friend was not looking in the right direction. But I am happy to accept what don Alberto says, as it pleases me to think I might have been invisible.

At the present time don Alberto accepts invitations to run for public office, not because he wishes to serve in that capacity, but rather to provide a role model for the indigenous community, particularly the youth. His most recent campaign was to be mayor of the good-sized town next to where he lives, but to his relief he was not elected. For the same town he recently organized, for the first time, a festival showing the work of indigenous craftsmen. The festival lasted several days and was highly successful. I was pleased to have been able to attend it.

In spite of injustices toward our ancestors, I am offering wisdom to people of the Eagle.[4] This is the value of spirituality. The normal thing for indigenous people would be to not want to give more of anything because many injustices still exist and will exist for my people. Injustice, however, isn't ended by injustice. Hate doesn't end hate. Darkness is ended by light and hate by love. It is easy to love people who love us, but it is possible and necessary to give love to people who have wounded us because this is where the spiritual opportunity lies. Give love to conquer hate. This is why spirituality is worthwhile.

The history of native people after the arrival of the Spaniards is very hard and ugly. When I was very young this reality filled me with sadness. I didn't really understand when my elders gave offerings of great love to those who had caused them sorrow. At times I confused this with cowardice because they never reacted to injustice. Many times I was watching from the tops of trees and saw that we outnumbered those who had caused us such distress, and I thought how easy it would be for us to unite and destroy them.

One day I understood from my grandmother that life is not just this body, and that a great opportunity for advancing spiritually exists when you don't return hate with hate. When we give something beneficial, we receive greater benefit. I have proved this in my life. When I lived on the street I received what I had previously given to someone. At that time I received food and what I needed. When I give more, I receive more benefits and support from others. This goes on, increasing more and more, indefinitely.

In my tradition old people are the light on the path. Our elders, male and female, maintain this form of living. In the typical Andean family the grandmother looks after the grandchildren. They all live in the same house. When a daughter or son marries, their spouse forms part of the family. The whole large family lives in one house; this is very important for us. Everyone contributes to the wisdom; grandparents, grandchildren, great-grandchildren, teach us a lot. This is a school; the first great school is the family. Thankfully this tradition has been able to survive. We don't learn much because someone teaches us or we read, but because we watch in daily life what each one in the family does. We watch as well what nature and the elements teach us, how they change from day-to-day.

I don't remember my grandfather saying to me, "Sit down, I am going to teach you something," but he always invited me to go along with him to do the things he was doing. I was very happy being close to him and helping him. I never thought that one day I would have the responsibility I now have. It never dawned on me that one day I would become a yachak. I really wasn't getting ready for this.

Our traditions are directed toward harmony with all that exists. Everything that exists, everything that we see is a manifestation of love—love that flows from the Great Spirit of Life. We are part of that spirit of love; we come out of that principle of love. This is our form of living: to love we first have to feel. Love is not a word; love is something spontaneous that comes from the heart without distinction. It is not possible to say, "I love this but not that, I love this animal but not the other one, I love my neighbor to the right but not the one to the left." It is very important in my tradition to maintain harmony with all that exists. Our elders have told us that in the same way that we give, so we will receive. And we are interested in receiving beautiful gifts. We want life to be good, lovely, happy, and for this reason we feel respect and love for all that exists.

Everything has life—minerals, vegetables, water, wind—everything is alive. It just has a different way of presenting itself, but the essence is the same. We all form part of the same existence. We are the crystallization of Mother Nature; we all belong to her.

It is the opposite of what we think these days. We think we dominate nature, that it belongs to us—that plants, animals, minerals, and the earth lie at our feet. No. We are a very tiny part of the whole immensity of life; we come out of her. For this reason we must feel love for everything that exists. For example, feel love for what we eat, eat with gratitude and feeling, not fill our stomachs mechanically. Feeling love also means not creating trash to be thrown away. If you love something you don't waste it or dispense with it. When you have love and gratitude for a gift of life, you don't set it aside and chuck it. In every grain of rice and each lettuce leaf, the power of Creation exists. This is love and the wisdom of the Great Creator. The power of the Great Creator exists in everyone. This is a belief that is highly valued in our tradition; it has allowed our culture to survive.

PART 2

· · ·

Teachings

9

The Eagle
and Condor Dream

The prophecy of the Eagle and Condor flying together in the same sky has already been mentioned briefly in this book. From don Alberto's account of his upbringing it is clear his father and grandfather were working to further this prophecy by seeing that he was exposed to Western religion and philosophy. They wanted to facilitate his future contact with the West, which, in their time, was by no means assured.

It's my sense that many people have acquired some awareness of this prophecy in the United States in the last twenty years or so. This has occurred not only through don Alberto's teaching but also through the work of many others. I asked him to elaborate on it and why he feels that there remains the need for it to continue to be taught at the present time. My impression is that many people understand, only on a superficial level, what is really a deep teaching and a dream for the future. There is a tendency to feel that one knows it all—Oh yes, the North is logic and the South is *feeling!*

He jumped at the opportunity to elaborate, and followed by giving his advice on how to achieve what he proposes. Key to understanding his advice is to realize that don Alberto experiences all elements as sentient beings. They do not have human sentience, but nevertheless it is possible for us humans to relate to these unique elemental sentiences on a personal level if we open our awareness to them (see chapter 11).

I believe this dream, this prophecy of the Eagle and Condor flying together in the same sky, at its deepest level presents a moral challenge to the United States. The challenge is to share its strongest attributes—to an extent not contemplated up until now—as well as to become receptive to another understanding of life. The type of sharing I am referring to is a radical kind of sharing and would entail a willingness to gift other less fortunate people with our wealth, instead of accumulating possessions for our sole benefit. In return we would be given the recipients' riches of spiritual and emotional understanding—of each other and of the natural world. Such a coming together of different life ways would represent an apex of reciprocity, which is a foundational value of the indigenous people of the Andes and those of the world over. This sharing of our strengths would support one another, enhancing and ennobling life, which will help our world to survive. At the heart of it all is gratitude for the gifts of life.

Here is *the dream* in don Alberto's words, as told to me in our 2016 interview.

The wisdom of the original peoples of the world is important. All the world's original peoples are making wonderful contributions by means of which the Western world, the world of rationality, logic, and materialism, may bring alive its other qualities. These are the qualities of seeing, perception, feeling, and flowing, which allow one to go further than the current paradigms, the established concepts for exploring and knowing what is in the beyond. This is contained in prophecies or statements by the wise ones of all the world's original communities. In our case, we, the elders of the Andes, women and men both, continue to affirm that the Eagle and Condor are going to fly together in the same sky.

Eagle represents logical, rational, mental, and material functions. Condor, the largest flying bird in the Andes, for us the largest bird in the world, belongs to the Andes. It represents the other abilities: the powers of perception, flowing, and intuition wherein people allow themselves to draw on their own wisdom, on their interior knowing from their cells and their heart. Their reflections flow beyond pure, logical rationality.

We consider Condor power to be important for the world of Eagle because if one only thinks and remains attached to logic and established paradigms, one is not allowing oneself to enjoy the other part of life that human beings have access to, which is to perceive and feel. By acquiring this other way, an industrialized society may benefit the planet without causing damage to the world or to nature.

When a society educates only from a material perspective or with respect to material riches and has forgotten or left in second place the spiritual and energetic riches that constitute the richness of being human, then it is a danger to the world. Our humble offering, given with sincere hearts, is that we may all arrive at a balanced way of living in this world and in daily life. This involves the mind and the heart, Eagle and Condor, flying together in daily life. Additionally, we ask that we have the use of those material things in this *pacha,* this time and place, that require logic and reason to understand and achieve.

People who are very developed intellectually and mentally, as they are in the world of the Eagle—the lands of the North—have the power of the Condor. Although all human beings have this power, in many it is not yet developed. This is because they don't often come across natural opportunities to develop this power of perception, feeling, and intuition in their familiar social contexts. But in my life, everyone has occasionally made use of and has flowed with these powers of feeling and perception. They may have done this many times. For example, if someone loves another person, it is not suitable for logic to be imposed, or for it to be allowed to meddle. They are going to lose their feeling, their love for this person if the mind interferes. We must allow our power of feeling to flow, which is different from passion. The passion one has for another person is different from love for that person.

In the world of the Eagle, people also have this power. They feel, they love, they perceive, they intuit, but what happens is that they do not have enough personal space or education or stimulation to continue to want this perception. Rather, they have a great urge to develop their mental and rational ability—in school, through other educational pursuits, in the family, in society. There is constant stimulation for people to become very logical and rational.

On the other hand, in the worlds of ancient cultures surviving today, what was most important was the development of perception and intuition, not that minds were not being trained or that we are not developing the mind now. We have minds too, and we do that. But the important thing at this time is—no matter how much academic preparation urban or rural cultures have or don't have—that we all develop as human beings.

So those who have the qualities of the power of the Eagle need to develop a bit more the power of the Condor: perception, intuition, feeling, flowing. And those who have developed Condor power a lot and lack the Eagle power need to cultivate qualities of logic.

Now is the time for us all to walk in balance, for Eagle and Condor to fly together in daily living; or for mind, reason, heart, intuition, perception, flowing, all to be together permanently in daily living without conflict, without struggle, and without looking for one to prevail against the other. It is time to be together without one of the powers quashing or attacking the other inharmoniously, each one in its own space and its own sphere of action.

What life needs is flowing, feeling, perceiving, love, intuition, and natural human feeling, especially for nature, for living in harmony, in balance. We need to understand open-mindedly that we live in a world where everything is interrelated, where everything flows, and there is mutual influence and connectedness of all feeling between all beings. At the end of the day all that we do, think, and say, and how we live, influences everyone else and comes back to us. And it has influenced ourselves as well.

Therefore, at this time when the world already sees and feels it requires a more humane society, one that is more just, more intimately connected with the elements and Mother Nature, this is our offering. It is the dream of more humane societies to be respectful of Mother Nature, to be mindful of the influence we effect and receive, and that we arrive at a society with technology that is developed and has wisdom. To say it another way, it is time that we gain a society with rational scientific knowledge and ancestral knowledge that contributes in the here and now to restoration and sustainability, not being destructive in a mindless way. If only we may understand better, may we learn to exist in a manner more harmonious with Mother Nature and the cosmos, with everything and everyone.

When we are connected to the elements, we can perceive the Creator of life. We can say, I feel God.[1] Many world cultures have their own directions for learning to feel; others, especially modern cultures, think it is necessary to have equilibrium, a balance in life. For those societies that focus on cultivating feelings, ones that are only feeling cultures, they need to focus on thinking. Both the powers of feeling and thinking are important at this time. When someone is focused only in one direction, empty places exist in his or her life. The easiest way of being in balance with ourselves is through contact with the elements.

It is through the elements that we have a direct channel to the Great Spirit of Life. Always remember that we are not outside Mother Nature, we are within her, and we must not forget that we are within the Great Spirit also. The mind has lied and convinced people that they are apart, separated, but it is not so, we are part of this. Not allowing oneself to feel this reality brings us suffering; many people in this present society are confused and suffer.

But everyone has a key. It can be practicing deep breathing or listening to water. In this way, wherever you insert it, you can activate your key—and many people have two or more keys. The mechanism is to feel wherever you are, all of the time. It's not a competition; feel little by little, for feeling the elements is to feel God. Feeling ourselves is to feel God because everything that exists is a part of the Great Spirit of Life; one has moved away from just *thinking* about God.

Depending on the culture, God is given different names but it doesn't matter. What matters is feeling Spirit in all the elements and in ourselves. If we flow with love, close to the elements, we will be able to "see" and will float toward the wisdom of God, which is how my people conceive of God.

Feeling this experience is something we need at this time. Beliefs can lead us to fanaticism and the fanatic can become dangerous. When we connect with and feel the elements, we also feel something magnificent. If we feel God, we will not be so far away; we will realize we are part of Spirit. We can describe a meal in various ways but if we eat it we will know it. We are not just believing that it is one way or another because we know its taste. No, we have tried it; we have eaten it. At this moment all the powers of life are here inside each one of us. Life force is in the earth, the sky, the water, in each cell of our bodies—in every aspect of this reality.

Capturing the wisdom of all that surrounds us, this is the teaching of our elders: to feel life and to love Mother Nature, little by little, slowly. And if we forget, don't stay forgetful but keep going and connect again with all aspects of life. This is the spiritual path, the path of wisdom, the walk of the wise. Wisdom is like a pristine butterfly in the light. It is inside all of us; it is in the connection with the elements, it is in joy, in our becoming childlike, it is in allowing ourselves to be free and fly like birds.

Feeling the power of the Condor is the response of our whole being without the mind's interference and without thoughts. What I mean by "feeling" is to perceive closely with our heart. Feeling, or sensing, is a different bodily function than thinking. We sense more when we are relaxed, not just when our body is relaxed, but our feelings, emotions, and thoughts.

The ability to feel, though, differs from the sensation that is felt through the five senses. We can touch with our fingers, but what we touch with them needs to be sensed both with and from the heart. This is feeling.

When summer comes we do not need to think; we just feel the wind, we feel the sun, we experience, we sense, we enjoy that summer has come. It is the same thing when we have intimate contact with the elements and with God. We then feel complete and remember to be complete. Developing our power of feeling becomes simpler and simpler all the time if we are alert to the four elements—water, earth, air, and fire. Great Mother Nature and the Great Spirit of Life work for us through the elements of nature.

As an example, in taking a shower or bath, you feel the water touching you: sense that this being too is feeling in its own way as well as touching your skin. Water's power enters into all our organs and makes us healthy. When showering at home in the morning, allow the subtle energy of the water to enter each of your cells with its energy, power, and wisdom, so that each cell comes alive. In the same way that it cleans our skin, it also has the power to clean our mind, our consciousness, and our interior state. Washing the impurities from our bodies, the water entering our pores heals our emotions, our falling spirits, our negative energy. Throughout, the only attitude we have to have, what we need, is a willingness to receive this energy, to be open to receive and immensely enjoy our showering or bathing—whether in the morning, noon, or night. In order to experience that it not only benefits the skin but is beneficial to our whole being, put all your emotion, intention, mind, heart, and love into the water.

We are part of the water and the water is part of us. Water is life and we are life. In this way we receive the power of water. It is the same with wind, earth, and fire. It is also the same with Mother Nature. The mind says, *Where, when?* Well, all the time, wherever it may be.

We can do this again when we receive wonderful gifts from Mother Nature, from Mother Earth; the food we receive at table when we have decided to eat. What we are doing is receiving earth transformed by means of all the elements of nature and cosmos so that it is distilled in an apple, lettuce, a tomato—in all the meals we eat when we are hungry. This is a very special moment of intimate contact with the gifts of Mother Nature, or intimate contact with the earth. Here I mean the power of the earth, the wisdom of earth that enters into our cells, our energy, our physical, chemical, energetic, and spiritual makeup, or whatever you want to call it.

The foods we serve ourselves are the product of transformation brought about by the days and nights. Through the participation of the moon, the sun, the nutrients in the subsoil and soil, textures, tastes, colors, and fragrances have been developed, all for us. So we politely make a meal and receive this food with conscious minds and hearts. In this we are not only receiving vitamins, minerals, carbohydrates, and amino acids but also the energetic part of the food—its wisdom, which is something more than mere material substance.

If we eat in this way, alert to what we consume, feeling and savoring nature's gift with thankfulness, the gratitude is going to take a natural form because we are immensely enjoying this gift in this moment while we are eating. And we are not doing it mechanically but in a natural way. In this we are receiving the essential part, the energetic part, the wisdom of Mother Earth.

This, then, becomes a beautiful, simple, and easy ritual of great power, for physical and emotional health, so that those parts of us that we are not using may be brought to life and may have more perspective, more intuition, and be more fluid without losing our intelligence or knowledge or anything else.

It is very important to have intimate contact with nature and it's not difficult. Thinking is difficult, although thinking is natural. Thinking about the wind is complicated, but sensing the wind is natural, easy. It's the same thing with the other elements. We ourselves are a part of nature. Our mind understands this, but now we must be able to *feel* it is true. It is important to think and know this truth, but it is more important to feel this truth. Many things exist that we can know, but at the present time it is urgent to feel what we know. In order to be able to feel what we know, we must feel everything; this is the path to follow. For example, we know how important air is. We know its physical and chemical properties. A way of feeling air is breathing in a conscious manner, and when the air is moving, it is important to feel and be conscious of when the air is touching us. Not many words exist that explain the feeling of the experience of air.

Up to 1989 emphasis was on the function of thinking, but from that year on, many things have come to the fore, and feeling is one of them.* This is the Andes' responsibility—to invite people to take part in feeling, to follow this path of feeling. It is not anything like a new religion or technique, but an invitation to take advantage of what we already know, to feel more, to make our lives complete with more intentional feeling. Feeling helps us realize that everything is sacred. In Kichwa there is no word for *sacred* or *profane,* all things from the smallest to the largest are sacred. Everything is sacred. Each one is a part of the whole and the whole is a part of each.

My invitation to you is to become a new being, to augment your power of feeling. Friendship with the elements is a portal through which you can enter and you will be able to find the power of feeling. When we feel complete, when we are feeling fully, it is like having encountered water. It is natural for the mind to say one has not heard or been given any message after this contact. However, this type of communication gives us a special feeling of tranquility, and afterward, when we go home, a solution will blossom.

---

*In the Andean understanding of the cosmos, after this date we entered into a period of pachakuti, the world turning over to a new five-hundred-year age. (For more on pachakuti see chapter 20.)

10

Sumak Kausay, "Abundant Life"

The Condor gift that don Alberto brings to the lands of the Eagle is *Sumak Kausay,* which means "Abundant Life" in Kichwa. It is the basic principle of living for the indigenous of the Andes. It requires a kind of awareness—a living in the moment—that entails a deep ability to feel connected to what is around us. In this we are able to appreciate the gifts nature and life bestow on us constantly. While we all have this ability, don Alberto's perception is more developed than that of most people, certainly more than those of us who grew up in the culture of the West. What follows in this and succeeding chapters is his continuing advice on how to live into this ability more fully.

All of us human beings are distinct universes, with preoccupations, joys, and sadness: we each have our own life.[1] Because the mind shoots off to one side or the other, our thoughts can lead us astray—we don't realize what we are doing.

I want to talk to you about a frequency that we need to find in our lives, one that can be compared to a radio frequency we tune into. Like radios, we human beings have frequencies also, and at times we tune into anger and at others sadness or euphoria. What we need to do is find a frequency that tunes into what in Spanish is called *conciencia* [awareness]; to find that frequency that allows each one of us to know what we are doing, to feel when the wind touches us, to feel every movement of our bodies. To be at that level of awareness is to feel, to be present.

I don't just teach thinking, I teach feeling; feeling when we move, consciously feeling when we breathe, feeling everything we smell, what we see or touch, feeling our heart beat. Our brains are all the time producing sparks and neuronal connections. This is what we are going to wake up to today. We are going to feel we are alive. I am going to know how I am, what I am doing, what I am seeing, where I am, for what purpose I do things and why I do things. We are here and now. *Kaypimi kani, kaypimi kanchik* (Here I am, here we are). Don't behave like robots, like automatic beings.

There are various levels of connection on the path. For example, one is to look; another is to look and listen; another to look, listen, and smell; another to look, listen, smell, and feel what you touch, noticing movement. Register all of these and then adopt and continue this all the time in a daily practice. When this is achieved I consider that one is at the best level of connection because it is a way of life we need to continue, to flow like the Great Cosmos, the Great Pachakamak.

In order to receive nature's gifts, it is important to feel the elements. As we know, we can feel water, air, fire, and earth. Everyone has a special element, an element with which we identify most, and this is the one with which we have to practice. Children connect rapidly because they live in permanent contact and because they are always playing. This doesn't happen to most people because they have already decided with their minds that things are serious. We may become bitter beings. I invite you to look at yourself in the mirror from time to time, and pay attention to the face you have. Perhaps you'll see a strong-minded face, or one that makes you laugh, or you'll see you have wrinkles, or how you pucker up your muscles. If your face looks serious or sad, smile at it and make yourself feel better!

Feeling is a very important attribute in our lives. Colors become more brilliant and our eyes begin to see better and with more intentionality. Life is not the way one thinks of it. No, life is the way it is. For this reason we need always to give thanks for the gifts we receive every day. And when we receive these gifts from the cosmos, we should also, in another way, return them to the cosmos. It is very important that this should come from the heart. Our Mother Earth, in a very generous way, gives us everything we need to live, and we don't say thank you—or worse, we don't offer any gifts to our Mother in return.

I want to give you an example. When we go to a bank and take out a loan, we give back this money with some interest, and it is the same in relationships between people: one feels happy to receive and also to give, and one knows it is right when one gives more than one receives. To feel happiness is to feel gratitude to life. Many times we are blocked because we think we must give thanks with our minds, but this doesn't always flow smoothly. Happiness flows naturally from people. This is a beautiful way of giving thanks: living happily is a way of giving thanks to life. The invitation is to make a fiesta out of every day of our lives. This doesn't depend on a calendar: it is in each one of us. We don't need a government decree. We just need to be awake and say to our minds and hearts, *This is another day to celebrate!* And then our minds will say, *What are you going to celebrate?*

There are many things we can celebrate every day. Every day we can walk, feel, we can appreciate the sunset, we can drink when we feel thirsty and feel refreshed, we can make love and be loved, we can talk, laugh; all of this is gratitude, and we human beings are all doing it. However, we don't realize it because to our mind these are not ways of giving thanks. What is loveliest is when our minds also enter into this circle of gratitude, when our minds understand that we are giving thanks with all our feelings and every part of our bodies. Again, this happens when we talk, cook, play, laugh, walk, and eat, even when we give thanks for crying, when we sleep, and when we rest.

To exist is a great gift. In other philosophies when they speak of ecstasy, it is no other than this feeling of plenty and harmony, of happiness to be prolonged for as long as possible. In Kichwa we call it Sumak Kausay, which we have discussed earlier. It means "Life fully expanded, fullness of feeling." I could die right now and that would be alright. In the same way that expressions of gratitude are offered when we feel things, expressions of love may also be offered: love toward oneself, and much love toward other people one's eyes see as well as those they don't. When we experiment with this feeling of gratitude and love, there is happiness. Happiness is not an objective we must reach for but a continual expression: it is comprised of feelings from within, and for what we receive from without. Happiness exists and happens. And happiness is linked to giving thanks, including giving thanks for difficult moments and for people who harm us, because this allows us to fly higher, to feel more, and have greater clarity and love.

In these times many people need to receive special gifts. But they cannot receive them because they are full of things that no longer serve them and as a result they lose themselves. Many people carry too much baggage that has become unnecessary. The mind thinks we need to be weighed down with many things, but what we need to keep in mind is that if we were going to ascend a mountain, the more baggage we take the more difficult it will be. Also, we would need to be ready to jettison entirely the things we did not need to carry further. We need not carry sorrow or sufferings, whatever it might be that preoccupies us. Let's hand them over and let them go.

The things we need to let go of are not necessarily bad, but are not useful at this time in our lives. We need to be grateful for those things that came to us at a certain time but not hang on to them any longer. We must say goodbye to them and allow them to leave. When we say goodbye to what preoccupies us, we will receive the things we need. Many times we suffer because we don't understand certain circumstances. Suffering brings many people to their knees but still they don't want to let their suffering go.

The different elements—*Waira Mama* (Wind), *Yaku Mama* (Water), *Nina Mama* (Fire), and *Allpa Mama* (Earth)—help us get rid of these difficulties. There are some difficulties and diseases that water can cure; others that the wind can help to distance; others that Mother

Earth can change; and still other problems and illnesses that fire can transform. We can let go of unnecessary baggage in many different ways, for example through laughter. Laughter helps us leave many things behind. To be too serious doesn't allow us to let go of things.

Wind is therapeutic because it helps us to clear our minds, to distance ourselves from unnecessary thoughts. The wind relaxes and frees us. When we are full of disturbances and sorrows, we can try to feel the wind. We need to allow wind to cleanse our mental blocks. It can take away many things in our soul and give us the things we need. It will only do this, however, when we let go of prejudicial baggage so that we will be able to receive the wonderful things that life wants to give us.

Water frees and cleanses us from things we don't need in the same way, because it too cleans us inside and allows us to flow, and it doesn't allow us to get stagnant.

Fire also allows us to walk away from our emotions and the sad situations that we may have experienced at a given moment. This prompting that sacred fire offers us enables us to give over to it all of our sorrows, illnesses, sufferings, vices, and to cleanse them, that is to say, burn them, get rid of this baggage we are grasping. This will be effective if we feel how the elements are working on these things, but it must not be done in a mechanical way. We have to see, feel, and listen to how the elements remove these negative conditions and turn them into things that are sublime.

For **Earth's** help, we need to lie on her, bury ourselves in her, feel her love; she too helps us be liberated from what we need to be free of. Earth feeds us, nurtures us, and we depend on her for our well-being. Without her gifts, brought to us through nature, we could not continue to exist.

If we don't clean out our home, if we don't have physical space, we can't receive more things. Our home is like our being, and the largest room is the mind. Many things exist in our minds that we don't need; we have too much anxiety and are too preoccupied. It is necessary to eliminate these things. Another lovely room is the heart, and here too we can have things we should not have. We have rooms filled with sorrow and sufferings when we have pictures in our minds of ourselves stuck in one pose. What I mean to say is that we see ourselves in static form being what we are and were. But perhaps we don't want to be like that. We may long to be another way that is more harmonious, more dynamic, and freer.

We need to clean out these rooms, get rid of these images. When we eliminate this, in our home, we have more space to receive gifts. None of us wants these gifts to be outside under the rain; we don't want them left outside our home. This happens a lot. We want gifts but we can't receive them because there is no space. And so I invite you to create new habits of connection to achieve contact with the Great Spirit of Life.

When my people go to a waterfall, we take an offering. We give her something to thank her. We leave gifts, we say and feel beautiful things for the river or the mountain, and when we leave we say goodbye. We do this in the same way that we would do if we were to visit a family member or a friend. Other times we bring music and dance; we share our happiness with the waterfall or mountain or lake, or with a tree. Spirituality and creativity are qualities of the heart; technique and method are qualities of the mind. We do not want to struggle against the mind; both mind and heart are essential—thinking and feeling—Eagle and Condor flying together in harmony and clarity with us.

We need to give thanks for food, and again, not waste anything. Food is our Mother's love. It serves no purpose to give a fervent prayer for food if we throw it away. We must give thanks because we have abundant food here, to have been born in a time and place where we have abundance. And if this abundance were not here, still we must give thanks, including for poverty, because it allows us to feel immensely when we receive simple things.

Poverty is a teacher. Everything teaches us, and everything demonstrates wisdom to us. Each person is born into the circumstances that he or she needs; we must give thanks for these circumstances and use them correctly. Material poverty can also become a blessing in that material things are complementary, they are not essential. People who do not have material goods think that when they have them they will be happy. People who have much, on the other hand, are bored, they want something simple. The essential thing is to feel gratitude for what we have and what we lack.

We need to give thanks also when we are going to sleep, for what we have learned and what we will learn while dreaming. For me, morning hours belong to the sun's day, and night hours belong to the moon. In the evening, as well, give thanks for the sun's day and that of the moon.

If we are open at every moment of our lives, conscious all the time, knowing what we are doing, and why, and for what we are doing it, it is easier for us to be aware when we are asleep and living in another reality, or what everyone considers dreaming to be. When we are aware of this, when we have awareness that we are asleep and dreaming, we need to grip something that is very close to us in this reality, and then we will know that we can take control of our dream. This could be something as simple as a pillow or a bedside table. Then we need to jump as if wanting to fly, and go up. When we are in this other reality the laws of physics that exist in this reality don't exist, and we can do unimagined things. This is what is commonly called the astral journey. This state is exactly what is needed for learning things in other realities. In dreams gravity doesn't exist.

We already have knowledge, philosophy, religion, technology, and all of this is important on our path, but now we must live it through habits of connection, through being open all the time, feeling all we do in the natural business of our lives. The invitation is to experiment with things that we already know in our daily lives. This will help us understand the lofty within the simple, to think about these practices and reflect on them, be thankful to the elements, be thankful for what we feel, and express gratitude before the sacredness of life, in each moment, in every place we go.

Then we will be full of happiness.

11

Building Habits of Connection

I invite you to create a new habit of life, new habits of connection, to achieve contact with the Great Spirit of Life.[1] Among human beings in ancient times, these forms of connections were open; children started out with clean and open channels, but now society and our way of living either helps or closes these channels. It is necessary to adopt certain habits to be successful in cleansing these channels; to create a culture that step-by-step guides us to harmony. This is different from the way in which we actually live now. Our actions and activities should be carried out with our hearts; they should have a feeling of significance and transcendence, taking us in the direction of feeling.

We should always give thanks, in every manifestation of life. We should give thanks also to ourselves, our bodies, because the body, its material, allows us to be conscious that we are alive. We need to give thanks to the five elements and all the directions, for they are our equals; they just have other manifestations.

My intention is to remove culture's blindfold for us to consider ourselves more a part of Mother Nature. We are her children and we are brothers and sisters to all that manifests life—that is to say, everything that surrounds us.

In my tradition it is important to have intimate contact with the elements of life. This guarantees that we have harmonious lives and promotes life and the cosmos entering into us and filling us with that life and happiness. When we are distanced from them, we are in danger of having problems with harmony and our health. When on our path we are united in relationship to the elements, every day of our life has significance. The four elements everyone knows are earth, water, air, and fire, and there is a fifth that we call *ushay*, which is the four elements that have come together in harmony. When we have the fifth element in our life we gain harmony.

If we eat something, and while we eat are conscious that it comes from the earth, then this "earth" feeds the earth that is our bodies. We are earth walking. To be in harmony with the elements means to acquire the power of healing our bodies, minds, and emotions, to fill our lives with happiness.

We can start being connected with any of the elements. It's not difficult; it doesn't require reading books. We just have to feel, feel that we are breathing, and receive the air with gratitude because each breath insures our body has life. When we breathe we are breathing in the power of life, and when we are conscious of this gift of air, then we are filled with the wisdom of air.

Wisdom is not so far off, it is not outside of ourselves, it is always with us. Greet the elements in the way we greet people we know. Understand that listening to nature's symphony is a way of being grateful—and smelling Earth's scents. These are ways of being grateful.

I think the trees, mountains, earth, and such are only different forms of life. They *are* all alive though. We should not think that we are different; we are all living beings. A tree has a different manner of being. We were formed with another one and we have ways of communicating with each other. A tree has its own ways of communicating, and this is what is so special about life: each form of life has its own characteristics. There are many things we can learn from this tree, as from each one of us. If I start to say hello to you and we open a channel of communication, then with my heart and mind I can learn from you. But if I don't open my heart, there is no communication and I will learn nothing from you.

The elements are not only outside of us, what is outside is also inside of us. We have fire inside us and as proof, our temperature *shows* that inside we have fire. We have water, we have air throughout our whole being, and we have skin. Our skin is our "sky," our muscles and bones are the stones, our "desert." Respect for nature starts with ourselves when we give thanks and have respect, when we open our hearts and minds, and when we begin to learn extraordinary things.

Inside each one of us and each of the elements exists the spark of life. Although we have a distinct appearance and have different organs for communication, the organ that allows us to talk with other forms of life is the heart. When we achieve this communication, although the mind may not understand, our whole being will because it has felt it.

Flowing and feeling allow us to advance on the personal path our life is following, even when we think we have lost our way. When we feel our lives flowing we are advancing. But advancing to where? Where is it that we shall arrive? Where is this place? It is exactly here, in this time and space. Everything is within each one of us; the only thing we have to do is help ourselves to feel. We have to be like children, spontaneous and natural. When people look at us cozying up to a tree and talking to it, they'll think we are crazy, but it doesn't matter. Those people won't be able to enjoy things like we do.

It is necessary to make the wisdom that is in each one of us come into flower. But the mind will say you are not wise. The mind will say you have to read more or that you need to walk further along your path. The mind is a great trainer; it is very useful. We need to talk even more with it because the mind is not our enemy. It is a power in these times. It is best to be friends with the mind, but when it tells us that we still have a long road to run and even now we're not wise, then we'll reply that we have everything that we need in life.

I'll say to you now that we are going to open the doors of our hearts and start to receive the gifts that life gives us. These are things it has given us before we were born and much more afterward. We need to feel the help of wind, water, earth, and fire, as well as the assistance of Father Sun and the whole of life that comes along in this moment. When we are connected then things that are outside of us are less important and the mind returns to being calmer and friendlier to us: it trains us and tests us and helps us on our path.

CONNECTING WITH EARTH

Every time we eat is an opportunity to connect with the Earth, or Allpa Mama: food is Mother Earth's love crystallized. We can feel her power, harmony, and wisdom whenever we eat: apples and lettuce are transformations of the Earth that express her love for us. If we eat with love, and not mechanically, we fill our hearts and stomachs with her love, nourishing the spirit as well as the body. Earth gives us many lessons. For example, she always gives—she transforms what is negative into the sublime. Another lesson is to share; she always shares her gifts. We must learn from her and be capable of sharing. She is in union with life in all its aspects. Remember, we have a body that is earth, just like everything that surrounds us—computers, cars, clothing, food—everything is earth. We have many opportunities to connect ourselves with her and communicate with her power. We can in various ways turn ourselves into apprentices of her wisdom.

What we eat is transformed earth, thanks to the great love of our Mother. This love is reflected in the whole of food's composition: its agreeable smell, attractive color, pleasant appearance, and delicious taste. Every meal is a great opportunity for putting us in intimate contact with the love of our Mother. When we enter into contact with her, we receive her secrets and wisdom.

Food has made a great journey to reach us, miracle by miracle as to its fragrance, taste, and form. It is a great gift of the Mother and the Great Spirit of Life. We are their children to whom they give their gifts. They love us very much. It would be wonderful if we all were conscious of how food is cared for, looked after, cultivated, transported, packaged, and prepared, and after that we could savor the taste that enters into us to nourish all our senses. If we were to understand all of this, then we would be thankful for this great miracle. If we were to understand this then gratitude would flow from us spontaneously, and gratitude brings happiness. We are turning ourselves into beings of light, of life, and wisdom.

Again, gratitude is an expression that brings us many gifts and we can practice gratitude three times a day. Eating with gratitude opens the door to wisdom. If you forget and you remember later, do it another time. This is the most real and permanent religion; it is spirituality without your having to say, "I am spiritual." It is simpler. Heaven is not up above, a long way away, it is here.

The entryway to wisdom is not far away, it is closer than you think. For the mind it's difficult if you think, *How am I going to do this?* You can't do it, but if you take grapes and bring them to your mouth with gratitude, savoring the taste and giving more thanks because they contain vitamins and please your pallet, then it is easy. You don't think much, you just do it. It is necessary when you eat to feel happy, to enjoy it. This is a way of giving thanks for the gift of food. In food all the elements exist together, and the harmony of these elements produces the fifth element, ushay. When we are connected to these gifts they have a very special energy, and this is how we are going to eat the energy that will fill our hearts and our spirit.

Give thanks before eating and after eating. If you have something to say, express it, and you will also savor the thanks through which food gives us energy. Each mouthful of food fills us with the special energy of Mother Earth, and for this reason we must not waste it. Not wasting even a nibble of food is a fervent prayer to our Mother.

CONNECTING WITH AIR

Do you think it's important to be grateful for breathing? To be thankful for the air we breathe? We are breathing all the time so we can take part in this. We must feel how the air, or Waira Mama, comes in by the nose and circles around in the head and throat, and feel how it fills the lungs. Allow yourself to enjoy the possibility of life that air offers. You can receive many benefits when you feel your breathing at every moment. Breathing is something we can do at every moment anywhere. If we feel our breathing it is very different from breathing without feeling. If we feel our respiration inside, we will feel it filling our hearts as much as it fills our lungs. We need to give thanks for each breath because air sustains our life. And step-by-step we will discover that all the activities of our lives are miracles, and we will be able to enjoy life's every moment. It's simple and easy.

When you breathe air in a feeling manner, you can bring to you everything you may wish for, so ask for what you need in your life. When air fills you, wait a moment, don't let it go, and after that breathe out through your mouth, very gently, but do it with feeling. If you do it without feeling, you will not be taking advantage of this exercise. When breathing, feel grateful because it is life you are receiving. This is a practice we can do continually with the consciousness of receiving life. It's important to do it with gratitude, everywhere, at every moment that we may think of it, because since birth we have been breathing. Now the only difference is to do it with feeling and gratitude. No matter what we happen to be doing—whether we are walking, cooking, driving, thinking, talking—we always need to breathe with gratitude.

This is possible right now. Close your eyes and breathe slowly. Feel your breathing, remembering that you can do this constantly without closing your eyes, because we are always breathing, all the time. We can always feel the air. It's natural for the mind to say to itself that it is necessary to be in a special place where we can meditate. My invitation is that we can do this at any moment, in any place; we need the benefit of air at each moment. This can be turned into a habit, and we will discover beautiful things because we will know as well the power of air, the power that is life.

Do it bit by bit. Be grateful, for to breathe with feeling is to connect yourself with the power of air. It's natural. I am no friend of techniques and complicated methods. For this we don't need an official school where we read a lot or memorize things we will never use in our lives. Are you going to go on feeling your respiration? It doesn't matter if you forget. What's important is that each time you remember to do it, do it. Then it will become a habit—a habit I have given you that makes it possible to know the power of air.

All of this shouldn't be a solemn practice but done like a child's game. Children play and perhaps don't do it well, but they go on playing and it becomes a habit and they repeat the game many times. It is important to find happiness in doing this. If you practice solemnly it is possible you will bring off the physical part, but you won't find the essence.

You can also feel air in another form. If someone feels the air around his or her body, it's similar to a fish in water. It's as if we are in a great fishbowl of air. Another way of feeling air is through a bird's flight, or when we hold a feather and let it go; then we can feel the quality of air. We can feel its power.

Listen to the air, to the wind blowing in the branches, breathing in the movement of the treetops. We can see it in the dancing leaves. It is lovely to lie down and see how the air moves the leaves. For myself, I am carried along very rapidly if there are clouds in the sky that move with the wind. When this happens, I feel as if I am carried in the opposite direction. Feel the air that comes in and goes out of your body and feel it all around you.

CONNECTING WITH WATER

Who cannot be in love with being near a body of water, a river, lake, lagoon, or the ocean? Water, known in our culture as Yaku Mama, holds a natural attraction for us. We are able to benefit just through the act of feeling ourselves near a body of water. I have already suggested a simple recommendation for feeling the power of water on a daily basis: take advantage of your shower or bath. Otherwise we may connect with water wherever we encounter it: swimming or standing

Giving thanks to water: don Alberto Taxo

in a pond, visiting a spring or waterfall, or at the beach. We can do this simply by feeling water on our skin, feeling how it takes care of us; we can feel water gently in the palms of our hands, feel how it circulates in the space between our fingers, and as often as you do this, express what your heart desires. We can even do this with snow. The most wonderful of things is the most simple when you start to feel.

Many times we look for sophisticated practices; the mind searches for them but does not reach an end to its search. What we need to do is practice, and we can do it when we feel what we are doing in the moment, causing feelings of transformation. The most ordinary ceremonial actions can have the most wonderful and magical effects. There exist many other ways of using the power of water, and we don't need ostentatious rituals. It is enough to get close to a river or a lake, and we also can take advantage of rain.

The Eagle with its books* says we are at least 50 percent water, depending on our age, and certain cells contain more than 75 percent water. We can use this information to transform water in a ceremony of feeling, to feel the water that runs through our veins. Water is very sensitive, it's transforming, and when we give water love it cleanses us. It gives us tranquility, helps, and cures us. When we meet someone for the first time, we feel apprehension initially, but little by little we turn into friends. We talk more and are thankful. This is the way a relationship with water should be, always conducted with respect and sincerity, a communication from the heart. In this way we will achieve friendship with water and all the elements. When we become friends with the elements, as when we have friends among people, if we have problems those friends will be there to help us.

We can look to many different ways of communicating with water: when we have a shower, when we drink, when we feel the water in our bodies and blood as a river that flows internally. Our relationship with water is not just outside but internal. Everywhere and at every moment we have an opportunity of connecting with it. When we succeed we will have fewer problems and our lives will flow like a river because water will respond when we communicate with it: if we communicate with love it gives us love.

Water has great power to accumulate information and exists in great proportion in all of nature. The wind has water and even the fire has water. Let's go for a walk with water. Look for connections with water and when you find them, allow your heart to feel what it wants to feel. The mind thinks it is easier to get close to a river to make this connection, but we need to remember always that the major part of our bodies is water.

Water doesn't just cleanse the skin; it also cleanses other things that we are not allowing ourselves to do freely. When water flows and there is an obstruction, water doesn't move backward but goes forward

---

*A reference to North American scholars.

and doesn't stop looking for another way to go. A small space gives it great power and in many cases it continues with more force. We need to know water's method of operating and its power in order not to stagnate in our lives. In difficult moments we need to remember how water does not go backward, and we also need to remember that water always looks for a way out. Rising quickly or slowly in a given space it looks for an appropriate exit and always finds it.

Intimate contact with water can give us everything we want in life, both material and spiritual. I believe that in different cultures, philosophies, and mystical arts, water has always held an important place. But in modern life people have become separated from the need to respect water. If we want to live a life of harmony and plenty, we need to act in a natural way with the elements. Practice this at every moment in every place. Let's wholeheartedly connect with water.

CONNECTING WITH FIRE

Each one of us has sacred fire burning inside of us, inside our persons and bodies. It gives us life because sacred fire gives everything a hue. This element, Nina Mama, makes us all sacred. To feel fire we can create various ceremonies or simple rituals; we can light a fire or a candle or burn incense. Look at the flame for a moment, then close your eyes but keep on seeing it. Repeat this by looking and feeling this flame inside your heart. This firelight is vital for our lives, as with all the other elements. We have it lit inside each one of us; we can appreciate feeling the warmth of our bodies and feeling passion through our emotions. Fire burns destructive things and gives us light. Friendship and love allow us to feel this sacred fire.

Fire also is therapeutic; we can throw in the fire everything that brings us problems, everything we don't need to keep. We can use interior and exterior means for connecting ourselves with fire. Often we think we need an open space to build a wood fire to connect to Nina Mama, but this is not so; each one of us has a fire lit in our interior.

In many ancestral cultures people speak of sacred fire. In my Kichwa language a word for sex does not exist. Everything we do with sexual awareness is called "sacred fire." This fire plays a part in helping us activate life because it transforms many things. In a fire outside, the circle of stones represents the female sexual organ. The wood represents the male aspect, and the union of the two brings about the kindling of life. Fire is active constantly and brings life to life. Fire illuminates our lives and makes us see ourselves in a sacred manner. It is very powerful, and if we don't know how to use it, we can burn. We need to give it respect because it allows life to continue and it allows us to transform from one state to another. With fire we can illuminate life and have faith. We need to feel fire's heat but not burn ourselves with it. We need to maintain the sacred fire but not allow it to spread and burn other things.

Sacred fire is not just the union of two people; it is also when two hearts feel something special. Everything in nature is activated by sacred fire; nothing exists in nature without it. Flowers are the sexual organs of plants, and the most beautiful colors and most delicious fragrances are concentrated in flowers. Flowers always turn toward the sun. When sacred fire is activated in a flower, fruit appears, and these contain the sacred fire of the plants. Each one of us has this fire inside us. We must give thanks for this, give thanks for the light we receive every day, give thanks for the presence of the sun. With its help we can transform things and eliminate other things that we now don't need in our lives.

This age is the Age of Woman and she is the only one who can use sacred fire in the best manner. Woman illumines the way with fire.

12

A Yachak Apprentices' Retreat

The top of Itchimbia hill in Quito is known to indigenous people as a sacred area. It is thought that an *intiwatana,* or Incan "Hitching Post of the Sun," was located there. This name *intiwatana* implies a stone or pole at places where, at the two equinoxes of the year, the sun appears to stand still for a while overhead. This gave rise to the idea that the sun had been seized by the Earth and attached to a hitching post. Perhaps the most well-known *intiwatana* is a stone at Machu Picchu in Peru. Ceremonies were held in such locations to help open vision to the spirit world. The Quito municipality has created a park on Itchimbia with patterns formed in concrete on the ground. These represent the Chakana or design of the Incan cosmos and the directions of the summer and winter solstices. They are comprised of small stone pillars for the lunar months and the high wooden pole of the *intiwatana.* On either side are circular stone enclosures, one that holds water, and the other, sand, for the placement of fires. Both are important for the Earth's fertility. While this installation emphasizes the sun, in don Alberto's understanding, Itchimbia is sacred to the moon.

Ever since I was seven years old my grandparents and parents brought me to this mountain, and afterward my own feet brought me until I was twenty-two years old. This isn't any old place but a special place to make the quality of the female come alive and connect oneself to it. This place is female, and Yavirac [the nearby mountain called Panecillo in

Spanish] is male. This is our Andean world; the serpent also represents the feminine aspect. They were wrong to put a statue of the Virgin on Panecillo because that mountain represents the male. The Virgin, who for people of the West is a symbol of the female, ought to be on this mountain, on Itchimbia, because it is the Temple of the Moon.[1]

Don Alberto took my friend and me to Itchimbia late one afternoon. He asked me to go and stand on a low earth mound on one side of the ceremonial area. This was the female mound, he told me. He then went and stood on a similar mound on the other side, the male one. I didn't know what I was supposed to do but, watching him, I saw he was praying and so I offered my thanks to be able to be in that place at that time.

Patricia Noriega Rivera describes a retreat for yachak apprentices that began at Itchimbia Park. At this retreat don Alberto addressed the group as follows:

Today is a female pacha. Because of this we are on a female hill, and we need to be fully conscious to receive the female part of this sacred hill. Let's feel that we become full of the *sinchi* (strength), *samay* (soul), and *ushay* (power) of our Mother Earth.[2]

The yachak apprentices' retreat took place over the course of a week for a small group in Ecuador that included at least one American. Its purpose was to further the apprentices' knowledge and experience of ancient indigenous practices with a view to these being incorporated into their lives, and to advance their ability to connect with the elements. Starting with a description of spiritual warriorship, the exercises recounted here include leaving offerings at sacred places, greeting the sun in the morning, and fasting to cleanse the body. They provided a further opportunity for feeling gratitude for food, and learning how to perform healing with plants (the subject of the next chapter). Reference is made to the indigenous practices on which these teachings are modeled. Don Alberto admonished his students in this way: "You are the ones who are going to remain here when I leave my body, and all these teachings I give you must be shared with others, as much as you can."

LIFE CHOICES AND WARRIORSHIP

Life always presents us with forks in the road.[3] We are on a particular road and right away we have to choose another one, this or that. To have clarity we need to invoke the Eagle and the Condor. We do this initially through head knowledge and using discernment. However, sometimes this is not sufficient; one has also to feel, breathe, let go completely, relax, and make a decision. It's possible we may take a road that doesn't bring us happiness, so we'll think we were wrong and will sorrowfully abandon that path. We can take the other path, the other option, and achieve happiness but not out of choice. We may find ourselves on a sorrowful path that was nonetheless necessary for us in order to learn. Chance doesn't exist, we are all in the pacha we need to be in.

By contrast, on whatever path a traveler feels held back, doesn't feel happy, or feels oppressed, then that path does not agree with them and is not for them. We need to aim to walk a positive path. The right path needs to be full; one needs to feel joy, pleasure, restlessness, a desire to learn more. If you choose a path of reflection, meditation, fasting, contemplation, and gratitude, it must be because this makes you happy. Jesus knew how to travel his path with joy even knowing he was going to die.

At times powerful things happen to test and strengthen our spirit. The cosmos shifts in such a way that our lives can alter direction by a hundred and eighty degrees, but that same cosmos takes charge of our precise situation in time and space. If something shifts, other things also shift to put us in the place we need to be. This is because we are warriors, and what is a warrior's approach? It is to be attentive, open, connected to the power of the Eagle and Condor in order not to be wrong at the moment of decision. For example, when we are at anger's gates we have two choices: to be angry or let it go. Emotions can make it happen that we lose control and fall, lose the battle, take the road we don't need. When we approach falling apart from an emotion such as anger, sadness, or jealousy, we need to breathe, exhale, and put the Eagle and Condor into action.

Pacha Mama gives us what we should have at the precise moment we should have it. Although it may seem ugly to us, although it may appear bad, it is for a reason. It is the right moment for all of us because we need to learn something from it. Within everything bad that may appear there is always something good to learn. We need to allow our lives to flow like a river, like water, because in spite of a stone being placed in the path of a river, water has options: it can go over the stone, open up a passage through other channels, or even destroy the obstacle. It never remains static.

A real warrior is not someone who walks along armed and full of courage. The warrior or rather the warrior of light has love as weaponry. By this I mean an awakened consciousness, light, solidarity, wisdom, intuition, and bravery. In addition to this, a warrior needs always to be alert and aware of all that is happening outside and needs to understand what the elements are telling him or her when danger or an enemy draws close. One needs to be vigilant but with the greatest weapon: love. This is the reason I am asking that we go to the place our hearts choose. You can go to a mountain or valley and I want you to do this. In so doing, have your eyes closed for most of the time so that the element of air may guide you. This will allow for hearing, touch, and smell to develop in a favorable manner.

TYPES OF RURAY, RITUAL ACTION

In a 2020 workshop don Alberto explained that *ruray* means "action" and implies ritual action. However, in the life of his people, daily living and ritual are so interwoven that they do not distinguish between them, unlike people in the West. Basically a ruray is an action to create connection with nature and give thanks for its gifts. Don Alberto encourages people to create their own simple ruray that come from the heart and can be built into their daily lives. Following are examples from Ecuador, some quite complex. He does not recommend following a step-by-step process. The fasting exercise described below is something that he only requires yachak apprentices to undertake. A ruray needs to be spontaneous and heartfelt and simple, such as lighting a candle, burning incense, singing, or dancing.

Mañay: Offerings at Sacred Places

Mañay in Kichwa means "petition" or "request." Don Alberto places emphasis on this ritual because it is a practice in which people can become connected to special places or objects that are felt to have a spiritual aspect. They are sometimes called wakas, a name encountered particularly in Peru. This practice of mañay is also found in the historical sources. This kind of offering has changed through time as animals were used in the past, but sacrificing animals is something don Alberto does not do. The kinds of offerings that he and his apprentices leave in sacred places are fruit, chicha beverages, sprigs of herbs such as sage, or leaves, feathers, maize, sugarcane cakes (panelas), flowers, and incense. These offerings may be left at springs or rocks or wherever in the environment one is moved to put them. According to don Alberto:

Mañay is giving thanks to the Great Spirit, Hatun Pachakamak Pachakutik, for all the bounties we receive every day. It is a very intimate way of connecting, a way in which one needs to connect with him through these sacred places. It is the ideal moment for giving thanks, but also for making petitions and prayers.

While in don Alberto's company, I have often left plant offerings in the landscape, and once had the opportunity to leave them at watercourses flowing through the masonry channels at Machu Picchu, Peru. I am beginning to do it at home as well.

Kuyuri, Morning Sun Practices

Don Alberto relates:

A long time ago our elders, at dawn while the sun rose, followed practices like we are going to do this morning. At present some wise people continue to do them but less frequently. In the past they would meet, always around large pots of water and food, and one after the other they would begin to talk in no set order. They talked about matters dear to the heart, that is to say, what they were feeling or seeing, or what they had to offer. The name for this group meeting is Council of Ancients or, in Kichwa, Tantanakuy (meeting). These were the ones who made far-reaching decisions for the community, for the group, or for their own life. Throughout these meetings, thanks to the element of water as linchpin, they would "see," and predict what would happen or make political, social, or spiritual decisions.

The description that follows is what was done at the yachak retreat in Ecuador, but don Alberto includes this practice in all his retreats when it is possible to be outside. Above he states that these indigenous morning rituals for greeting the sun with feeling and receiving its energy are ancient. Morning sun rituals are recorded in seventeenth-century literature of the Incan Empire, but not enough is currently known to understand to what extent modern practices reflect those of the past. Patricia Noriega Rivera relates that according to don Alberto, indigenous people, before going on their daily tasks in the fields or at home, leave their quarters generally at 4:30 or 5:00 a.m. to conduct these practices as a symbol of respect to the sun and to receive it on the new day. Don Alberto describes them as follows:

Kuyuri consists of a series of physical exercises with spiritual content that can be done individually or collectively. Generally we do them in a circle. They are spiritual because one has to do them with the heart, connecting to the sun, the elements, and the directions. It is the main way for us to connect with *Tayta Inti,* Father Sun, because it is when he has scarcely started to shine on a new day.

According to the Kichwa dictionary, *kuyuri* means "swaying" or "moving." Patricia Noriega Rivera states that many times these movements include vocalizations with various letters or with the names of the elements (fire, air, water, earth, and ushay—the essence of all of them). The most common kuyuri practice is to vocalize the elements looking in the four directions. One makes a kind of basin shape with one's hands, inhales deeply while raising one's hands up to the sky from the ground toward the head, passes one's hands with all the energy received from the ground over one's whole body, and exhales slowly, saying the name of the element that corresponds to the direction in which one is facing. East represents Allpa Mama and Inti Tayta (Earth and Sun); South represents Nina Mama (Fire); West is Waira Mama (Wind); North is Yaku

Don Alberto greeting the sunrise, Rhode Island

Mama (Water); and above and below are Ushay Mama (essence of all). Once one has captured the Earth's energy and raised it to the head and over the whole body, one continues the movement to form an arc in a backward direction and holds it for about five minutes in this position to receive the sun's energy. When one is holding this position don Alberto might say: "Father Sun gives us life. From him we receive his energy that brings us to life."

This description sounds complex, but don Alberto has told me that there are many different ways of doing kuyuri, and that one can create one's own movements. I have experienced a much simpler form using just arm movements, stretching out toward the sun and then bringing its energy in toward the body and over the head without vocalizations.

Fasting

Don Alberto explains to his apprentices:

The food this morning was the last until two days from now. I am very happy that you are all eating with such gratitude. I have told you that fasting is important because the digestive system needs to be without eating for a while to detoxify. What we ate recently this morning will be cleaned out in two days' time. Food stays in our stomachs for two days. And generally food attaches itself and solidifies on the walls of our digestive system. This can stay there for years and cause stomach or colon disease. This is why it is necessary to cleanse it with fasting or with certain fruits that are able to detach those remnants that pervade the intestines. These include pineapple, papaya, and dragon fruit (*pitahaya*). In other retreats we have eaten these fruits sparingly, but today we will make a total fast. From this moment on we will only take herbal water and a little unrefined cane sugar.

We need to fast not just to cleanse our bodies but our spirits. We need to learn about hunger in order to feel nourishment, to give thanks and understand the importance of it in our lives, and to understand the magnificence Mother Earth offers us.

13

Learning Plant Healing

Plants are very important to don Alberto's practice, and his teaching on plant healing at the yachak apprentices' retreat in Ecuador is summarized in this chapter. The *limpia* ritual is one that he conducts extensively in the United States as well as in Ecuador to clear negative energy that can lead to all kinds of disease. Ideally the practitioner conducting the limpia ritual collects the plants while giving thanks and establishing a personal connection with them.[1] This is usually not possible in the United States. In this case, don Alberto uses flowers brought by the client or provided by the host; the client's act of choosing them has already created an emotional bond. This chapter ends with a long section on plants of psychedelic power and how don Alberto feels that the way he teaches is much more important than the brief psychedelic opening that they offer. He, in fact, considers all plants to be plants of power.

THE LIMPIA RITUAL:
HEALING WITH THE ELEMENTS

This is one of the practices most used in the Andean world, but we need to learn how to do it well.[2] I have asked Patty to be the volunteer sufferer because I am going to do a limpia, a cleansing. Before starting a healing we need to connect ourselves with Hatun Pachakamak Pachakutik, Creator of everything. However, it's unnecessary for everyone to use this name; you can do it with Jehovah, Yahweh,

Krishna, Mohammed, Buddha, or whatever name you want because all of these deities are the same, only the names are different. The important thing is to be connected with the Supreme Spirit that allows us to be a channel between Spirit and patient. I have no power and neither do you. In order to heal we simply have to allow the supreme energy to flow through us; that energy takes charge of the healing.

I know many people who heal and who think and say they are powerful, but they don't realize that if they operate in this mode what they extract from the patient permeates them. Many *curanderos,* healers, have come to me asking for my help and for me to cure them of terrible diseases they have acquired through bad healing practices. This is in addition to feeding themselves badly, eating meat, imbibing alcohol, and smoking—all this helps absolutely nothing. This has the effect that these people are unprotected. And so I tell them that they have to stop doing this, don't drink, eat good food, and above all, don't take on the energies that are concentrated in the illness of the patient. But they pay no attention to me. Then after a little time they return to me with terminal diseases and die in an inhumane way.

So, having made clear this first point, which is to connect ourselves and become a channel where we can manifest the power of Hatun Pachakamak (or whatever name you want to use), we need as well to connect with the elements of nature, and choose one, some, or all to effect the healing. At times I make use of the five elements, and at others one is sufficient. At times I don't use any because it has happened to me that just by connecting with the Great Spirit of Life and talking a bit with the patient, the healing is achieved immediately.

We can use any of the elements of nature, but we have to do the same things we did with plants yesterday. First draw near them with respect, communicate with them, and ask that their energy may purify the patient. I generally use plants that are both bitter and sweet and that represent Allpa Mama, Mother Earth; feathers that represent Waira Mama, Mother Air; pure water or water from a spring or sacred lake that is Yaku Mama; and sacred fire, Nina Mama, which can be created

The limpia ritual: don Alberto
prays with the drum

The limpia ritual:
plant cleansing

by burning palo santo wood or using incense or aromatic charcoal; and an essence or oil that represents the element ushay.

Illness is caused by a person's imbalance with Pacha Mama, the cosmos, with the different activities that develop in his or her life, and by becoming disconnected with the elements of nature. Our conception of illness, different from the Western one, is one in which emotions may be connected to organs such as the liver, the kidneys, the brain, or the amygdala. For us the human being is a whole that is complete. Symptoms are not the illness; symptoms are the pain in the liver or forehead. But this is not the illness, it is only a symptom that shows that your ushay, your life essence or energy, has been damaged for a long time. And so organically or physiologically one may be well but still feel bad. Illness starts in the ushay, in the breath of life, even though initially there is nothing wrong physically. Then later it's going to take shape and materialize in different organs of the human body.

There are elements whose energy cures people's sick energetic aspect, for example, herbs that often one does not even have to eat because it is not the active chemical element of the plant that cures. What one needs is the plant's energy, the ushay of the plant. For this reason, this is called healing, *limpia* or *limpieza* in Spanish, and *pichana* in Kichwa. One passes the plants over the body to restore what is missing so that the person is again charged with energy.

How to Conduct a Limpia with Plants

We are going to learn how to make limpias with these plants we brought with us. It is important for the person conducting the limpia to collect the plants in order to communicate and have an intimate connection with the energetic parts of the plants for successful curing. Afterward give them to the fire so that they are charged with purifying what we have extracted from our bodies, minds, and spirits. All plants have a spirit and energy like us. Everything is alive, everything deserves respect, everything that exists is in essence the same, but presenting itself differently, it simply changes its skin. Everything that lives on planet Earth, whether animal, vegetable, mineral, protist [these have animal and vegetable characteristics like mushrooms], all are the same in essence. If we think something and convey it to some manifestation of nature, this energetic charge, which can be positive or negative, will arrive at this element in a pure way because it doesn't have the human conception of good and bad.

If we go to a mountain and ask something of it in correct form, that is to say, we make a heart connection with the mountain, it is going to listen to us, and what we ask for happens. I want for us today to ask a plant for good and lovely things for our path. We are going to ask for what we need to be happy, to walk in a purposeful way. The plant doesn't know what is good or bad and it is going to be charged with the intention we put on it. Many people will say a plant is nothing more than that, but that is not so. Like everything that surrounds us, it is a being full of life. This plant also has awareness [consciousness].

As I learned from don Alberto, plant cleansing through the limpia ritual is energy healing. Precisely how it is done depends on the intuition and training of the healer, so the details of the method, while following a generalized format, are in fact variable. Don Alberto respects the intuition even of a novice and does not insist on one way of proceeding. The ritual will vary according to what a client is judged to need, which will determine what elements are employed and in what order. A basic outline might be as follows:

- With plants held in the right hand, the healer starts at the face and sweeps sideways working down the body to the feet. The same is done at the back. (In the following text don Alberto says to sweep from left to right. Not knowing this, I have swept from the center to the left and to the right working down a central line, or used a serpentine motion across the body. Don Alberto did not correct me.)
- If air is invoked, similar movements may be employed, using a feather.
- For fire, the movements are made with smoke from palo santo wood or sage, or a lighted candle in a safe container.
- For water, don Alberto, like other yachaks, has learned a method of taking water into the mouth and spraying it out. (He does not use the traditional alcohol.) A feather may also be used to flick water.
- For the fifth element, ushay, an essential oil may be used for anointing.

Philosophy behind the Limpia
In doing a cleansing, a limpia or *pichana,* there are certain things everyone knows that can't be denied. For example, it is well-known that we all have a right and a left side. From an energetic point of view,

the right hand gives and the left receives. This is why we must always do cleansings with the right hand. If we give with the left one we will receive what the plant or the element extracts from the patient. This is not at all advisable. This is why I hold plants, feathers, and essences in my right hand. For the same reason it is necessary to start the cleansing from the left side of the patient and end with the right because the left side receives. It is not necessary for someone to believe in this kind of healing because the elements have energy and their energetic capacity, even more the connection of the healer with the Great Spirit, works in a natural and definite way. As you have seen I have performed this ritual (as they call it in the Western world) in this way with plants, feathers, and essences. And afterward I have gone on to burn the plants because they are permeated by the energies extracted from the patient. The best way of neutralizing this energy is in the fire known as Nina Mama. You can also neutralize the energy afterward by placing the plant or element in a trash heap or someplace no one goes, although it is better to burn them in fire because it purifies.

As I poured water from a bottle you saw air coming in; the same amount of air enters as water leaves. This happens also with human beings. The same amount of energy that we need for our existence comes into what is emptied out, that which leaves. Our being is never empty; it's never lacking to any extent. The space that can be occupied by negative things in our lives, that we empty out is immediately occupied by things we need for our path. This is what happened just now during our limpieza. The plant helped to clean out that thing that was creating trouble in our lives, and in place of this negative thing that left will come beautiful things for us.

On Animal Diagnosis and Curing

It isn't necessary to sacrifice our little animal friends, which is why I don't do so in my rituals. The guinea pig beats all else as a tool for diagnosing where illness is to be found. But it's not necessary because all illnesses are the same; they happen when a person's energy is not good because of various habits they have in their daily lives. The limpia cleansing ceremony serves as cure for all illnesses. It is not necessary to diagnose or kill an innocent animal as part of the healing ritual. Alcohol too has a lot of energy and can cure, and also tobacco, but I prefer to use more natural elements, like water, fire, plants, and feathers.

I have done limpieza cleansings with guinea pigs because it is an animal with a great deal of energy that absorbs energies that are doing damage to the patient, and removes the illness. But I do not agree with their being sacrificed. What I was doing was curing the patient with the guinea pig and then curing the guinea pig, because it obviously was much debilitated. For this I had some cages specially conditioned for warmth, airiness, and feeding, by means of which, little by little, the guinea pig recovered. Perhaps after a while I would use this same animal again for curing other patients.*

PLANTS OF POWER

We are not here to learn things about plants [in the Western way], for example chamomile, which we know has curative, digestive, antacid, and analgesic powers thanks to its active principle. The indigenous people didn't know this. We knew plants by connecting with them through our hearts, allowing communication to flow, and we would cure only with their energetic presence.

I have ingested plants of [psychedelic] power very few times. In Mexico I took peyote, and here in Amazonia, ayahuasca, as part of my path. But I didn't use it as it's done now without any kind of preparation, with doses that are not appropriate for those who take them. For now, it is not possible for me to enumerate the sierra plants; there are very many plants of power that exist at every step. I have not

*The only animal healing method that don Alberto teaches does not have physical ramifications for the animal, as described here, but is solely a shamanic energy method for those who have that orientation (see chapter 23.)

taken them, but yes, I aim to. In the actual ritual of my initiation, I did not ingest any plant, and I ate nothing, including breakfast.

Personally, I don't approve of how the plants are used now. It really must be done with preparation, not just with physiological fasting. Rather, one should have consciousness of what one is doing and be conscious that this plant is a being and a special being at that.

These plants of power are not ordinary, they are full of potentialities. One has to befriend them, pass days and nights with them, before asking for a part of it to prepare. It has to be a long process, and it has to be understood by the person who is going to eat it. When I first drew close to a plant, in Canelos in eastern Ecuador, I took seven months to befriend it and prepare myself in various ways. I did this with a *tayta* and *mama* (male and female mentor), day and night, living with the plant. Afterward I prepared it myself with the supervision of a tayta and a dose appropriate to my constitution, which fit my manner of life. With such assistance, for me, ingesting the plants is sacred.

After eating it, I first had a very beautiful sensation of traveling to six sides at the same time, that is, shifting to the left, right, front, back, above, below, like the rose of winds [shown on a compass] but all around in three dimensions at the same time. Then I had a feeling of I don't know what exactly, not exploding, not coming apart in pieces, but of expanding. It was very lovely. I performed this exercise within a ritual where I was the only one to ingest the plant, but there were ten taytas and mamas, more or less, accompanying me. The effect lasted a night and a day. While everyone was conversing the following day, I was continuing to float.*

In other countries the same plants and things exist as in our

---

*Psychedelic plants are used to expand consciousness and the specific experience is unique to the individual. Yachaks may take them as part of their training. The experience may produce insight that is life-changing or not, depending on what is needed and whether the person is already on a positive path or not. To achieve a positive result, whether or not of great import, guidance from a psychedelic plant specialist is extremely important. An example of an unintentional ingestion of a hallucinogen is in chapter 25.

culture, but with other names. They are all used for the same end. The same thing happens with the use of symbols: they depend on place or climate. For example, in the Amazon they use plants from that environment, bird feathers that are only from that place, and free-form songs and prayers. On the other hand, in the sierra, one cannot always be outside, but may have to find an appropriate room with suitable conditions for having a ritual or healing. All these things vary depending on the place, but only the formal part. In the end it is the same.

Right now, we are in an epoch awaited for centuries, an epoch in which everything is open. It is now that we must make the most of it with gratitude and clarity. We must always be open, not just for a few moments, not just when the plant acts on us. We must be conscious intrinsically within ourselves and in our daily state of being. Because of this I don't approve of consuming these plants indiscriminately as this tends to result in people becoming lost. It is like a substance for unclogging pipes. When one throws this into the pipeline it makes an explosion and opens the pipe up but not in a natural way. The pipeline is not stopped up with water or a liquid but with something dense—some material thing that got in there, or with water itself that thickened and became a hard substance. This happens in the same way in our lives. We fill ourselves with negative things, impurities in our bodies when eating or impurities of spirit, and it clogs our pipeline, our intuition, our sensibility, and our intelligence.

And so what is it best to recommend? Is it to take a plant of power that would act like a substance for unclogging pipes, one that opens us for a moment after an explosion and after a bit returns us to being closed? Or is it one that in a natural manner makes these impurities leave us so we are open throughout our lives? The latter is what I teach. It is good for things at this time to interact in a manner that is suitable, mature, and conscious, and to act with gratitude, respect, and appreciation. These plants are sacred and must not be used unconsciously; it would be better not to consume them at all. At this time, we must just open our eyes a little more. Human beings are not in darkness as there is light and clarity already.

If someone ingests a plant of power without adequate preparation, it can cause unwanted effects, including for those who have not taken it. If they want to take a plant of power but there is harmful residue in the digestive tract the plant can act in a negative way. At a minimum, the digestive tract must be clean, without any residue, and also the emotional, affective, and spiritual preparation must be strong for the plant to act in an adequate way, the way that Pacha Mama generously gave us. If there is a lack of preparation, it doesn't work; rather the plant can make people ill or harm them, or is likely to disappoint.

Many indigenous cultures, on the other hand, have used these plants without being harmed because their youth were raised to know about the plants at hand and respect guidance in using them. Thus, they did not use them in an irresponsible way; we learned to respect the plant. But now the youth, often of other cultures, do this and are lost because they think they can prepare the plants themselves without any knowledge of how the plants function. These plants can achieve magical results but do not work by magic: knowledge is required to access their secrets.

Some people appear unable to understand that there are more things in the world than we can see with the five senses. When it seems that person has no possibility of coming to an understanding that this is erroneous thinking, there is a view that one can give them a plant of power to ingest that will change their understanding. But this is not the path, not the method, not the only way. I not only propose but rather insist that the path I teach is the better way. Specifically, we should walk in an open way, in a natural way, feeling and living, because we are in the epoch of being awake. This pertains to every one of us human beings, because everything in the cosmos is open and Pacha Mama is helping us, so this is really essential.

There's no law that everyone who wants to transcend must ingest some plant of power. No. Now we must do it in a natural way, by sensing, and being in contact with the elements of nature. I advocate doing it by breathing, through adequate food, by visiting a hill or spring, for instance. There are many forms that can be engaged for this. Many think that if someone can't consume plants of power they cannot manage to enter into the mysteries of wisdom, or believe that if someone already entered, that person has already gone through a portal. We can see in everyday life there are people who have ingested not once, but a number of times. How are they living their lives? Where are they, what are they doing with their lives? Wisdom is built through daily living.

These plants of power, through the simple fact of being present, radiate a huge energetic field, and can modify our lives. They can help not just other plants, but people, animals, and minerals. These plants help even more if they have special characteristics. As I've said, I didn't only have to ingest but at other times had to absorb, perceive, be in exclusive contact and sleep by them, touch them, feel them, and communicate with them. They don't just have a physical-chemical effect when one ingests them. They are plants that offer up their energy only with the act of seeing them and touching them.

Plants of [psychedelic] power are magically wonderful and potent, giving us power and opening doors of feeling for us. Taking them is not bad, but they can't be consumed irresponsibly. One needs to put in years of preparation, at least seven years. Taking a plant of power is too extreme a shortcut. Why isn't it better to walk the whole path with feeling? Isn't it better to do it with full, conscious awareness? Plants of power uncover our feelings momentarily. The path I teach is to be awake all the time, at every moment of our lives—to have open awareness every moment of our walk.

14

Resolving Conflict: The Nature of Good and Evil

BAD HABITS

Should we discover some habit we don't like, one that is not good for us, or some defect of ours, we shouldn't demonize it, because this is a spirit that is living in us and by doing that we are giving it more force energetically. Struggling against what we don't like nourishes it so that it grows and can take possession of us. What we need to do is increase what we like, leave the bad on one side, not even hate it, just leave it be. Do you remember what I explained about the bottle of water? When water comes out of it, immediately air goes in because space is always occupied by something. So if something goes out something else has to come in. The following is what we want to attain: in order to be filled with the good things we need, we need to not allow what harms us to increase its girth, but rather eliminate it. To achieve this, our approach to life has to be one of joy, thankfulness, and contemplation, that is to say, we must be open and aware.[1]

We need to keep the ideas good that we have in mind because we can do damage if we think negatively or with revenge or hate. We can influence how the cosmos is arranged in such a way that a bad desire can reach someone. This would not be prudent because energetically it later falls back on us. We need to be aware of what we think and what we say. Often because of anger we say something without thinking. That sound is reproduced, that is to say it does not just last for the moment. Our ears notice the audible resonance but the sound waves that occupy a place in the energetic field expand infinitely into space. It is because of this that we must be careful of everything we utter, and it is why it is said that words have power. We also need to be careful of what we write and how we do it as well as what we think. Everything we say, or write, or think is replicated energetically in a way that can have repercussions in our reality.[2]

Conflicts exist. They have always existed, and will always exist, but because they exist it is not something to beat ourselves up about. They are not due to some intrinsic wickedness in the human being.[3] What is happening is that when some people or a group of people are not in balance in the development of the two powers [Eagle and Condor, mind and heart], and act solely by means of one power, there is extremism. This is a belief that what that person or others like them think is the only way. There is no tolerance, no openness, because they have developed only this one vision, this one way of seeing the world. And so there are conflicts, and at the bottom they start with social conflict but there are also individual conflicts.

In family conflicts, conflicts between parents, sons with mothers, daughters with sons, and other members of the family as well, each person who is a member of the family has his or her own personality and they are going to develop their own characters and opinions. And there may be no continual sharing through discussion. When a family talks a lot, and members of the family, parents with their children, spend a lot of time sharing, conflicts are minimal.

Whenever there are families where both father and mother have to work or have their own activities and the children don't have them present, the children grow and develop without much contact. There isn't much conversation between the parents. They don't share long moments together, and each one starts to see the world differently, with different views and ambitions that cause collision among family members.

And so the first thing we naturally have to do is converse more and share more. This should be without trying to impose one person's thinking on the other. We need to open ourselves, be more tolerant of each other, be more understanding, in order to arrive at well-being in the family because we all gain or we all lose.

Practices that help us to have harmony are: Have a glass of water in your rooms or living room, wherever you believe it is convenient, and with sufficient care, a small burning fire. This can be a candle even. Plants, flowers, and different elements of nature that can be inside the place are good to include; these help a great deal. In the same way if you can do this outside, if the weather and circumstances allow, have a plot where the family can care for a flower or a plant. Have a common garden and have barefoot contact with the ground or a hand touching it. An hour or two at least is enough; whenever one can. What this contact does is it allows the earth to absorb any energy that is charged with ecstasy, shock, or conflict. And so people quiet down and their nervous systems come into harmony. When tired, walk a while when you can do it on a path outdoors or on the beach. Allow your skin and feet to make contact with water, air, wind, wherever there is sun. If you are inside and it's sunny outside, go outside to take in the sun, the wind, and the colors. The color green helps to harmonize and heal a great deal, as well as a purple, lilac color.

It can also help that when we bathe, we allow bathing to penetrate our cells, our minds, and our feelings, and our nervous systems that are negatively charged with conflict or disharmonious thoughts. We may have disharmonious feelings, emotions, intentions. If we walk when tired, touch the earth with the palms of your hands or your feet, or for example, lie down on the beach with as little clothing on as possible. All this helps a great deal. This allows your troublesome emotions that are static electrical charges to be absorbed by the earth. They can find the earth like the static in a broken electrical instrument needs to do.

We are the same way. Our body is a marvelous machine, a wonderful gift from our Mother Nature who is also alive. She works with bioelectric impulses so that when conflicts produce short circuits, bad discharges, ugly things, we have to use water, fire, and the different elements to harmonize our feelings and our thoughts. These elements are those of the sun, beach, sand, earth, and wind, among others, and they allow our marvelous system to balance and cleanse itself.

THE NATURE OF GOOD AND EVIL

The concept of good and evil does not really exist.[4] Everything depends on the culture and those in power who want to influence the thinking of the populace. Precepts, laws, and commandments are the parameters that establish what is good and bad. However, Pacha Mama [the cosmos] has offered this great power to all of us, plants, human beings, and animals. We are beyond good and evil.

At times, when someone is contaminated with negativity, we in the Andes say—in line with our vision of the cosmos—these things that belong to the Uku Pacha are manifesting in the Kay Pacha. But if there is positivity, we say that these are Hanan Pacha things that are benefiting the Kay Pacha. Know that the Kay Pacha is what is here, what we see, the place where we function. The Uku Pacha is what is below, the lower world. The Hanan Pacha is the sublime place of the divinities. But the Uku Pacha is not, because of this, bad or negative. It is simply necessary for the existence of life.

I do not like to use the words *good* or *bad, positive* or *negative.* Everything is a part of a life force, part of the whole existence of the cosmos. However, many people have self-identified with darkness rather than light, like people who have a greater affinity for sweets than salad, and this has repercussions. If someone eats a lot of sweets or a lot of salt they are going to have problems with their health. Similarly, there are people who are always thinking they are going to become ill, who are defeatist, sad, or thinking they will upset someone. These people may always be critical and see the defects and mistakes of others. They are particularly in contact with the Uku Pacha because these people help in recycling energy. Rather than being bad, they help others cleanse themselves, wash away mistakes, purify things. They are components in an energetic recycling system.

In 2017 I asked don Alberto to expand on *how* people with negative attitudes could serve as recycling agents for others. His reply: If they have *false* negative thoughts about others, they draw that person's negativity toward themselves, thus providing a cleansing function for the other person. One needs to be careful not to wrongly badmouth others, but if they are bad enough, it is alright, their negativity will not be attracted. All this is a natural function.

There are people who mostly live in Uku Pacha locations, such as cities that drain your energy or draw your emotions into conflict, but these people do have places for transformation. In cities there are drains, latrines, sewers, places that are outlets or vents for eliminating waste on the physical level that may also be used for energy cleansing. If people come close to these, they have an opportunity either to release their problems or fill themselves up with more dirt if they so choose. If people realize they are more inclined to Uku Pacha, or "dark" things, and want to change their energy, one option is to go to a spring and ask the spring to cleanse them—not just their skin but also their energy. The shower is also a place of cleansing. In places where nature has been banished to largely inaccessible parks, people may support their cleansings by nurturing an indoor plant such as aloe vera or whatever plant may appeal.

Again, this recycling of energy is natural and necessary: it is a part of life. It is not something that should disappear. It is not a rejection of "the bad" to be defeated by "the good," or an overcoming of evil by the eternal light of religion. According to my way of seeing, it is not like this. All of this is a part of life. It would be like saying that the only part of the body that serves it well is that which goes from the generative organs upward, while the part going down (which is the Uku Pacha in humans) does not serve it. Or to say that the only good part of the intestine is the upper part where food enters and the lower part, the anus where all the contamination leaves that we take in through the mouth, is useless and bad, and belongs to hell and sin. If we did not have this outlet, what would happen to our bodies? Both of these parts are essential for the body not to fail, for it not to cease to exist. And so for me the Uku Pacha is not bad, it is necessary. It is the same with the Hanan Pacha, because without these two nothing would happen in our reality, the Kay Pacha. As with cold, heat is also necessary.

I am not justifying, nor do I believe anyone ought to justify, anything that harms other people. I am not justifying anything that attacks their life, health, integrity, or loved ones. And not just human beings, but any being that exists in the cosmos. No one should harm anyone or anything. But beneficial damage does exist. For example, in nature if there are small plants needed by another plant, they will be absorbed. One is not about to say that the big plant is bad because it eats the little one, nor that the little parasitic plant does damage to the bigger one. From a rational Western point of view, one is bad and the other is a victim, but for nature the flowering and life force that happen are necessary.

With this, I don't want to justify the behavior of many yachaks who, because of their unconscious ways, do harm. The yachaks who are conscious on behalf of the Uku Pacha do not do such things as to make people ill, or cause them to leave their bodies so that they cease to exist, but devote themselves to other more important things. It is the devotees [witches], the bad apprentices of the Uku Pacha, who apply themselves to these things for money. They offer their services to people so that they can take vengeance, do harm, and more. These people receive with the same force or worse. Everything they do is against others. They become ill, and ugly things happen to them because nature in the same way has to look for equilibrium.

I also asked don Alberto if yachaks belong to a particular pacha since what he has expressed seems to imply that they do. He said yes, that those who belong to the Uku Pacha are involved in recycling the "dregs" or what is "bad." Dregs can be material or spiritual; bad or evil behavior is composted so there can be new growth. I asked him if he belonged to the Hanan Pacha and he said no, the Kay Pacha, with aspirations to the Hanan Pacha. This means he works with all things of this world, which includes plants, cooking, and so much more. There are different categories of being a yachak in all three pachas, such as types of angels in the upper world. During training, apprentices show tendencies one way or another; whatever makes them comfortable points to a particular pacha.

DEATH AND REBIRTH

Death does not exist. Stone, plant, earth, sand—they are all alive. We in the Andes have a different way of knowing about death. I have already said, *Waranga waranga kutin shamushun:* we will return thousands upon thousands of times because energy is eternal, it's not destroyed, it just transforms. The whole body is energy. Life is not only represented by how we are now in our human form. Life is displayed in different forms—mineral, vegetable, animal, spiritual—and all these are formed by microorganisms that also are forms of life. This is not just in this reality or only on our planet: the universe is infinite. There are millions of forms of life and other kinds of beings of greater transcendence. Energy just changes when we leave our bodies, we never disappear.

In this reality there is this form of life and in other realities are other forms of life. The whole cosmos contains an infinity of forms. Every night we leave our bodies while we travel in the dream dimension, but we come back. Now when we leave our bodies for good, when we definitely die and become disincarnate, we are living in another reality and we don't understand that we are dead. When this happens, the being inhabits what we Andeans call *llaki kausay* (life of distress), something that approximates to what the Catholic religion calls purgatory. When someone leaves their body for good and crosses to this space, because they don't realize they are dead, they return to physical space and no one can see them except those people who are very open and whose perception is very elevated. This happens until the person understands that they have left their body. However, until this happens, they will be traversing *llaki kausay*—that is to say, a state of uncertainty and sorrow.

Only when someone realizes they are outside their body will they abandon their physical form, transfer out of their frame, and feel radiant with just a silhouette that later will become energy. And so a mathematical process is engaged in, like perfect equations, until an energetic result is produced and one is newly placed in another body. That can transpire in this reality or others below or above, in this time period or future or past times.

The *runa* or human being who succeeds in having clarity and transcendence can also choose the place he or she wants to return to in order to incarnate with absolute awareness. They can communicate and encounter their kin through dreams to give messages to their loved ones. This can be achieved if we have an open awareness to the realities in which we live. Death is something lovely and marvelous, so for us death does not mean sadness and lamentation, death is not understood to be as it is conceived of in the West.

15

Medicine Wheel of the Four Winds: Life Lessons Drawn from Nature

Shortly after don Alberto had visited my home in Massachusetts the first time, I was startled one day to find a foot-long live snake by my chair in the dining room. A snake had never appeared inside my house before, but I managed to ease this ring snake into a cereal box and place it gently outside on some leaves. Don Alberto and I had recently been visiting what appeared to be huge representations of serpents in the local landscape. Identified by a local archaeologist, they were created by indigenous people of the past who modified eskers, or built snakes that seemed to be stone walls unless one knew what features to look for. I asked don Alberto the meaning of all this and he said the snake in my house indicated wisdom and that the ancient serpents were built for this time now to help Mother Earth gain power. The following material tells more about snakes and how they connect to other aspects of the Andean symbology.

On a more recent visit, don Alberto handed me a six-hundred-page volume in Spanish, *La chakana del corazonar,* and suggested I might find something of interest in it for this book. The Chakana is a symbol of many meanings central to indigenous Andean thinking; a description of it follows in the next chapter. *Corazonar* denotes a way of living out of the heart. Having nearly finished a first draft of *this* book, I did not relish having to submerge myself in such a tome, but dutifully thumbed through it quickly to see what part I might want to read. Some months later, knowing I was including a small part, don Alberto looked at me in awe and asked, "You really read all six hundred pages?"

"No, just the part I was interested in," I could truthfully reply.

La chakana del corazonar by Patricio Guerrero Arias is an expansive coverage of the development of indigenous philosophy in recent times in Andean history. Many indigenous leaders and yachaks are quoted, not least don Alberto. Most of his quotes come from *El vuelo del águila y el cóndor*. What really caught my attention was a compilation of the symbolic connections of an Ecuadorian medicine wheel. This was a matrix of symbols put together by a group of yachaks from the Pichincha region, the area around Quito, at a conference in 2009. Suddenly, various aspects of my own experience, both in the United States and Ecuador in the years since I met don Alberto, which I had not known how to interpret, began to make sense to me. I began to understand the indigenous thinking, which then ushered me into deeper insights about the direction my life had taken. Many of those experiences are described in this book.

The Medicine Wheel material I encountered helped me see a wider cultural context for what don Alberto teaches. It tied into a symbolic Andean system. Thus I decided to provide a shorter version here that includes many direct quotes from the insights of indigenous Ecuadorian sages.[1] The Medicine Wheel section in *La chakana del corazonar* starts out with a note to the effect that while the assigning of directions to the four winds, the power animals, and the *saywas* (symbolic matrices) may be approached differently by different yachaks, there is an Andean commonality in that these are always summoned or invoked in ceremonies and represented on healing mesas (altars). These powers and energies revitalize life and give it meaning by raising the level of heartfelt living.

Moving through the Medicine Wheel's sacred spiral of life corresponds also to the stages of our own existence. It is important to note, however, that in the yachaks' understanding of the cycle of life we do not go through these stages linearly, but rather in the dimension of Spirit. All these stages are interwoven and complementary; one aspect predominates, but it is linked to the others. Similarly, their sources of energy—play, song, dance, and meditation—do not belong exclusively to each life stage, but move in the same way as life: spirally. It follows that being able to synchronize these stages depends on the spiritual level reached. Children may have deep wisdom, or the lack of ability to play or love at any stage may result in all kinds of deep human problems. At whatever stage of life, it is important to know that spiritual forces make the spiral of life fully alive, like a sacred game.

To overcome problems at least one of the attributes of the spirit of water is needed, to flow over, around, or through obstacles, and in the Andes, as we have established, water is viewed as a very important element.

THE PATH OF THE WEST: WATER AND SERPENT

The spiritual journey through the Medicine Wheel of the Four Winds begins with the Western path, the path of ushay, the power of spirituality. Just being born is already a manifestation of the power of a benevolent life spirit. We start the Medicine Wheel here, naked, and it is to this spiritual direction that we will eventually return but in a different way due to the twisting spiral of existence. The Western path is where the female energy of Mama Yaku's spirit, Mother Water, dwells. The fecundity of her ushay or spirit makes possible life's harmony: each time-cycle has a specific vibration and water's vibration transmits peace, harmony, and a time to prepare to be fecund. To make life fertile we need water's vibration.

The water path is the direction in which one meets *Mama Cocha*, the great ocean, since it was there that life began. Some consider it the direction of death because it is the region where every day "the sun is swallowed by the sea." But it is also thought to be the direction of the rebirth of spiritual power, *ushay*, since Father Sun wins in his struggle against the shadows and is reborn each day to continue gifting us with life. At every dusk, water meets the spirit of fire, Father Sun, who sinks into the waters to struggle with obscure forces, then sleep and rest so that there will be another day when life will have the transparency of water. That is why the West is the direction of spiritual rebirth.

When we begin our cosmic journey, we spend nine months in a watery microcosm, in the tender ocean that stirs in our mother's belly. During this time in the belly we have everything: food, and our mother's protection, and we hear the rhythm of our mother's heartbeat, the internal message not only of our biological mother but also of Mother Earth.

Mother Water's spirit is charged with a profound wisdom for orienting life, and teaches us she is the primary symbol of transparency, of crystal clarity, the power that flows, of flexibility, of the capacity to unite, to bind together what is separated. But she also dissolves. Water has the power to transform and change itself into whatever form it has within it while keeping the energy of its being intact, continuing to be what it is, always itself. Water shows us the necessity of opening a path for ourselves so that our lives may flow. Clean water has cleansing power and so the spirit of life lives in her.

Water does two things: she cleans and carves up the land. When she carves it up, she has her own path, the *yaku ñan,* and when she needs that path there is no one who can tell her it can't be here or there as she goes this way or the other.

The spirit of Mama Yaku teaches us also a path of infinite transformation and that there is "cyclicity" to life, where life occurs in cycles and nothing disappears. In our culture we think we come and we go, are born and die. But human beings are like the flowers of life: if one day the petals drop, the seeds remain alive; our body can die but not our spirit.

Mother Water's wisdom also teaches us that there is a nonstop, perpetual growing and flowing toward being more. However, this transition, being an act of supreme love toward "otherness," can only be reached with others. It is this capacity to join with the energy of others that is water's true power. While water starts as a little drop working loose from the sky or from the snows of the Father Volcanoes, it joins with others to make a rivulet and then others to make a stream. And it continues joining, flowing, growing, until it becomes a river, a sea, a powerful and boundless ocean. In this way water's wisdom teaches human beings that our destiny is to learn to flow toward growing greater, everyone moving together.

Water's wisdom also teaches us the strength of fragility and patience, since within its apparent weakness there lives a powerful spirit that, through acting wisely and with patience, is able to perforate the hardest rocks and oxidize the strongest metals. By acting with patience, indigenous pueblos have had the know-how to preserve their way of life through the insurgent struggles of history. This is the same way that water goes on flowing, opening a path little by little, letting flow an inner spirituality to confront the perversity of power. As mama yachak Nicolasa Toctaguano says, "Little Mother Water's wisdom invites us to have crystalline hearts, full of transparency and light."

The wisdom and power of water offers us further profound lessons so that we can sow in our hearts a cosmic ethic necessary for daily life. When we have to confront difficult situations, the healing power of water cleanses not only the body but also the heart and spirit, as tayta yachak Alberto Taxo makes clear in his teachings (see chapter 11).

For the indigenous people of the Andes, the wisdom and spiritual force of Mama Yaku are very powerful, since she is the Creator of life who births and rebirths anew. She is not a resource as in the Western capitalistic conception but a holy spring of life, a fountain of spirituality and strength for struggles. It is for this reason that she is in the horizontal axis of existence, the Kay Pacha. Water, not as an element but as a being of power and life, is present on the mesas of the yachaks who ask that she grant them her healing energy. Mama Yaku is the compass of indigenous people's struggles, and it is for this reason they say, "Water is not bought or sold but fights," since they know she is the sacred spring of life. The indigenous of the Andes have always felt reverence for her since her spiritual force is very great; her flow cleans, calms, and heals the heart.

The sacred animal that lives in the spiritual house of *Mama Agua* (Mother Water) and facilitates passing along the Western path is the serpent, *Amaru,* the primary sacred symbol of the Andean world. The serpent uses a flowing motion to go forward, and in the same way, small streams and great rivers demonstrate snake-like movement. They transmit energy from the periphery to the center until they arrive at the vastness of the sea. The ocean consists of snake energy from the flowing water of many rivers that embrace there. For this reason, water, for the indigenous world, represents "the integrative spring of life's diversity." The serpent's wisdom has deep symbolic meaning: the snake is an animal that pulls itself along. We too start out life pulling ourselves along like a reptile, creeping before getting up to walk on the Earth. It is important to crawl because each child that does so learns to defend himself or herself. It has been shown that such children already have arrived at solutions needed in adulthood.

The serpent symbolizes light, flexibility, and transformation, the latter being a very important attribute because the snake is always changing its skin. The process of changing skin is painful, not easy; the same with transformation. The snake looks for a thorn, throws itself on it, and on feeling the pain, shucks the old skin so that a new one may be grown. This is the wisdom of the serpent, and we have to find our own thorns to get rid of our old skins if we want to transform our lives.

The path of serpent wisdom invites us to shuck, or let loose, past suffering. In a similar way, the spiritual path requires us to jettison the dead clothing of a past that keeps us asleep so that we cannot wake up. We human beings need pain to be able to advance in our internal transformation, and we need a thorn to be able to exorcise the past.

As yachak Ricardo Taco has said:

We will be able to grow and change the skin of our soul like the snake if, after having plumbed the depths of our own suffering, we learn from the wisdom we encounter in pain and failure. We will need to see these not as problems but as opportunities for transforming ourselves so that bitterness and resentment do not obscure joy, and the weight of pain does not prevent us from continuing life's journey. From childhood we are taught to be afraid of pain and don't talk about it, and so we are afraid of death. We can't tolerate the pain of death, but we have to learn that pain holds wisdom; this wisdom being not to forget to see the beauty of life in spite of the suffering.

The Western path, the path of the snake, allows us to divest ourselves of the old skin of reason, since reason's irrationality has impeded us from being able to look at, listen to, and describe life and its mysteries with the eyes of the magician. Reason has voided our capacity for astonishment, the power to be amazed at the beauty of simplicity that is displayed by the miracle of life. Reason has pulled the sacredness from reality and has made us forget the sacred, transcendental, and spiritual feeling that dwells in the universe. It has made us strangers to these things. In the name of reason, we silence the heartbeat of nature and the cosmos and stop conversing with them in love and respect.

We have distanced ourselves from nature and given her death-dealing wounds to such an extent that today she is in pain. And so we have to jettison the old skin of reason that has fed this civilization that is sustained by violence and death, and start to "derationalize" and "decivilize" ourselves. For only in this way may we rediscover the magic of life. We need to deeply revisit our errors as this will allow us to shuck all our old skins that prevent us from growing, transforming, rising up, and walking the world resolutely. Worse, they prevent us from flying in the direction of liberty, and simply being better and happier.

Changing skin like the snake can also be seen as a symbolic and political act if we loosen the skin of overpowering ego and Cartesian reason to have new eyes, and be open to the wisdom found in meeting others with kindness. This includes the poor, the downtrodden: Earth's condemned. This is not the snake of the Garden of Eden but the "plumed serpent," Quetzalcoatl, the Divine Duality. This is why indigenous wisdom teachings of the heart have always known the spiritual power of the serpent teaching.

The serpent path is also the way to get started on the path of wisdom. Thus it implies a shucking of the skin of what we have learned in order to open us to unforeseen wisdom, and can only be felt out of the heart's potentiality. This unforeseen serpent wisdom is especially important to the Shuar of the Amazon who access it by means of a plant of power, ayahuasca.

The yachak path is one of "enheartening" life (*corazonar*), and as the yachak uncle of the author Sairy Lligalo said to him:

> I want to know if you can stay on your feet when no material things are near you; if you are going to stand strong and firm in those moments of emptiness like we are passing through now, strong in heart and mind. If you do this, the power of the universe will come to your aid as long as you persevere with heart and mind together. Always walk with courage when you have doubt and your faith has gone. In the way that clouds envelop the sun for a while and then dissipate, no doubt it will be the same for you, so go forward with bravery knowing that nothing is clouded over forever.

THE PATH OF THE NORTH: EARTH AND JAGUAR

The second direction is the path of the North, whose cosmic being is the Earth Mother, Allpa, who symbolizes the wisdom of the matrix of life: fecundity, fertility, supreme generosity, abundance, industriousness, ruray, practicality, and concreteness.* All our wisdom traditions understand through their senses that Earth is the Great Mother who seeds life, and therefore they call her Pacha Mama [Cosmic Mother Earth] who is made fertile by the love of Pacha Tayta [Cosmic Father]. He, through his semen as rain falling from the sky, makes her womb fertile, allowing life to continue giving us more gifts.

The great diversity of existence has been brought about by the joining together of their love. Mother Earth teaches us that generosity is the supreme expression of love. She is the motherly loving power that sustains and supports us, keeps us in balance, and is always creating life. She is the sacred uterus whose fertility brings life to birth, and to whom we will return after walking her body. Earth, who has been here since the beginning of time, is the supreme fount of wisdom and invites us to have generous hearts, fertile and solid, and to feel that the continuity of existence depends on her.

As mama yachak Maria Simba says,

Little Mother Earth is certainly our mother, and like every mother is infinite love, is good to all her children, doesn't prefer one over another, whether good or bad she wants the same for all. And so, she feeds us, nourishes, and sustains us day by day without asking anything in return. She has a generous heart toward all, but her ungrateful children forget this and treat her badly, they are killing her, and don't realize that we cannot live without her, but she, on the other hand, can go on living without us.

Another expression of Mother Earth is that her power gives us the energy and harmony to root ourselves in life so we may find our own heartbeat. As yachak musician Néstor Karal tells us:

*Being in the southern hemisphere, people in the Andes experience North and South in the opposite way from those in the northern hemisphere who associate North with cold and winter, not with summer and fertility.

Earth shows us the vibration of life's energy, the heartbeat of our Pacha Mama, and our drums and percussion instruments reproduce the heartbeat of Mother Earth to generate a strengthening effect on human beings, not just in their heads, but rooting them in Mother Earth. This is from the heart; this vibration that strengthens you.

Giving us food to eat daily is a supreme expression of her love, so that eating becomes a sacred ceremony that allows us to feed our bodies, but especially our hearts and spirits. As tayta yachak Alberto Taxo says, "Every time we eat is a great opportunity to be connected to the Earth, Allpa Mama, and receive her blessings." (See chapter 11.)

Making eating a sacred act allows us to understand the spiritual dimension of the spiral of life whose radiating movement generates vital energy. We have forgotten this because the rule of soulless reason sees only chemical components in foodstuffs, and not that they are inhabited by the powers of the guardian spirits of nature and life. By merely eating bread we can discover the miracle of the dance of existence.

Eating in a hurry without awareness provokes not only physical but spiritual illnesses. As mama yachak Nicolasa Toctaguano says:

How sad that people seek miracles in extraordinary things when in ordinary life miracles are in front of our eyes but we don't see them. How can it not be a miracle that bread starts out as a small seed that has to face sunlight and darkness to germinate into a life form, wheat. This wheat then must be cut by working hands, and it takes more strength and work to turn it into flour. After that there are yet more hands, those of the bread maker who kneads, and those that put it into the oven until finally, after all this energy and work making up the spiral of life, we get to eat it. How sad that there are people who don't realize this. We must teach our children from babyhood to see all this, but above all that they be thankful and have gratitude for life and give thanks for the generous gifts that Mother Earth gives us daily.

The sacred animal of the northern path that brings change into life is the jaguar. This animal doesn't slide along the ground but walks firmly on it with sure step, and sharp, watchful eye. It knows its goals and methods, knows what it wants, and what it needs to do. This is the ruray path of doing, of recreating and maintaining oneself, sowing and building. Without this power nothing can come into being. The jaguar knows its very survival depends on these actions: it is constantly making decisions on how to act. It knows its past but is not imprisoned by it and has overcome it to concentrate on how to live in the present. It lives intensely in the here and now, has jettisoned its old skin like the serpent, has stopped crawling and started to get up. It walks firmly on its own four feet on the Earth.

On the northern path's walk the jaguar's wisdom and spirit push us to overcome fears, to face death knowing that we want life. It is a walk in which we die consciously to a life without meaning and start to weave a different life, to have an encounter with the meaning of existence. What is our sense of meaning? we ask ourselves. Why are we part of the bioverse? Why are we here in this time and place? What is our mission in the cosmic order of life? In light of this, the jaguar path is also a time to start training warriors to be the guardians of Mother Earth and life. Those with jaguar power make their own decisions and do not need to go along with the rest to get along; they are free and do not need to take orders. Rather, they have perspective, objectives, and missions, not for themselves alone but for society as a whole.

THE PATH OF THE EAST:
FIRE, HUMMINGBIRD, AND DRAGON

Traveling the path to the East comes next. It is considered the path of birth since this is the direction in which *Tayta Inti,* Father Sun, rises and births the light of a new day, giving illumination, color, energy, and life to the whole of existence. His wisdom teaches us about the primordial matrix of complementary duality (*yanantin*) because in light's heart there also beats the heart of darkness and shadows: through light we discover shadows. Fire, *nina*, is what frees the sun's energy; fire is the essential manifestation of the transforming power of love's spirit, the *munay*, or caring intention of the cosmos.

As shared by Hilario Chiriap, a spiritual leader of the Shuar of Amazonia:

> For us fire is a vital fount of energy; we know it is the fire of life. What is love? Love is a feeling, an emotional, psychological, spiritual, and physiological vibration that comes from the spiritual power of fire: from it come deep internal vibrations. We know that this energetic force of fire's spirit is expressed through love. It is expressed through love's power, through passion, bonding, and an expression of well-being. Fire is a superior and supreme transforming energy.

The path of fire's wisdom is a symbol of will hardened like stone, of passion that propels us forward in the struggles of life. As the yachak musician Néstor Karal says:

> Fire must give force, so to call it up we take our wind instruments, our horns that call up all this cosmic energy, this internal fire for us to take hold of, to seize its force to go on struggling, go on living.

Fire symbolizes the power that transforms everything, that consumes to ash what it touches, something that is necessary to renew life. This is why we call it *Wilka Nina* (Sacred Fire), *Enka Nina* (Essential Fire Energy), or *Nina Mama* (Mother Fire). All indigenous cultures here know about the transforming power of fire as this is an irreplaceable part of their ceremonies and sacred spirituality. Fire illumines and opens, and from earliest times has brought about brotherhood as people sat around it feeling its sacred dance. They were able to share with others their wisdom and dreams, committing to each other so that they might continue living. Fire has illumined and given shelter to ceremonies of word and memory. Fire's wisdom demands that we awaken our internal fire, that we always keep alight the passion of our spirits. We should always be "guardians of heart's fire and never let it go out," as the Amazon's ancient Guarani sage Karai Mirí Poty has taught us, because without passion in our hearts we cannot transform life.

The wisdom of the yachaks teaches it is important to feel consciousness that fire is a sacred power that lives in all existence. It is not outside us but lives in our interior selves reminding us of the cosmic and sacred dimensions we possess, as does everyone who lives in the bioverse. Tayta Alberto Taxo's teachings expand on what is said here. We have the fire of life within; it burns away destructive things and is also therapeutic. It makes us see ourselves as sacred and allows us to transform; however, we must know how to use it and not let it burn indiscriminately. We must give thanks for it and for the sun, and as we come into the era of woman, it is women who know best how to use sacred fire (see chapter 11).

For some tayta and mama yachaks, the spirit of fire's sacred animal of transition is the hummingbird as messenger of the gods. It is the hummingbird that enlightens us with wisdom, and as mama yachak Maria Chiluiza says:

My grandmother told me when I was a little girl that the *kinde* (hummingbird) is a little sacred bird because it brings us fire, and that it is a symbol of the wisdom of the ancestors' words. They said that the hummingbird makes us catch a little on fire, for it enlightens us and makes it possible for us to fly lightly, as *it* does. Nothing has ever been seen as beautiful as the speed with which it moves its wings, hovering over the little flowers and giving them fire.

For other Ecuadorian yachaks, as in Peru, the animal that corresponds to this eastern direction is the dragon. The wisdom of the dragon tells us we have to put down roots and allows us to know who we are and what we want of life while never losing the magic of our dreams. According to yachak Ricardo Taco, it is considered a Chakana or bridge animal between earth and sky because the dragon both walks the earth and flies with its mighty wings. The dragon's path lets us walk with the wisdom of the ancestors who now walk among the stars but used to walk the earth. It helps us access this knowledge.

It is also a bridge between reality and fantasy as the dragon walks and flies in both worlds. The dragon is a mythical and mysterious being who tells us we have to hang on to our myths, because if they are extinguished we give up our wisdom that tells of these things. The dragon is the guardian of Wilka Nina, sacred fire, and fire is a symbol of transformation that illumines and gives color. In the past to allow a new year to be reborn we burned all that no longer had value from the old.

THE PATH OF AIR:
CONDOR AND EAGLE

The journey along the paths of the Medicine Wheel ends with the southern path, the direction where one encounters the four winds, for its spiritual and cosmic being is the air, the wind (*waira*), the breath of life itself, the energy that sustains our spirit and all that lives. This direction is that of the *saywa,* or symbolic matrix of wisdom (*yachay*). Air is light's medium, the symbol of subtlety, transcendence, supreme liberty, of all that cannot be learned except in a higher dimension of spiritual wisdom. Air has the power of giving advice, of opening to the living power of what is invisible, our dreams, to show us the paths we need to follow in our lives.

As mama yachak Nicolasa Toctaguano says:

> Without this life force, without this *sinchi*, we couldn't exist; in our ancestral spirituality, waira is the first gift the Great Spirit gives us at that moment when we are first born into this life. It is also the last breath that we give back when we have to leave this material envelope to unite with the breath of the cosmos. Doesn't this seem to you to be divine reciprocity, and how can you not give thanks for this miracle? Air is the most powerful element so we try to teach our kids from when they are very little to listen to the wisdom of the four winds. This is because the wind is a sage, a counselor, if you listen to it from the heart. Our children will know how to walk through life, and if they become lost, they will find their way back home.

The wind that blows from the West will tell them to learn to look and listen from within their hearts. The southern wind will teach them to be humble in order to arrive at wisdom, and to know how to listen to and learn from the grandmothers' teaching. The wind that comes dancing from the North will bring them the teaching of Mother Earth. It will tell them that she is sick and suffering, that ambition has taken us away from her. Because of this we have to learn to walk with love and respect on her body because inevitably, sooner or later, we will reap what we have sown. The wind from the East will teach them to learn to hold on to spiritual peace in their hearts to be happy.

The simple act of breathing is a miracle we need to rediscover through awareness, because each inhalation and exhalation is proof we are alive, as tayta yachak Alberto Taxo tells us (see chapter 11).

The wisdom of air tells the heart that it may always fly free, and that nothing may imprison it in chains. The subtleness of air's liberty leads us to fly toward the unfathomable, the unforeseen—

we are beings made for liberty. As yachak musician Néstor Karal tells us:

> Air builds liberty, because tell me, what has more liberty than air? It creates enjoyable melodies for the meaning of music, and in the community, or in gatherings of family and elders, air is connected with wind instruments.

COSMIC ETHIC OF THE FOUR WINDS MEDICINE WHEEL

For yachaks, after they have reached liberated flight from following the southern path, the Condor and Eagle vision does not imply the end of the journey, but the start of a new one as life's spiral continues to turn. From here one returns again to where one began—but transformed, different, other, reborn. We start this magical journey from a natural spiritual dimension and return to it transformed, to be able to continue the transitioning with more wisdom and heart gained from the wisdom of the wind's four directions.

Whoever has learned to fly, look, and listen like the Condor and Eagle from the depth of the spiritual wisdom of heart and reason, whoever has learned to live out of the heart, has a cosmic ethical duty governed by the *saywa* (matrix) of reciprocity (*ayni*). He or she has the responsibility of sharing with others how to live and learn this. We must not forget that one of the key fundamental ideas of indigenous cosmological understanding is relationship, reciprocity that is both actual and symbolic, which makes living possible.

And so the Medicine Wheel makes possible an *ayni* of wisdom. Only in this way does the collective seeding of cosmic knowledge have meaning so that others may start on the same Medicine Wheel journey to cleanse existence, heart, soul, and society. With this they will be able to see the beauty of life's cycles seen in seeding, gestation, birth, growing, letting go, death, rebirth, and flight. Those who reach this wisdom become multidimensional beings, bridges, Chakanas to a different existence—spiritual warriors of heart, wisdom, and tenderness. They become guardians of the Earth, with love, hope, and joy. They become warriors of life.

In the whole infinite cosmos beats the heart of life so that the journey of the spiritual directions of the four winds and life's Medicine Wheel is a pathway to heartfelt living and can only be followed from the heart. So by walking the paths of water, earth, fire, and air, accompanied by the spiritual wisdom of the serpent, jaguar, hummingbird, dragon, condor, and eagle, we may be able to reach the heart of life itself, and thereby bring more heart to life to transform it and ourselves with it.

16

The Chakana and the Staff of Gold

The Chakana, or stepped cross of the Andes, is a symbol familiar to many, but few are likely to know the extent to which its elegant geometry represents the Andean indigenous vision of the sacred cosmos. It is what anthropologists call a multivalent symbol, a symbol of many meanings, and those meanings are often added to or even changed through time. *Chakana,* in the related Quechua and Kichwa languages of Peru and Ecuador, is derived from a word meaning "to cross over," "a bridge," or "a stair," but what is it that the bridge or stair is connecting and for what purpose?

Chakana is not the only name for this cross in indigenous Andean languages, suggesting its meaning probably varied at different locations along the Andean chain that is thousands of miles long. The Incan Empire extended from present-day Ecuador to central Chile, but lasted less than a hundred years, so the wisdom often attributed to the Inca is likely to be much older, belonging to the pre-Inca peoples. The Andean cosmic view was applied by the Incan Empire to the landscape of its territories, creating a sacred geometry that still exists and is still recognized as sacred.

In chapter 2 on Grandparent Wisdom, don Alberto gives a brief outline of his understanding of the Chakana and the three levels of the Incan world: the upper, or Hanan Pacha; the middle, or our world, the Kay

Pacha; and the lower, the Uku Pacha. Here he elaborates on these basic concepts that are still relevant to the surviving pre-Inca societies of today. Following his account is material from Peruvian indigenous writer Javier Lajo, a friend of don Alberto's, to whom I was honored to be introduced in Lima. Lajo elaborates further on the complexity of Andean cosmological and philosophical thinking. Don Alberto also holds a vision for a new society that is understood in terms of the story of the founding of the Incan Empire with the staff of gold, and it seems fitting to end this section on his teachings with that. Don Alberto's description of the Chakana follows here, as told to me in a 2016 interview.

The Chakana is a tool that our ancestors used to codify the wisdom and scientific knowledge that were developed in their times. One of the easiest ways of understanding it, to read this symbol or tool, is to orient oneself in the four directions that we know: North, South, East, and West. If we look at the Chakana from above, we will see it is a cross with sides of equal length. No arm of the cross is longer than any other: they are symmetrical. We also notice, continuing looking from above, a square whose corners have been turned into steps—stairs with exactly three steps to each side—so that the square, now a stepped cross, fits inside an outer circle. There is also a circle in the center. Some representations, especially those used for hanging around one's neck, do not have an outer circle enclosing the square. The Chakana is really a circle, and a square within a circle, the circle containing the square (see facing diagram). The circle is essentially female, the square essentially male. The female essence, Pacha Mama, holds the male within her, thereby creating a dynamic catalyst to generate life that in turn fosters the continuance of all aspects of the cosmos.

If next we look not from above but from the side and imagine that this object has three dimensions—length, width, and depth—and then project onto that three planes of consciousness that comprise the mineral, animal, vegetable, and human worlds, this model symbolizes how all knowledge and wisdom intimately connected to the macro cosmos is

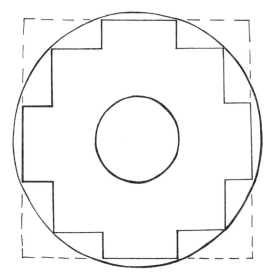

Basic diagram of don Alberto's Chakana
Drawing by Gabriela Ansari

created. Further, the Chakana, as we observe it in the constellation of Orion, may be viewed as a fan or as a winnowing fork.* The Southern Cross, as it is known, is also an expression of the Chakana that can most clearly be observed in the month of May in our lands in Ecuador.

The Chakana, to be best understood intellectually, has to be seen in all its dimensions. You have to imagine it as a moving object suspended in the air and view it from all sides. In this way, perceiving it from all directions, a fourth dimension is then achieved, and the continuous movement produces the other dimensions. The Chakana also contains, in our pacha, our Kay Pacha, knowledge of mathematics, astronomy, and agriculture, as well as social, economic, and political orders. In all, it is a great collective system, a codification of the knowledge and wisdom of the Andes.

---

*A winnowing fork is like a fan with a handle or a leaf rake. Don Alberto did not elucidate their meaning, but to me these objects suggest the Mayan understanding of Orion's central three-star cluster and smoky nebula as the focal hearth of the cosmos (Freidel, Schele, and Parker, *Maya Cosmos*). Might the purpose of these objects be to fan energy into the flames of the fire of life?

Don Alberto also explained the three pachas in terms of a spiral plant metaphor. The seeds are in the soil, the Uku Pacha, and grow up into the Kay Pacha. The plant grows up in the Kay Pacha to flower and seed in the Hanan Pacha, when its seeds then fall back down into the soil of the Uku Pacha and the process starts all over again. But the succeeding processes are not identical with what went before, so a spiral is a more accurate metaphor than a circle.[1]

Aspects of don Alberto's Chakana description are not easy to follow, and conceptions of it in Peru are equally challenging. To start with the antiquity of the cross and the name *Chakana,* while both have ancient roots, the length of time of their being associated is uncertain. The stepped cross is found on Incan buildings at Machu Picchu and in the Sacred Valley near Cusco, and in the older Tiwanaku culture of Bolivia. Cusco was the center of the Incan Empire in the Peruvian Andes. The earliest known description of a cross in Cusco in 1609 was not a stepped cross and was appropriated as a Christian symbol. It was a large, equal-armed cross of finely worked and polished red-and-white mottled marble (or jasper) that had been venerated in a shrine (*waka*) in a royal house.[2] On the other hand, in a 1590 text, the word *Chakana* was known to be the name of a star,[3] and in recent times it was found that in two villages near Cusco, one in the Sacred Valley, the word was applied to two different clusters of stars. These are the belt of Orion and three stars of Canis Major.[4] The Orion association connects to don Alberto's description.

In the last twenty years or so, the Chakana cross has become important to the resurgence of indigenous cultures in the Andes. The Peruvian indigenous writer Javier Lajo made it the subject of his book *Qhapaq Ñan,* where he analyzed and described it extensively. Lajo interprets it in terms of his understanding of indigenous concepts learned from his pre-Incan Puquina heritage, a people considered ancestral to both the Quechua and Aymara. A brief summary of his major interpretations is given here to further demonstrate the complexity of Andean cosmological philosophy as it is now being interpreted.

Javier Lajo's argument provides a window into Andean cosmovision, the Andean view of the workings of the cosmos that includes our daily lives. Following is a description to elucidate how two main principles of Andean philosophy, parity and the three pachas, are represented by the stepped cross, a symbol of many meanings. To understand this it is necessary to pay attention to the cross's internal geometry, shown here as even more complex than in don Alberto's description (see diagram below). There are three sets of circle/square pairs. Starting at the center there is a circle inside a square that fits inside a second circle. Outside this second circle is a second square that also forms part of the stepped cross within a third circle. The stepped cross is in fact a third square made to fit within the largest circle since its dimensions are the same as if it had been a simple square extending beyond that circle (as demonstrated in the diagram).

The principle of parity is basic to the indigenous Andean worldview, and the cosmos is seen as a pair-verse, not a universe, where interconnectedness is supreme. Everything has its complementary and reciprocal partner whether it is two different worlds, or man and woman.

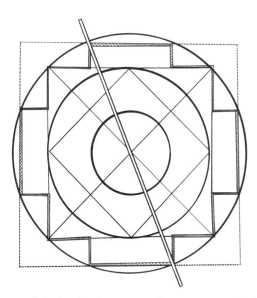

Diagram of the levels of meaning of Javier Lajo's Chakana
Drawing by Gabriela Ansari, after Lajo's drawing No.11 in Qhapaq Ñan

The Chakana bridge is what holds the pair together. In the Chakana diagram, the circle is female and the square male, and circles and squares not only fit within each other but relate to each other proportionally. This female/male symbology even extends to paired circular and square temples on Amantani Island in Lake Titicaca, Peru.

Somewhat similar European symbols may be found in the work of Carl Jung, who stated that the squaring of the circle and a sphere divided into four were once important symbols in Western alchemy. Through their appearance in dreams Jung came to recognize them as archetypes of God in the collective unconscious. In alchemy there was also a concept of parity through a female partner or *soror mystica,* a mystical sister.[5] Intersecting squares and circles were also important to Leonardo da Vinci and his fellow fifteenth-century artists and architects in their drawings of floor plans for churches, a design feature they attributed to Roman architect Vitruvius of the first century BCE, who in turn referenced earlier writers. They saw such geometry as expressing a divine proportionality that related to the human form, as expressed in Leonardo's Vitruvian Man.[6] Although the female is not mentioned, it seems likely that a fuller male/female symbology was the original intent of this proportionality.

The double diagonal line that cuts through the diagram from northwest to southeast also refers to parity, given that it cuts the symbol exactly into two halves. Parity and proportionality do not exhaust the possible meanings of the diagonal line, however, since it may relate to the angle of axis of planet Earth. Pre-Incan knowledge of astronomy was extensive, and still plays an important role in the present. The diagonal line also represents the southeast-northwest line that may be drawn to connect many towns of ancient Peru, and beyond that Lajo hypothesizes it is a Qhapaq Ñan, or "sacred path of the just."[7]

Further symbolic meaning beyond complementarity is expressed by the three circles shown in the Chakana diagram. These represent another basic principle, that of the three pachas that encompass our existence. In a different nature metaphor from don Alberto's spiral plant conception, these worlds are seen as moving outward like ripples in a pond caused by a spring bubbling up.

The central, smallest circle represents the Uku Pacha,[8] the world within or below, out of which new beginnings seethe and flow to create the future. This is the place of new beginnings, of wisdom and knowledge, and the locus of sexuality. One astonishing gallery in the Larco Museum in Lima is filled with pre-Incan erotic sculptures, many representing the sexuality of the skeletal dead, a visualization of the Uku Pacha.

While the inner circle, the Uku Pacha, is symbolized by the serpent that represents renewal through the shedding of its skin, the outer largest circle is the Hanan Pacha, the world outside, and becoming the past. It is both an upper spiritual world symbolized by the condor and a past world that in some sense is always with us but which we cannot change. The middle circle or Kay Pacha, symbolized by the puma, an animal of strength and power, is our present, the world in which we live, the only one in which we can act and create. The urban plan of Cusco is that of a puma, the head being the fortress of Sacsayhuaman. While in Peru, don Alberto gave me a small bronze statuette of these three animals together.

These three pacha worlds within the Chakana cross suggest that the Chakana provides a bridge between them. The northwest-southeast diagonal line in at least one current shamanic path drawn from past Peruvian traditions is viewed as the direction of flight of the royal hummingbird that connects the worlds.[9]

THE STAFF OF GOLD:
ENVISIONING A NEW SOCIETY

An Incan founding legend from Peru survives in similar form among the Shirys, a pre-Inca people living at the present time in Ecuador. In the Peruvian story, Manco Kapak and his sister Mama Ocllo, children of the sun and moon, were sent by the sun to bring advanced culture to the hunters and gatherers of the Andes: agriculture to provide better food, as well as weaving and laws. Starting from Lake Titicaca, they were given a staff of gold and told to search until it sank easily into the ground, and to settle there. This place turned out to be Cusco in Peru, which became the center of the Incan Empire.[10]

In the context of this story, the significance of the staff sinking into the ground would indicate that the ground was fertile and ripe for the introduction of agriculture. Recently, a Kichwa yachak assistant to don Alberto, quoting a saying of Andean elders, posted the following on Facebook:

> At each high point on the road, whether one is sleeping, eating, or resting, try to place the staff in the ground. Not every place is right for planting the staff of gold; only that place where the staff sinks in, as if in water, is the place appropriate.[11]

While this was an obvious reference to the Incan foundation myth, I had no idea what he was talking about, so in 2018 I asked don Alberto for an explanation. These were his words:

All wisdom teaching is gold, and having the staff of gold in hand is to walk with wisdom. The place where it sinks easily into the ground is in whatever place or with whomever that wisdom may be shared.[12]

In the following text, don Alberto applies both the Incan legacy of the mixing of peoples and the symbolism of the staff of gold to cultural values and social relationships. In a reversal of how the story is presented in Peru, Mama Ocllo is mentioned ahead of her brother, a position that is consonant with the Kichwa understanding that the female principle is the more powerful. It reminds us that we are now entering an era of the rise of female energy. What follows applies explicitly to Ecuador, but it is not difficult to apply the principles to life elsewhere.

According to Padre Velasco, here in Ecuador there used to be various tribes or groupings of families and *panacas* [priestly lineages].[13] They exchanged products with each other and experimented and so forth, and created the Kingdom of Quito.* Now, among the Shirys, it was said that at an earlier time Mama Ocllo and Manco Kapak left Titicaca and walked toward Cusco, their staff was buried there, and they founded Tahuantinsuyo [the Incan Empire]. In these two stories [from Ecuador and Peru], communities, villages, and groups of people intermingled with other groups of people, and all benefited. The Inca did this, and it is not that they were all wise, but they joined with the Waris, another knowledgeable ancient people, and also shared in other kinds of understanding that arrived in Ecuador.

Now at the present time, we already know about the former violent, ignorant, and savage interference of the Spaniards in our lands as a result of which we are likely to repeat the atrocities committed, and it will have a consequence. The consequence is social and there will be two elements to it, because things always originate through both female and male progenitors. This is how a process unfolds. However, for me, purity goes beyond the physical, beyond the external. Purity is food and fragrance; these are things that sustain a population. It may be the two elements will be cultural values that could of necessity intermingle with each other, and I don't consider it good or bad if this happens.

All this goes beyond human control and beyond intellectual fancy. It is real, a living force of life, and in my way of seeing things, it would be a beautiful thing if two peoples were to exchange cultures in a respectful manner that would be advantageous to them in mutually bettering themselves. Rather than one harming the other or absorbing the other, both should benefit and create a third. May it happen that this third people in all ways be a beautiful creation and that they overcome the difficulties of one or the other people and raise up children and grandchildren to be a society that has the best of each culture. I believe that at this very moment we are in this reality, or at least in its first steps.

---

*Juan de Velasco, eighteenth-century Ecuadorian historian, described a pre-Incan "Kingdom of Quito."

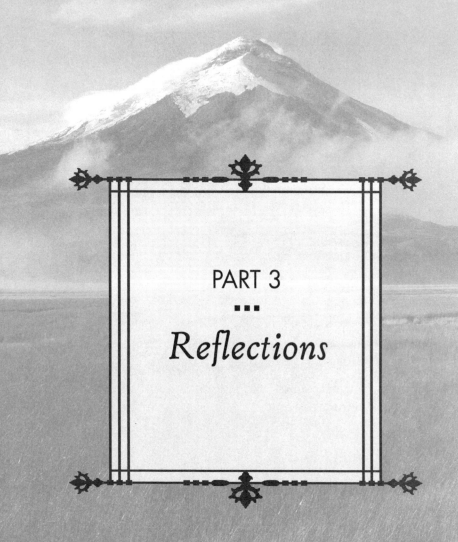

PART 3

...

Reflections

17

Beginnings Stateside

Susan Cooper

Susan Cooper grew up in the wooded mountains of Stony Point, New York. After graduating from SUNY Binghamton she spent four years teaching high school English electives, including filmmaking. Later, following one year of law school and three years of "clerking" in a law office, she passed the bar exam and became a lawyer. Susan has practiced law in New York State for four decades, and for two decades has explored the mystical realms. In recent years, with Nassim Haramein's online Resonance Academy, she has enjoyed learning about the interconnections of quantum physics and Spirit. The following interview was recorded during don Alberto's retreat in Vermont, June 2018.

◆◆◆

Shirley Blancke: Susan, could you tell me please about the early days of don Alberto in New York and other places in the States, and what you know of the roles of Helen Slomovits and Martha Travers, who were early associates of his in supporting his work in the United States?

Susan Cooper: For me it started in New York and Ecuador. I met Alberto at the Omega Institute [in Rhinebeck, New York] where there was the first gathering of shamans brought up from South America by John Perkins and his Dream Change coalition. He had brought up ten shamans, many of whom had never been out of their villages before, unlike Alberto who had been many times to the States and to Europe. I didn't know what a shaman was, but for some reason I felt called to go to this gathering. Each of the shamans introduced their own particular healing style, and in fact, a triple translation was needed for many of them, as they only spoke Kichwa. So somebody first translated what had been said in Kichwa into Spanish, and then someone translated the Spanish into English so that everyone could hear from each of them. Alberto spoke in Spanish (although Kichwa is his mother tongue), so it was slightly more direct. Healings were offered to those of us who were there, and if we weren't in a healing session, we could listen to one of the shamans give an address in the main hall. In any event, we put our names into a pot to choose who we wanted to have a healing with, and I just knew it was Alberto I wanted; his grandfather was a yachak, his father was a yachak, and he is a yachak. Then I realized that because many other people had put their names in already, I might not get to have a healing with him. As it was, I pulled out something for Sunday, the day we were to leave.

SB: When was this?

SC: In 1999, October, I think. I was sitting in the main session, and I guess it must have been Friday or Saturday, and I was thinking I might never get to see Alberto because of the timing. But suddenly I got an intuition that if I went up the hill where he was, I'd get in. I didn't usually follow my intuition, so that was the beginnings of my journey, to follow that intuition and go up. And indeed, I did get in, because the way he was handling it then was, instead of doing everyone individually, he had a group of us lie down on the floor with our feet in the center in a circle, and he would move around us. He uses the elements to put you in balance. If the elements are balanced in you, you will feel in balance. The four elements in balance create a fifth, which is called ushay. So he did that with all of us. He used feathers, incense, and water—I can't remember if he blew water on us—but it just felt beautiful. You can't know what I felt, and I don't have ways to describe this: it just felt beautiful.

Afterward I went outside and walked in the labyrinth at Omega. It was one of the times in my life when I felt I *had to know* where I was going and what I was doing. It was just one of those pressured times. So I was walking in the labyrinth and I suddenly started laughing because I realized that the beautiful thing about a labyrinth is that you just put one foot in front of the other and you will always come out the other end. And I laughed because I felt that was the balance he gave me, to recognize that I should just keep doing what I'm doing, just keep walking, just keep moving one foot in front of the other. Wherever I got to would be just fine. This took a lot of pressure off me at that time.

So I knew I wanted to go down to Ecuador and learn from him, and at that time, Dream Change was planning to host a program with Alberto and other shamans in Ecuador. I was waiting to sign up for it, but I never got any information and finally discovered that communications had broken down. Turns out that Alberto was going to be working with someone else and there was no trip. I was *really* disappointed.

SB: John Perkins of Dream Change was going to send someone else?

SC: No. The communications between Dream Change and Alberto broke down, so it wasn't going to happen. I was very upset because I was trying to find out how to connect with Alberto. I wanted to go down and thought, *I don't care, I don't speak Spanish, but I'll find my way there and I'm going to study with him.* Then I saw that there was something happening in Massachusetts with Alberto, and I figured, alright, let me go look and see what's going on. That's when I discovered he had something happening in September in Ecuador that sounded more exciting and interesting than Massachusetts, and I could contact the person who was coordinating it. That was my first trip to Ecuador. I think it was September of 2000, and Martha Travers was there but Helen Slomovits was not. Helen's connections came a little later. There were quite a lot of people and it was a beautiful, beautiful gathering.

We arrived at the Quito airport very late at night, and they had a bus bring us to Quilajaló where Alberto lives and where he was going to do with us whatever it is he does. He said, "Okay, I'll let you sleep in in the morning, as it was a very late night for you, and after you have breakfast we'll do something." We went outside after breakfast and I think he probably gave us a little talk because a lot of us needed to have answers to our questions. (At least we did then; I think we are easing up a bit now.) We were sitting in a circle around a firepit on his family land and again, just like at Omega, he had us lie down on our backs in a circle with our feet in the center.

SB: This was his original ancestral land?

SC: Yes. There's a huge circle for a fire, and there were tree stumps all around, which is what we sat on for a while, and at one point he said to lie down. Again, we had our feet in the center and from above I am sure we would have looked like a flower with our heads fanning out. One of the reasons I wanted to go down then to Ecuador was he wasn't doing just a trip or a visit, he was doing what he called an "initiation." This turned out to be the first initiation, very powerful. We were lying down and he was chanting and doing similar cleansings like he had done at Omega, but he was much more powerful in Ecuador as he resonates more naturally with the earth and everything in the cosmos there. Of course, he resonates here too but there's more interference here. Regardless, it's an extremely beautiful and powerful experience here too.

So we were lying there and all of a sudden, I heard beautiful drumming and flute music that was moving all around us. I didn't even open my eyes, it was just so exquisite. Eventually when I did open my eyes, I saw three beautiful Kichwa brothers whom we came to know as Oscar, Rumi, and Guillermo. They were musicians whom Alberto had known for years. They just decided it was time to come visit Alberto from their home way up north, and they arrived during the ceremony and just started playing. It was so exquisite and it was so beautiful that when I finally opened my eyes I thought, *Oh, that was our initiation as it was so very magical.* After that every day we did different things; we walked up mountains and visited special places. It always felt like Alberto set the energies when we arrived in those places to maximize our transformation.

That was my first trip to Ecuador, and I returned maybe three or four times after that. Alberto's first trip to the States after that was to Colorado, and we all went there because there was this sense that he wanted to follow up on what had happened in Ecuador. That was also a beautiful trip in Colorado. Over the years different people brought him to the States, and there was a time when I started bringing him to New York, but I don't like organizing, so it was very hard. I turned it over to others, who did it for a while and turned it over to others, who likewise did it for a while, and now we have Caty [Laignel] doing it.

Martha Travers I met down there, and Martha was a beautiful, slight, almost butterfly-like woman who became an extremely good friend of Alberto's, and she would bring him to Michigan. She's at the University of Michigan where she teaches meditation and is a writer. Those were beautiful trips where we would come and spend time with him and learn from him, and my feeling always was that it didn't much matter what he said, but that I transformed in his presence. It's hard to understand this, but I really feel my small mind understands what he is saying no matter what language he is speaking in, Spanish or Kichwa. But it's not my mind; my mind doesn't get it. I couldn't tell you really what it is, but it's being in his energy field. Any person whose energy makes them special like that causes you to transform in their presence. And so I just came whenever I could and went down whenever I could for quite a few years.

SB: You continued going to Michigan?

SC: It was often to Michigan. There was also someone who did some Ohio organizing, bringing him to Ohio. I brought him probably only once to New York. I brought Oscar up more often, the musician with the two brothers, and then turned it over to somebody else. But it was

Martha Travers who started Winona University with him. It's still functioning but differently from what we thought it would be. When Martha stopped sponsoring Alberto, as everybody does at some point— you've done what you've done and now it's time for somebody else to do it—Helen Slomovits came on board. Helen was always quite special to me because she was responsible for introducing me to a lot of people who didn't know Alberto but with whom I wound up having a great connection.

She told me about *The Eagle and the Condor,* written by Jonette Crowley. The title, of course, was exactly what we had all been talking about with respect to the Andean prophecy we had learned about from Alberto. It was a beautiful book, and I wound up on Jonette's trips. They were spiritual trips, if you want to call them that, where we worked with the energies of the place, and I traveled with her frequently on her trips. Helen also introduced me to someone she told me about. This was Lucia René, who wrote a book called *Unplugging the Patriarchy,* about the demise of the patriarchy on an energetic level. She became somebody I was very active with on the Internet, in meditations and things like that, which also contributed hugely to my growth. All of that connected me with other women who got together to make something called—I forget what it was called—something like the Women's Academy, also online, with the richest teachings. Incredible.

But I never lost touch with Alberto, who was dear to my heart and obviously helped me move to a level where I would be open to these other people and these other teachings as well. Alberto's teachings have always been the same, they just might have different words or sound a little different sometimes. For me, his teachings were about paying attention to the senses, what is observed by the senses—sight, sound, hearing, and touch. That was his message for basically getting us out of being solely in our minds. And for me I think it broke that disconnect we have between heart and mind, or at any rate that I had between heart and mind. It worked for me. It was very simple but it was always the same. No matter how complicated your question got, the answer was always very simple. It involved tuning into the sensations and tuning into the elements, and it worked for me; it smashed the grip that logic had on me.

SB: You're a lawyer, right?

SC: I'm a lawyer, yes indeed. And there was a long period of time between working with Alberto and then these other people whom I mentioned, where I was walking in two worlds. I had the legal world and I had this world where I was so connected to Spirit. But over the years it became the same world because it was always the same person who showed up—me. It was always the same Susan who showed up to each world, who did different things in each world, but it was me and I didn't change. I think that reflects what we all are a part of now, which is that when we change how we are in ordinary places, we change the people around us and the things around us just by being the way we are.

SB: I'm becoming more aware of that, given what he's been saying here in Vermont.

SC: Yes, you plant yourself somewhere and your energy transforms things around you.

SB: So then that raises for me the question of when one's energy gets low, which happened to me this winter, how do you get it back again? I wasn't very successful at doing that.

SC: Those elements he has taught us about, they are always there, the shower to stand in, for example, to absorb the power of water.

SB: Yes, I was aware of that but somehow it wasn't quite enough—a candle and the fire when it was really cold—and there were health issues too.

SC: Well, there are times when you're swimming upstream and it is a little harder, but you kept your consciousness because that is what you wanted to do, and eventually, I guess, you rode through that storm.

Alberto is not always in an exquisite space, and when he comes up here it's hard for him. The energies here are much harsher, and there were times if he was here for two or three weeks it was really pressing on him hard, not that he couldn't do what he did for all of us, but it took its toll on him.

SB: He was tired.

SC: Yes, and I think it is probably lonely to be a yachak, certainly one with the sensitivities and powers that he has, because you don't have many equals to be with. I know he's often said his path is to walk with the eagles, but he doesn't always want to do that. There have been many times when he asked the elders, "Is it time to stop?" And they would say, "No." And he would lovingly keep coming back and never give us anything other than love. Always his pure lovingness was and is his power.

SB: I agree.

Could you tell me more about Helen Slomovits? I have heard such glowing reports of her from those who knew her; what a wonderful person she was.

SC: Yes. Helen went often to Ecuador and she began sponsoring the Michigan gatherings and continued for a long time.

SB: She was in Michigan, was she? I assumed she was in New York.

SC: No, she was in Ann Arbor, and Laz [Laszlo Slomovits], her husband, is still there and the two of them wound up building a home in La Loma [Quilajaló] where Alberto lives now. They went down quite frequently, and she became very close to Alberto. Helen walked a unique path. She wasn't well, even though she seemed to be, and she was always extremely thin. In her later days—I saw her just before she ultimately died—she was actually doing the most extraordinary work. She was basically working energetically with the painful energies of the Holocaust, and I just looked at her and I remember saying to her, "This is going to kill you." But after she died, I realized there she was gathering in all this stuff to bring it with her and transform it. That was my take on what happened. She took it all in and took it with her and transformed it when her time came. She was extraordinary.

It was obviously part of her path to deal with those energies, but during all the time in Ecuador, I think that she and Alberto saw what was coming for her, and by the time she was ready to die he had taught her how to transition. Laz has written about how beautiful it was; how she was just so peaceful in telling him and telling their son what she wanted for them and how she loved them, and not to be afraid for her. She was in a very beautiful place, knowing she was about to go.

By the time Helen needed to go, she had all the lessons she needed to have, and she had transformed her own vibration and energy to where it needed to be. I feel her every now and then, and I'm sure Alberto connects with her still. She was a very special woman.

To sum this all up, my first meeting with don Alberto Taxo in 1999 began my journey of reuniting my heart and mind, reconnecting me with the flow of the natural world. I continue to walk with don Alberto as my teacher and dear friend, along with other transformative teachers who have appeared along the way. I am now seventy-one years old and will continue researching and writing briefs for attorneys until something else presents itself. I plan to live to one hundred twenty in good health and with a clear mind, walking gently on the Earth with an open and full heart.

18

Connecting with Awareness

Martha Travers

Martha Travers, PhD, was given the title *mama yachak* by don Alberto in 2007. A teacher of meditation and nature-based contemplative practice, she has been teaching Contemplative Studies at the University of Michigan since 2005. She is the author of *The WayCard Oracle: A Guide to the Inner Journey,* and *Return to Earth: Encounters with the Mystical Traditions of the Andes.*

◆◆◆

When I first heard the Ecuadorian healer and teacher don Alberto Taxo inviting me to "feel," I thought he was telling me to feel my emotions.[1] It was a cold spring evening in Michigan in early May of 2000. Don Alberto had traveled from the Andes Mountains of Ecuador to share the Condor teachings of his elders with those of us who live in the North. In the ancient prophecies, we in the North are called Eagles. Those who live in the traditional way in the South are the Condors. For don Alberto and many other spiritual teachers of South America, the time has come for the Condor and the Eagle to meet to exchange wisdom. Condor brings the gifts of the heart to the North while Eagle offers the gifts of intellect and technological know-how to the South. The Condor prophecies promise that as Condor and Eagle exchange these gifts, partnership, healing, and love will increase on the planet.

About thirty of us were gathered in the main room of what had once been a one-room schoolhouse but now is a family's home. We sat on chairs and cushions and looked toward don Alberto and his translator, Silvia. Beneath us the polished wood floors gleamed. Along one side of the room, long high windows ran the length of the wall, letting in the evening dark, while a small fire burned quietly in the woodstove.

In Kichwa, his native tongue, don Alberto is called a *yachak* that, loosely translated, means "one who has walked a long way." As I sat listening to don Alberto's words, my mind and heart began to travel through many times and places. I found I was listening with something akin to memory. The ideas don Alberto was offering were simple and familiar—as if they belonged to my past.

Don Alberto was dressed in white, his long black hair and graying beard neatly combed. Though it was a cold night, his feet were bare.

"Ask me anything you want to know," he said in Spanish. He smiled at us, and Silvia translated into English.

Alice, who was sitting near don Alberto, began to raise her hand. Don Alberto turned toward her. "It is so difficult for me to stay centered," she said. "My life is very, very busy, and I experience many pressures all day long. Sometimes it is easier to cope with the day if I close down. There is so much stimulation. Sometimes I just go numb."

Silvia translated Alice's question while don Alberto listened attentively, his eyes gazing toward his feet and his head tipped slightly in Silvia's direction. After listening, he was quiet for a few moments. Then he looked toward Alice and made a brief gesture with his right hand. Flowing his hand through the air, don Alberto said, "*Siente . . . siente.*"

"Feel," translated Silvia, "Feel." Don Alberto turned toward a small ivy plant growing in a pot near him and caressed the leaves. "*Siente las plantas,*" he said. Then he motioned toward those of us seated in the room, as if touching our garments with his outstretched hand. "*Los colores,*" he said, smiling. Then, forming a circle by touching his hands together, don Alberto said slowly, "*las formas.*" Next, putting the tips of his fingers toward his mouth, "*los sabores.*" He then lifted his face toward the ceiling, closed his eyes, and inhaling, he said, "*los aromas.*"

As I listened, I felt the moist green of the ivy plant on my fingertips. I saw bright colors and auras of light in my mind's eye. I sensed the perfection of the circle and felt its presence inside my body. I smelled the aroma of the earth in the spring. For a few moments I forgot to think. I was existing in my body's sensations and the intuitive connections those sensations invited. Then my eagle mind awakened, and I thought, *Ah, he is not talking about emotion when he says "siente"; he means something else.*

For don Alberto, activating the senses provides a foundation for developing awareness of many levels of reality.

In the North, many people today are called to shamanism. Don Alberto does not call himself a *shaman.* He believes the word is too general and that using it can lead to misunderstanding. Yet often the students who come to him are seeking lessons in shamanism. These students often seek access to a type of knowledge that cannot be learned in schoolrooms or from books. They seek an experiential and spiritually based knowledge that they hope will teach them how to heal themselves and others. To gain this knowledge, many students seek techniques that will help them cross the threshold between daytime or everyday reality and the reality of nonordinary states, such as those one enters when dreaming.

For don Alberto, ordinary and nonordinary states are both reality, and both are sacred. The yachak becomes aware of the many levels of reality that are present in every moment. To assist people in connecting with the sacred, don Alberto invites his students to feel the four elements—earth, water, fire, and air—through activation of the five senses. As we deepen our connection with the primary elements, a fifth element, which in Kichwa is called the ushay, is enabled to grow.

Connecting with the elements requires attention and practice. It is challenging to undo habitual patterns of thought and behavior. The trick is to playfully engage in the practices—not straining or forcing, not putting forth great effort. Instead, whenever we notice that we are "off," we playfully return. We simply relax into what is already present.

This effortless approach reminds us that these practices assist us in removing the veils that separate us from our true nature. We are not trying to change ourselves; we are letting go of those places in the psyche that interfere with our whole self being known.

19

Furthering Dream Change

John Perkins

John Perkins's roots are in New England where he attended Middlebury College and Boston University. Shamanism saved his life on a trip to Amazonia, and Perkins has used shamanic practices to help individuals, corporations, universities, and governments the world over. His ten books have been on the New York Times best seller list for extended periods, and he has made fourteen documentaries. He has lectured at more than fifty universities around the world. He has been featured on numerous media outlets and in major newspapers among other publications. He was awarded the Lennon Ono Grant for Peace 2012 and the Rainforest Action Network Challenging-Business-As-Usual Award 2006.

◆◆◆

John Perkins's best-known book, first published in 2004, is now out in a new edition titled *The New Confessions of an Economic Hit Man*. He has written extensively on his experiences with South American shamanism in books like *Shapeshifting*. These experiences caused him to come to understand that in his role as a high-flying, world-traveling economic adviser, he had become an agent of a destructive and unsustainable worldview that needed to change for the future health of the planet and all its inhabitants, human and otherwise. His change of heart created a desire to shift humanity's consciousness and inspire new ways of living, and was expressed through his founding of two nonprofit organizations, Dream Change and the Pachamama Alliance, which help others achieve that shift.

In the original edition of *Confessions* there is a clear statement of his understanding of the Eagle and Condor prophecy as follows:

> It states that back in the mists of history, human societies divided and took two different paths: that of the condor (representing the heart, intuitive and mystical) and that of the eagle (representing the brain, rational and material). In the 1490s, the prophecy said, the two paths would converge and the eagle would drive the condor to the verge of extinction. Then, five hundred years later, in the 1990s, a new epoch would begin, one in which the condor and eagle will have the opportunity to reunite and fly together in the same sky, along the same path. If the condor and eagle accept their opportunity, they will create a most remarkable offspring, unlike any ever seen before.[1]

Perkins's encounter with shamanic perspectives that honor nature led him to found the Dream Change organization (as noted above), whose purpose is to take Westerners to meet shamans in order to learn from them how to create a sustainable future for ourselves before it's too late. This organization was founded in the 1980s, and don Alberto Taxo was, and is, one of the shamans who participate in it. Following is an interview I conducted with John Perkins at don Alberto's request.[2]

Shirley Blancke: Don Alberto Taxo told me that he had worked with you at one time and wanted me to contact you. I have been wondering how you met. I was thinking at first he might have been one of the South American shamans (you have mentioned in your books) who influenced your life, but from looking at *The New Confessions of* *an Economic Hit Man,* I see that don Alberto would only have been fourteen years old when you first visited Quito!

John Perkins: Well, I met don Alberto sometime in the '90s, probably the mid to the late '90s. He was introduced to me by my partner and fellow leader of trips, Daniel Koupermann. I took many groups to visit don Alberto for the next eight years or so, and he also came to the United States and participated in several gatherings of shamans. These were organized by Dream Change and occurred in places like the Omega Institute and the University of Michigan. Don Alberto was there with a number of other shamans. Then he and I did a couple of events in the Boston area together.

SB: Do you know how Daniel Koupermann met him?

JP: No, I don't. At the time Daniel introduced me to him we were already taking people to a number of other shamans in Otavalo, in the Andes near Quito, and to shamans in the Amazon region. So he was just one of several shamans that we would visit on these trips.

SB: If you were working with don Alberto in the late '90s, it seems that you probably knew him after his involvement in the *levantamiento,* the uprising of the indigenous people in Ecuador in 1990 to obtain political rights, during which he was on the run for a period of time?

JP: I wasn't aware of that.

SB: Were you influenced at all by his philosophy or was it more that you were taking people to learn from him?

JP: More that I was taking people to learn from him. We would stay at his facility in Salcedo, Ecuador, for a night or two. I think we learned from each other to a certain degree. He would listen to my lectures and I would listen to his. I wouldn't call him one of my primary teachers because that happened before I met him. However, he gave some very beautiful talks during all of these trips, and I found a lot of the things he had to say about climate change and the indigenous people to be very insightful.

SB: Yes, I've been interested to learn about him by translating from a book, published in Quito, for the purposes of this present book. It seems that his father knew that he was going to have to make contact with the West, and he gave him an education about it by sending him around to different groups who were practicing different kinds of Western religion and philosophy. He finally came to the conclusion that he preferred his own indigenous religion. He said to me that he would like to know what you thought of him.

JP: He is an extremely knowledgeable shaman who has a great deal of wisdom about shamanism. I think that's how I would sum it up.

SB: It seems that one of his assistants, a yachak, was calling him a Hatun Yachak, which I think is the highest level, isn't it? Do you know what the levels are?

JP: Yes, but it depends on the culture. Many of the shamanic cultures don't believe in so many different levels. They believe it's a matter of whatever people get out of it. I think Alberto is part of a culture that is evolving. It's in a way modeling Western traditions where you have these various degrees, almost like in the martial arts, with first-, second-, and third-degree black belt. In the ancient traditions, which I like very much and have studied all my life, there is only one black belt. You can just get better and better and better, but you don't have to keep aiming at levels. Likewise in shamanism. I believe there is this kind of evolving tradition that follows a Western hierarchical protocol, but I've never felt a need to say that one shaman is better than another.*

---

*Sometime after this interview had taken place, I had the opportunity to ask don Alberto about yachak organization and what the different grades signify. He described three yachak levels and made it plain that to view these in terms of a vertical hierarchical model would be a misconception, as they are nested horizontal circles that involve increasing responsibility, not privilege, and there has to be a willingness to take on that responsibility. He does not see this mode of organization as "modeling Western ways" as Perkins interpreted the question. Don Alberto's description is in chapter 4.

JP: I consider that the shamans we go to are all excellent. They're very good at healings, at sharing teachings and wisdom, and helping people and societies become empowered to change. Alberto is a healer and also particularly good at expressing the myths, the legends, and the wisdom of shamanism. I'd say he is that kind of a shaman as well as a deep healing shaman.

SB: Really? Here in the United States he is doing healings, though, and I have not heard him say anything much about myths and legends.

JP: Well, maybe he's changed then, focused more on healings.

SB: I think he must have, or perhaps he is just different with different people.

JP: The last time I was with him was about a year ago when I took a group of about twenty people to meet him outside of Quito. We were in some caves, and he didn't really do any healing there; he just lectured and answered people's questions about his culture and shamanism in general.

SB: Well, here he does the limpia ceremony in the retreats he gives.

JP: Seems like there are two aspects of him. I guess what I would want to say about Alberto is that he is a very knowledgeable teacher and knows a great deal about the traditions of shamanism, about the legends of the Eagle and the Condor, and many other legends and prophecies. He can be wise in terms of the advice he gives to people. He is both a healer and one who gives inspiring lectures.

SB: You studied a long time ago. Did you go through a series of initiations as a yachak?

JP: Yes, I did in several countries, as well as with the Shuar in the Amazon and with the Tamayos in the Andes of Ecuador. Have you met the Tamayos?

SB: No, I haven't.

JP: They're very powerful. Don Esteban Tamayo and his son Jorge are from Otavalo and are extremely well-known by people from all over Latin America. Don Esteban and I were compadres; we worked together for many, many years. I went through an initiation in Otavalo at a place called Tundo Povio, which means "spring of the beating heart" in Kichwa. It's at the bottom of the mountain Cotacachi, a sacred mountain where the water comes bursting out of the volcano of Cotacachi into a cave. To be initiated you have to go into the cave. I was told that during the past year, out of the eleven people who had gone in, only eight had come out alive. I later learned that what actually happens is that poisonous gases explode out of the volcano into the cave. There's a little waterfall in the cave, and you have to go in and sit and pour water on yourself and offer sacred ceremony to Pacha Mama, Mother Earth, and make offerings. It was very scary, knowing that people died there, but I was assured that I was well enough prepared and I guess I was. I'm here to talk about it now!

I was, as I mentioned, also initiated in the Amazon by the Shuar shamans. Those represent two very different cultures in close geographic proximity to each other.

Following are excerpts from three of Perkins's newsletters that invite people to participate in the journeys he leads. They show very clearly his understanding of why a grasp of the shamanic perspective toward nature is important for us in the Western world. In particular, they reveal why plants are important, including—but not limited to—those that can change one's consciousness. His view is similar to that of don Alberto, who thinks that reaching that consciousness without the help of consciousness-changing plants is slower but preferable because it is longer lasting. Perkins also mentions *shapeshifting*—the subject of one of his books. Here he applies the term to a wide range of activities—

from the ability to vanish in one's surroundings to changing the nature of a society as his Dream Change coalition is aiming to do.

I've written in previous newsletters that you and I are incredibly blessed because we are part of the greatest revolution in history: the Consciousness Revolution.[3] This revolution has come none too soon. Because humans are navigating our fragile space station, Earth, toward disaster, it is imperative that we reboot our navigational systems—our consciousness and perceptions about what it means to be human on this planet.

Many years ago, as I've written in several of my books, my life was saved and forever changed by plants served by a Shuar shaman deep in the Amazon rain forest. I'd never heard of ayahuasca at that time. All I knew was that it had a profound impact on my consciousness. For me, the most important thing I learned that first night and many afterward, as I trained to be an ayahuasca shaman, is that plants have a consciousness and they are insisting on sharing it with us humans.

Plants teach us to alter objective reality by changing our perceptions of reality, making the impossible become possible—to shapeshift. Just as a tiny seed breaks through cement, we can break through the "cement" that has imprisoned us in destructive patterns—individually and globally.

In recent years, ayahuasca has become popular in many parts of the world. While I have deep appreciation for the plants that are used to concoct the tea that is ayahuasca, I also am concerned that many who partake are missing the real point: plants—all plants—are our teachers. They do not have to be ingested nor do they have to transport us to hallucinogenic states in order to teach.

Some plants teach us about art (roses, tulips). Some teach about nutrition (avocados, almonds). Some teach about healing injuries and diseases (aloe, turmeric). Some teach us respect for nature (poison ivy, thorns). Some about consciousness (ayahuasca, San Pedro). Every plant is a teacher if we are just willing to listen.

Plants, like the seed that breaks through the cement, empower us to do what the Shuar and other indigenous shamans refer to as "touching the jaguar." We confront our obstacles, our blockages, and use the energy of those obstacles to make the "impossible" become possible.

When I was in school, everyone I knew—except my parents and grandmother who were plant lovers—scoffed at the idea that plants had consciousness. The plants themselves have since shown us otherwise. A few of many examples:*

- Plants illustrate that energy, nutrition, and everything needed for life can be created directly from water, air, and sunshine in the sustainable processes known as photosynthesis.
- Scientists at the National Center for Atmospheric Research (NCAR) discovered that plants in the wild medicate against pain by emitting methyl salicylate—a form of aspirin.
- Research published in the journal *Oecologia* conclude that plants warn each other against predators and potential enemies. A plant network receives external signals of impending danger and transmits it to other members of the network.
- Studies indicate that some plants emit chemicals that deter herbivores from eating them.
- Experiments have shown that plants learn to use musical scales and are able to make music with the use of a synthesizer.
- It seems that, during this moment in history when our space station is starting to spin out of control, the plants have stepped forward to help us save ourselves—and them. Our scientists are legitimizing plant intelligence and confirming that they not only have consciousness but can also help us touch the jaguars that have kept us caged in unsustainable lifestyles. Plants are becom-

*See Paul Lenda, "The Consciousness of Plants," Wake Up World (website), May 26, 2015.

ing our allies in making the transition into global systems that are themselves renewable resources.

◆◆◆

The question has been asked: Why does a guy who writes books on global economics also give workshops on shapeshifting and sacred plants and guide people on trips to experience such things with indigenous shamans in Latin America?[4]

The answer is one that is best experienced for yourself—although I offer a short version below.

The short answer to the question: Once I dropped out of my economic hit man job, I committed to doing everything in my power to transform the type of failing economic system that I'd helped create to one that will work for my daughter, grandson, and future generations of all species around the world. Since I've written extensively about the need to convert a Death Economy into a Life Economy, I won't go into details about that here. Suffice it to say that the key point is to change perceptions, mindsets. A Consciousness Revolution is waking people across the planet up to the need for systems that maximize long-term benefits for all (Life Economy)—rather than short-term gains for the few (Death Economy).

The indigenous people we visit during our trips to some of the most spectacular forests, mountains, and coasts on the planet have prospered for thousands of years by embracing Life Economies. Their shamans tell us that we can focus on systems that clean up pollution, regenerate destroyed environments, and utilize technologies and processes that rejuvenate resources. Traditional economies are themselves renewable resources. We've moved a long way from that; now it is time to create a Life Economy that is itself a renewable resource and that maximizes long-term benefits for all.

It has become apparent that the plant world is participating in the global Consciousness Revolution. Recent interest in ayahuasca and other consciousness-raising plants, as well as organic foods, natural medicines, and nature in general, is a necessary part of this revolution. It is also something indigenous people understand and advocate.

In his groundbreaking book *How to Change Your Mind,* Michael Pollan discusses "the critical influence of 'set' and 'setting'" when taking consciousness-altering substances. He writes: "Set is the mind-set or expectation one brings to the experience, and setting is the environment in which it takes place." This is evident during trips to Latin American shamans—ayahuasca is taken in natural environments where it is a native and among people who prepare participants with mindsets that benefit from centuries of interconnectedness with the plant.

I teach workshops on shapeshifting and lead trips to indigenous shamans because those teachings are so powerful and so needed at this time in human history. They are guiding us into the Consciousness Revolution.

I also do it because it is fun! I love the rain forests and the gigantic pyramids of Guatemala, horseback riding through the forests of the Colombian mountains, tubing down rivers into the Caribbean, and rafting and psychonavigating on the magical Punta Mona ("Monkey Point") peninsula in Costa Rica. I love the birds, the monkeys, the butterflies, the jaguars, the plants—and the people!

◆◆◆

Most environmental degradation is the result of predatory capitalism.[5] . . . Our hearts break to see children separated from their families at the US-Mexican border. It is time to ask ourselves what we can do to stop people from feeling a desperate need to flee to the United States (from Central America, or to Europe from Africa and the Middle East).

Answering the tough questions is essential because if we can't cure the disease that is destroying the world environment and forcing people to leave their homes, all our children will face crises that dwarf those of today.

I spend time in Central America. . . . I used to be an economic hit man (EHM) whose job was to corrupt government officials so our corporations could exploit natural and human resources. I see that what has happened in Central America during my lifetime is a microcosm for much of the world. Predatory capitalism, global corporations, and US government agencies have used the stick and carrot—EHM methods—to coerce governments to promote economic systems that enrich the wealthy and drive the poor and what used to be the middle class deeper and deeper into poverty. The titans of industrial agriculture and infrastructure projects, and the retailers of sporting goods, clothing, and other sweatshop-oriented industries, have ravaged and chemicalized lands that once supported thousands of small farmers. At the same time, they've created working conditions akin to slavery.

Some questions to ask ourselves are: Where does corruption originate? Who buys the drugs? What motivates young people to join gangs or become terrorists? What drives the businesses that are ransacking the environment? And who benefits from political instability and warfare?[6]

It is the perfect time to ask such questions because there is a new consciousness rising in the world. People are waking up to the fact that we live on a fragile space station. The problems in Central America and other parts of the world that are behind the waves of immigrants and those that ravage our ecosystems are symptoms of the virus that has infected the navigational system of our space station. It's time to reboot that navigational system.

The answers to those essential questions involve the stories behind the official stories. I've told some of those stories in my books. Indigenous shamans and the plants themselves are working hard to open our hearts and minds to new realities . . . , a new consciousness that is evolving through the wisdom of ancient cultures and the plants.

You and I are fortunate to be living in this extraordinary time of great challenges and amazing opportunities. Let us look at each of the problems we face as a message that it's time to transform a failing economic system into one that is itself a renewable resource.

When we come together, we can solve seemingly insurmountable problems.

20

The Teaching of Yachak Tayta don Alberto Taxo

Itzhak Beery

Itzhak Beery is an author, shamanic teacher, healer, speaker, community activist, and trip leader. Since 1995, Itzhak has bridged the spiritual and practical wisdom his indigenous and Western teachers entrusted to him. He was initiated into the Circle of 24 Yachaks by his Quechua teacher in Ecuador and by Amazonian Kanamari Pajè. Itzhak is the founder of ShamanPortal.org, the Andes Summit, and cofounder of the New York Shamanic Circle. He is on the faculty of major spiritual centers worldwide. Itzhak received the Ambassador Peace Award from the Universal Peace Federation and the United Nations. He was born in Kibbutz Beit Alpha in Israel and lives in New York City.

◆◆◆

It was on a crisp morning at the beginning of April of 1997 when I first visited Ecuador and met don Alberto. It was in his modest home in the middle of sprawling fields bordered by big eucalyptus trees and sloping bare mountains of the High Andes. I'm forever grateful for his teaching and friendship. We were a group of eighteen curious people from the United States who traveled with John Perkins, the cofounder of Dream Change. With his tall, slim frame, long beard, black wavy hair, simple clothing, strong bare feet, and endlessly smiling sun-drenched face, Alberto was impressive, just as John claimed. He looked to me like a biblical prophet. No wonder the Dalai Lama called him "Jesus of the Andes," a term Alberto, in his humility, doesn't like people to use.

Later in the fall of 1998, I returned to Ecuador and met with him again for another round of teachings and healing. We met a year later when he was invited to participate, as one of the Andes shamans, at the shamanic gatherings at Omega Institute and also in the following years. I also had the honor of hosting him in my home as I organized a big workshop for him in New York City and assisted him in the many healing sessions he offered to our community. I continued to meet Alberto with the groups I bring to his now Cotopaxi home, and I am honored to have him as one of the ten most powerful teachers at the Andes Summit, a yearly event I founded and have held in Ibarra [Ecuador] since 2017.

In 1997, don Alberto was just in the middle of constructing a new building on his property to house his growing groups of students. He had already built a few cabins where we shared rooms, and a large round healing room—resembling a kiva—with a firepit in its center. Precisely at noon, as the sun was above our heads in the cloudless blue skies, we gathered in his yard under the shade of a large tree, in front of the family kitchen, to meet him. I can still hear don Alberto greeting us with his soft, humorous, and loving voice.

TEACHINGS

In his presentation, Alberto shared with us the principles of the Andes shamanic knowledge and wisdom. A few of those themes became central to my life and my shamanic practices. He talked about how we need to befriend and intimately feel—not merely think—the four elements: earth, water, fire, and air. He described how when we truly feel and connect with all of them from our heart, we then reach into the fifth element, the ushay. It is only when we connect with this elusive element, which contains all of them, that we can enter into full harmony with nature and ourselves. When we have an intimate relationship with nature, we are happier because we are in harmony and are less likely to become sick, as all symptoms of illness are the result of a lack of harmony within our physical and emotional bodies with nature and Spirit.

He said that in Kichwa there is no word for the sacred, because when we start truly feeling, everything becomes sacred. He mentioned that his culture sees life as a circle, not like in the Western world where life has a beginning and end. This perspective allows them to integrate everything that they do or experience.

"In our tradition," Alberto said, "we do not learn by listening to other teachers. We learn by observing what our elders do. We observe how nature changes from day-to-day. Our tradition is directed toward harmony with all existence. Everything that exists everywhere is a manifestation of love—love toward the Great Spirit, as we are part of that Spirit Love." Alberto looked in our eyes to see if we were absorbing his words and smiled with love.

He continued. "That is why gratitude is essential. Gratitude toward all that is: to Pacha Mama for allowing us to plant *mais* (corn). Everything we do is an opportunity to show our gratitude. We shouldn't think that we *should* give gratitude. If we understand the love of nature, we don't need to think; it comes naturally. It is necessary to have a spontaneous attitude of reciprocity with the gifts of nature. When we express joy for what we have, the food that we eat, the warmth of our house, that is gratitude."

He paused and said, "When I was young, a grandmother told me— no one circumstance in life is negative. It might be very difficult, but when we've passed it, we're left with learning, as the condor waits for the resistance of the strong wind to fly him up."

THE TWO PROPHECIES:
A NEW TIME CYCLE

It was the first time that I heard about the two ancient Andes prophecies. The first event was to occur on December 21, 2012. It was said that the old 5,126-year Mayan cycle was ending on that day, and a new cycle would begin at midnight: a time when the Earth's magnetic field would change by a sudden Earth axis shift.

Alberto held his hand up as if holding a ball and tilted it dramatically. He described it as a shattering and transformative event that would change our collective consciousness. A time when the land would become sea, when nonbelievers would perish, and a new mindful civilization would emerge.

I was in awe and frightened. "No, don't be afraid," Alberto said and laughed, as he saw the fear in my eyes. "It's the natural cycle of life, here in the Andes we are safe. We call it pachakuti, a time when the world turns over. This is not the first time it has happened." In the Mayan tradition, as I experienced it in Chichicastenango in Guatemala, on that day, it was called "the new B'ak'tun."

Alberto has a similar understanding to that of the Maya but based on different calendrical calculations. For Alberto's Kichwa people, this date marked the end of five hundred years of ruthless occupation by the Spaniards, which started at the conquest of the Incas and that was connected to male energy. This pachakuti is a correction of time/space that ends the previous era of domination after the killing of Atahualpa, the last ruler of the Incas. We are now, Alberto says, entering a new five-hundred-year cycle that presages the growing strength of female energy, a time of peace, cooperation, and harmony in the world. It is important for Westerners to recognize that while nothing dramatic happened on that date, the date itself is of huge spiritual importance to many indigenous cultures around the world that still have a similar belief.

THE CONDOR AND THE EAGLE

And then he shared the Condor and the Eagle prophecy, a further elaboration of the meaning of the current pachakuti. This era started around 1993 and would be a time when the heart-centered, Earth-honoring Southern cultures would integrate with the logical, industrious Western cultures in a peaceful, harmonious coexistence. This would be a time when the Condor and the Eagle would fly together in a dance of harmony in a bright blue sky. This would be the time when the feminine energies would return to our modern Western life, and they would adapt to our technological achievements. I looked up into the blue sky—imagining that dance—when two black vultures soared above us: an omen.

CITY SPIRITS

One early morning, Alberto invited us to walk to the sacred spring that fed his community, where he would perform a cleansing and healing ceremony for all of us. Alberto invited his young son to walk with us. As we crossed the field on the long way, I told Alberto, "For you, who live surrounded by this beautiful nature, with those mountains and springs, filled with spirits, it easy to practice shamanism, but what about us who live in big glass and cement cities, crowded by traffic like New York; how can we connect to nature and Spirit?"

He stopped, surprised, and smiled widely. "Don't you think buildings have spirits, don't you think cars have spirits? Connect with them. Everything around us is alive and has a spirit." And he continued happily on our walk. I tell this story in many of my workshops for people who ask me the same question.

WHY "TAXO"?

"Alberto," I asked him one day when we sat on the grass lawn in Ecuador, "Taxo is not an Ecuadorian name, right? Where did this name come from?"

Alberto giggled; he put his hands on my shoulder and looked me in the eye. "I'll tell you. It is all because of my mother," he said, roaring with laughter.

"Why?" I pressed. "Because when I was a child, I loved to eat passion fruit; I only wanted to eat passion fruit. So my mother, who was also a *curandera*—healer—and in many ways my first teacher, named me after my passion. You see, in our Kichwa language, *Taxo* is the name for passion fruit. That name stuck to me. Sweet."

INITIATIONS

"How did you initiate into becoming a yachak?" I asked him on one occasion over dinner in my home.

Alberto was laughing and fished into his memory. "I spent many years studying," he finally said quietly. "My teacher told me to devote one year to feel each of the elements. Once I did that, I spent one year as a homeless person on the streets of Quito without identity, money, food, or clothes to change; living off the mercy and generosity of others. It was one of the most humbling experiences of my life. I learned to surrender to the will of the Creator."

"Is that what you teach your students also?" I asked.

"Yes, of course. But my main intention now is to remember the simple, plain things that have the power to transform our lives and that we can perform anytime. The keys to most things are inside us."

HAPPY CHILD

As we all gathered in Alberto's circular Healing House the day after our arrival, there was a buzz of excitement and anticipation in the air. For all of us it was the first introduction to a real shamanic healing ceremony, and we did not know what to expect. The room had a magical ambiance. In the center was a big burning firepit surrounded by a low stone wall in a perfect circle, on which we all sat quietly. The heavy smoke was rising to the tall conical ceiling top, as the bamboo walls filtered the last rays of the setting sun. Leisurely, Alberto took his place by his altar. Curious, I looked to see what was on the altar. It featured different stones of various sizes, bottles of unfamiliar liquids, plants, flowers, and bells and other items, all of which had been set on a colorful fabric. He placed a large animal skin between himself and the firepit. It looked like that of a mountain lion.

Alberto welcomed us and explained the principles of limpia, the ancient healing and energy purification ceremony he would be performing on each of us. We gasped when he asked us to strip naked for the ceremony so that he could work with the elements of fire, smoke, and water. And so one by one, we stood by the firepit, buck naked in front of him. While he was performing limpia on one person, his four-year-old son burst through the door on his red tricycle, loudly singing a native song, breaking our sacred silence, and circling us happily.

I immediately felt upset. I thought to myself, *I would never allow any of my children to do that, and I would discipline them. Alberto is a weak father. He has no consideration that we are paying him, that it cost us so many thousands of dollars to come here for this once in a lifetime opportunity to have a healing with him.* My blood boiled. I followed that little rascal with my angry, judging eyes. Then he stopped. He got off the tricycle and went over to his father's altar! He picked up the sacred objects on it one by one and played with them like he was the shaman. Imagine! He took the feathers, then played with the bells, with the stones, as if we were not there.

His father, the great don Alberto, lifted not even a finger or an eye and continued his healing and chanting as if nothing had happened. I was mad. *That's it,* I thought. I wanted to leave. And then the boy got bored and left, leaving his tricycle in our sacred space. *Great. Now that he ruined it for me he leaves?* I thought. I let my blood cool off. And then I started to think about this interaction, and I got it. Alberto had never said no, nor shushed him as if he was disturbing us. He never told him that he was a bad boy and never reprimanded him. I had another hour before my turn to reflect on my way of raising and educating my three kids, and then I understood Alberto's lesson. To this day, I am so grateful for it.

The lesson was one of education by personal involvement in experience: deep knowing. It was the idea of encouraging children to say "Yes!" to life, and to let life teach them what is best. It was not to disrupt the natural curiosity of a child through over-discipline, which transfers your fear to the child. Children learn boundaries that are created through deep respect and understanding of a ritual, not by fearing the father's discipline.

Twenty years later, visiting Alberto's home in Cotopaxi, I met that young boy. In front of me was a happy young man, confident and open-hearted, just like his father. This time, though, don Alberto's long hair and beard were gone; he was smoothly shaved. I was surprised by this radical transformation. Someone told me that she'd heard that when he visited Native American elders in California, he did not have offerings, so he gave them his prized hair. Long hair is considered the conduit to Spirit, like leaves on a tree are to the sun. Someone else told me that he'd heard that don Alberto donated it to children who'd lost their hair to cancer.

HEALING AND BURIAL

Alberto's healing ceremonies are a privilege to witness and assist in. He accepts his client with love, hugs, and smiles. He sings and chants melodically in a soft voice while gently drumming, almost making love to the client's body and soul. He uses only herbal teas instead of the traditional alcohol-based Trago, the sugarcane rum, for purification. He allows a large amount of smoke to carry the worries away. He also gently caresses the client with green bunches of herbs, all to open the client's heart and bring him or her into a peaceful and harmonious existence with the cosmos. He is, in my opinion, an example of the perfect integration of masculine and feminine energies that healers must use.

One day, after a few healing sessions in New York City, we took a lunch break and strolled to the East River. Alberto was tired; exhausted and a bit depressed. "How do you feel?" I asked him, worried.

"I want to go back home," he said, pleading. "I can't do it any longer. I am old." I was surprised. He was only in his early fifties. "I think a lot about my death lately," he said. We continued to walk in silence. He breathed deeply of the fresh smell of the river. "That is why I don't like New York City. It depletes my energy. You see, after every trip like this one, I get sick." He sighed.

"So how do you heal yourself?" I asked him.

"When I get home, the first thing I do is go to the field next to my home. I dig a deep ditch in Pacha Mama, and bury myself overnight. The next morning I feel good." I looked at him in disbelief. "Yes, it's our old tradition to let the Earth take all the negative energies and sickness away. Try it," he said, and laughed.

MAN OF ACTION

What I believe makes Alberto a unique teacher and example for other shamanic leaders is his ability to smoothly shapeshift from his role as a spiritual teacher of Andes wisdom, a life of harmony and love, into a powerful warrior, a man of action. As mentioned previously, in the early '90s—five hundred years after the brutal occupation of Ecuador and South America by the Spaniards—there was a powerful movement, an uprising—*levantamiento*. This was a uniting of the indigenous people from the coast, sierra, and the Amazon, who demanded recognition of their heritage and language. He was one of the indigenous leaders who organized the oppressed and discriminated indigenous population across Ecuador at this time. They blocked roads and shut down the country for a whole week, forcing the government to address issues of land access, education, economic development, and the self-determination of the indigenous people. This powerful uprising was one of the most significant events in the recent history of Ecuador.

Tayta don Alberto is still very active in this movement. In many ways, we are the beneficiaries of this uprising, for the indigenous people are now proud to own who they are and share it with the Eagles.

21

Initial Impressions

In this chapter are accounts of the impacts that don Alberto and his teachings made on three individuals. The first is by Christiane Gottwald, a German psychologist who is a longtime student and friend of don Alberto's, having met him in 1990. She had already heard of the prophecy of the Eagle and Condor at that time and had gone to Ecuador in search of it.

More recently, in the summer of 2016, don Alberto was invited to give a workshop in a lovely garden on the banks of Narragansett Bay, Rhode Island, to a group that had spent a number of years studying Peruvian Quechua spirituality and shamanism; Jeanne Dooley and Susan Martin are both members of this group. In her account that follows, Jeanne uses some Quechua terms that differ somewhat from the Ecuadorian Kichwa of don Alberto found elsewhere in this book.

Christiane Gottwald

Christiane Gottwald was born in Colombia in 1940; her parents were German. In 1990 she went to live in Ecuador until 2000 when she returned to Germany. She worked as a psychotherapist at the Psychological Institute's Center for Integral Development in Quito with Dr. Vera de Kohn, a psychotherapist who had come to Ecuador in 1937 from Czechoslovakia. The Quito Psychological

Institute is in the tradition of the great German master Karlfried Graf Dürkheim.

———————————— ◆◆◆ ————————————

In 1990 I went to live in Ecuador after I'd raised a family in Germany, and I went there expressly in search of the Condor and the Eagle, a prophecy that resonated with me.[1]

I arrived in Ecuador knowing that I wanted to have contact with Ecuadorian shamanism. This happened quickly. A friend invited me to Quilajaló to meet Alberto Taxo, a shaman in that village. There were five of us women friends, and Alberto and his family entertained us with great kindness. I remember I was surprised at how young he was and how easy his speech was to understand.

During that first visit Alberto gave a teaching that has stayed with me throughout life. He taught us by means of the Maguey cactus, a medicinal plant that has large spikes that curve backward. He ran his hand over the spikes and said, "This is Nature. If you go *with* her, she does you no harm, but if you go against her, you will injure yourself."

That day a friendship started that has lasted years. Alberto used to go to the psychologist Vera de Kohn's house where I was living, to hold conferences, and we had long conversations, feeling as we did that Condor was meeting Eagle.

With Alberto I learned how to experience nature in a *feeling* way. For me it was a uniting of Spirit with body and thought with feeling. Still today after so many years, when I go out into the street in the morning, I breathe and "greet" the air. In the shower I feel the water, and my feet tread Mother Earth.

I was in Ecuador from 1990 to 2000. During that time we took trips together, Alberto and his family, and I and my children—whoever happened to be visiting me. We took long and adventurous journeys through Ecuador, Peru, and Bolivia. Like Condor and Eagle we "flew" together, and as we made our way through those countries, we received great teachings without the need of books or apprentice-ships. I learned to trust; all would be provided.

In 2000 I returned to Germany but continued to feel loyalty to Ecuador, so the Eagle flies every year to meet with the Condor. This meeting has become a constant in our lives.

Alberto's teaching and my experiences with him have helped me live my life more consciously. That is the thing that is the most important, I think. During the journeys with him I arrived at a new way of being, seeing, and thinking—the way of Alberto, his friends, his ancestors, and his indigenous people. This entails living in the moment without planning anything the way we do in Europe; it is a way of living that expands my awareness.

Jeanne Dooley

Jeanne Dooley is an executive director of OUT Maine, which works toward creating a welcoming and affirming Maine for all rural young people of diverse sexual orientation, gender expression, and gender identity, also known as LGBTQ+ youth. She is an owner of Body, Mind, Spirit, LLC, a private practice using shamanic skills for personal and organizational transformation.

◆◆◆

As I appreciate this foggy, rainy Maine summer morning, remembering my experience with don Alberto brings tears to my eyes. I am thinking about the sadness and grief in our world these days, the disconnection from others and from the world around us as many seek connection and information, meaning on our smartphones and computers. We live in challenging times. For those of us who are parents it is a double whammy, pondering what the future will bring for our children.

In the middle of a serious life transition myself, I approached the weekend workshop with don Alberto Taxo wondering, *What will be the teachings? What will I draw from the teacher, from the group? What*

will I draw into my heart from the weekend and take forward as I return
to my life afterward?

I was struck by don Alberto's early admonition: I am not the teacher
here, we are having a conversation. And so the weekend proceeded with
"conversations" abounding, and not just through words.

I have been on the shamanic path for over a decade now and it truly
has changed my life: how I think, how I engage (or don't) with others,
what is important to me in the way I spend my time and in what I
choose to pursue, how I connect to myself. My current transition is a
direct result of this work—rooting into the core of myself to determine
what the next phase of my life should entail. I believe it is important to
live our lives consciously, even if it is not comfortable!

Yet a big piece shimmered on the horizon as the weekend began,
and its teachings came home through every one of my senses, thanks to
don Alberto's gentle guidance. In the shamanic path we are gifted many
rites. One of the most important is that of the "Earth keeper," tending
to this amazing home of which we are stewards. While I have tried to
walk in balance with this beautiful planet of ours, there was a way in
which I just didn't get it.

Thanks to the weekend with don Alberto, I now "get it" in a different way. With invitations and activities to explore this world of ours
through all of our senses—sight, sound, touch, smell, and taste—*Pacha
Mama* (Cosmic Earth Mother) came alive in a new way for me. We
engaged, in turn, with the four elements—fire, water, earth, and air—
by making complete use of our senses and by learning how to source
ourselves from the gifts that they are offering, always.

I have in my heart our beautiful opening fire ceremony with
Mother Fire—a different connection with fire than I had experienced
in all of my many fire ceremonies. It was softer, more caring, more
open, more healing. I sat by *Mamacocha* (Mother Sea), our ocean,
tuned in differently, and felt the connection with all of the waters of
the Mother around the world. I walked the beautiful labyrinth, appreciating the stones, after rooting into the earth and wrapping myself

around the strong, grounded trees, integrating my connection to the Mother. I felt the air upon my face and body, bringing its cleansing caress and feeding the flame of new beginnings. I welcomed *Intitaita* (Father Sun) at sunrise over the water, drinking in its light and power to feed my new phase, thanking it for coming each and every day to share its gifts.

I felt more alive and more aware of how this amazing planet is forever pulsing with life force and energy around us. I began a new way of connecting with the beauty around me, letting myself be sourced from it and thanking it and appreciating it always in return. The conversations that we began that weekend will continue in so many ways.

It was a powerful, reclaiming weekend for me. I send deep gratitude to don Alberto, whose gentle wisdom and humor was the perfect invitation for me to reconnect to my knowings and to the Mother. I send special thanks to our hosts for their generosity of spirit and place in hosting the weekend; hugs to all of our *allyu* (group) who held the weekend with such sacredness and sharing.

And most important of all, I am so deeply grateful to be living in a time when we *can* reconnect to ourselves, each other, our wonderful planet, and our reason for being here. In this way, we change the world.

Susan Martin

Susan Martin grew up in the quiet town of Berkley, Massachusetts. After earning a degree in chemistry Susan's career segued into biotechnology, perhaps with an unknown longing to see into the unseen worlds of scientific discovery. Intrigued by the question of defining "medicine," or "healing," she is called to work in the worlds of ancient, modern, and future healing to improve life on Earth today. She has studied shamanism with the Four Winds Society and Sandra Ingerman, and herbal medicine with Sage Mauer. Susan is a lifelong learner who follows her family tradition of creating what is needed as it is needed. As well she is a singer and an inspired writer of poetry, prose, songs, and short stories.

--- ◆◆◆ ---

The Rhode Island weekend with don Alberto was amazing: I was ready for amazing! I have been on a healing path studying energy healing, plant medicine, and shamanic techniques since 2008. I love to travel, and I often visit Peru to meet master healers on their turf. The Amazon rain forest in Peru holds a special place in my heart.

I met don Alberto in 2013 in the town where I live in Massachusetts. I am familiar with his kindness and gentle ways. I feel like sunshine when I am with him as he teaches class. Having him in Rhode Island with an experienced group of shamanic practitioners set the stage for a higher level of teaching and learning than I experienced with other groups of people in other locations. This class was ready for takeoff. I missed the Friday evening talk and fire ceremony, but I attended all day Saturday and the second half of Sunday. We started with some review as we all got comfortable with him and the translator working together to get his message across to us.

I know some Spanish and the ideas behind what he was saying, so I was ready to move a little faster. His first unspoken message, however, was to slow down and relax as we got started. He gave us 100 percent of his attention always while teaching. This is a rare quality that I did not appreciate until then. Second, he spoke directly to us, on many levels, always. There was no American "guide" leading the show and letting him talk now and then. In my experience, few other shamans come from South America "unescorted."

He has proven that he can teach in the moment that we are ready to receive. We as a group (and he reads between our eyes) are the collective student. The pauses between his speaking and the translator talking and our response must be part of his lecture plan. I have only seen him teach this way. It must be like breathing: inhale, pause, exhale, pause, repeat. What is he bringing in before he speaks? As he applies his knowledge to teaching us, we receive and absorb on many levels, like paint on a canvas.

I am focused and excited to learn and experience more about the elements: earth, air, wind, water, and fire. These beings that surround us every day are so vast, so huge, that we don't even see them. They are like the canvas that the picture is painted on. What is visible and what do we see? What can we sense in our surroundings using touch, smell, taste, sight, hearing? What is invisible that we need to believe before we can see it, or experience it? Is it easy for us to learn because we are remembering, not learning, for the first time? Is it déjà vu?

I felt that a veil was removed from my mind and perceptions that weekend. My heart was opened up and stretched so much that it hurt a bit as my ribs and lungs adjusted. In the totality of the healing work I had just done I felt reborn and awake! I could receive the gifts of the teaching and the elements. I could converse with the earth and trees, and sing with the water and air their songs. I could feel the love all around me and inside me. I more easily could go with the flow; it was as if my feet could follow a yellow brick road that I couldn't see. And I was free and authentic, fearless and without boundaries. All possibilities were open to me and I received the best of the best. I got the rainbow without the storm, and I would not have minded if the storm came with it.

In learning to honor the elements, each had a new value to me that was priceless. The understanding of the universe and teaching on that topic was welcome as a reminder that we are a part of a huge Oneness. Even so, we each are creating our own "space" to live in; our own destiny and journey through this lifetime. Mentally I was asking him for "more," and it was given with this teaching and with the experience with the trees.

Don Alberto directed our attention to a small cluster of four trees with an open space between them that one person could stand in. [The number four had cosmic significance that related to the Chakana.] He led us in an exercise to greet these trees mentally, telepathically. We made this connection with our hearts, so not quite mentally. We set our intention with our hearts, and we used our minds. Perhaps it was a way to exercise our sixth sense for feeling and communicating. Once we acknowledged and "believed" the tree communication, we asked their permission to approach them, to come into their energy field. Don Alberto instructed us in the most respectful way to come close to the trees: to keep feeling for the "welcome."

We were planning some meditation with the trees, and it was important to ensure that the trees were willing to participate. We practiced and practiced and practiced feeling the energy from our surroundings . . . from the elements. The trees would have much to teach as they are directly connected—with their roots reaching deeply into the earth and water, and the trunk and branches standing and reaching up into the air. Even cut, dried wood has a connection to the fire as it burns! Through the weekend we expressed our gratitude to the cluster of trees. Each time I looked at those trees they appeared lighter and brighter.

After that weekend I connected to trees in many places, especially those close to my home. The practice of tree communication is in place with me; and the gratitude continues to grow with the gifts I acknowledge and observe. During a recent storm one pine tree deflected the broken top-half of another pine tree as it fell, slowing the descent enough that my wooden shed beneath was hardly damaged. I was reminded yet again to give the gift of gratitude to the local trees.

The wisdom that surrounds us is hard to believe, but that is what we must do. We must believe it so we, and others, can see it as everyday reality. Food as a gift from Earth is a great reminder. In the end what I could embrace is that I am part of a bigger whole and I am the bigger whole. I found my wholeness and completeness—if that is possible. My mind is still catching up with the experience of the weekend.

A month after the workshop, I was working with each one of the elements for my healing and in giving gratitude. In some quiet realizations that "we" are not so unlike, I connected to them as one being to another. We are all part of the same universe, or *unisphere* (Earth). (I don't know if *unisphere* is a word, or if I just created it!) To help release and relieve emotional stress, I have connected to the elements (nonemotional beings) as they have an unlimited capacity to take this energy. I know they will have no judgment or story or drama around the emotions as people often do. So, in a way, I have befriended the elements.

Then I ask for "what I need now" and . . . I get something; but again, no drama, no story. Similar with the trees, but I talk and listen more to them. The trees, however, have some engagement with my mind, and that is also useful. Elements I feel more in my body and heart, trees more in my mind and heart. When I go to Walden Pond I connect quite well to the elements there, and I have started connecting to people there, in curious ways, also.

I had a chat with the trees at a friend's house a few weeks ago. They said something like: "We have been watching you over the years that you have been coming here: keep up the good work."

What?

I hadn't noticed them until don Alberto said how special they were and until we had the experience with them.

Mostly I connect as one being to another being. The next step is to connect "as one being"—in other words, to become water and release the energy, without the emotional aspect.

22

Connecting with Springs

Shari Parslow

Shari Parslow is a shamanic practitioner with more than twenty years of experience in energy medicine and integrative bodywork. She is based in New York State. She has been certified in ancient wisdom teachings, training with esteemed healing teachers and elders in Ecuador (don Alberto), Peru, Tibet, Australia, and the United States. With a theatre arts degree from Northwestern University she has also worked as a professional actor and singer.

❖❖❖

Shirley Blancke: Shari, you mentioned that you had wanted to know more from don Alberto about how to connect with the springs where you live.

Shari Parslow: Yes, our town is renowned for its healing springs. They are mineral springs that people drink and also bathe in, as they each contain different supportive elements. Some have iron or natural lithium, others have healing digestive properties. I was aware that they are extraordinary and had been held as sacred for healings by the indigenous nations long before the arrival of Europeans. At the turn of the century and beyond they were clinically prescribed by allopathic doctors for treatments of many ailments; this was called "taking the waters." I was aware of their extraordinary energies, and having learned water healing chants from an elder, I had offered them ceremony in awe.

Yet something awakened in my consciousness on that very first meeting with don Alberto. After his long day of travels and his introductory evening talk, before retiring for the night, I brought him to have a quick viewing of one of the springs that sits in a manicured park, spouting under a charming gazebo. Don Alberto immediately got out of the car and walked directly over to the spring. He then said, "*Hola te! Hola te!*" (Hello to you!) This felt familiar for I had been taught to approach the element of fire and introduce myself to it in such a respectful manner.

Don Alberto then got onto his knees and prayed to the water. He thanked her over and over again with a connection that was genuinely playful. He asked to go onward to another spring, and another. It was close to midnight when he was done touring as many springs as we could access in the pitch black.

What shifted for me that night in his presence, and what I find to be so profound in his offerings, is the depth of personal connection he shared with these beautiful springs. They were his new friends and the relationship was humble and playful all at once. This experience stirred something within me. The springs had been a part of my life for many years but my relationship with them has never been the same since that evening with don Alberto.

The cultivation of a reverent relationship with all of nature, in gratitude and reciprocity with the sacred web of life, has been a core teaching of all of my mentors in the healing arts. That night my relationship with the elements began to open and transform into a far more personal and direct experience. Don Alberto later shared that he felt it necessary for him to introduce himself to the springs before he taught the people in our community. He needed to genuinely meet this vital force.

The essence of this water is available as a teacher and healer that resonates through our bodies, through our community, and beyond. We too have mutual responsibility to protect the land we steward.

SB: I am always aware when I am with him just how deeply connected he is and however much I try, I know that I am not really in that place at all. I think I am moving a little bit more in that direction now. Still, I find it really hard to do, particularly at this time of year, in winter, when you can't be pleasantly outside. In Ecuador you can be outside most of the year, so I like to think it is a bit easier there, but maybe I'm wrong.

SP: Perhaps there is a reason don Alberto comes to visit us in the summer. We know that Mother Nature always has teachings for us. At this time of year water takes on so many forms. We're called deep inside the quietude beneath the snow. I walked with my four-legged companion today, my dog, which in truth may have been the only reason I went out into the dreaded bitter cold. Once I surrendered to the walk I was moved by a beautiful pine tree among many lovely pine trees, and so I greeted them in their stillness. They warmed my heart . . . "Hello, Great Mother. Hello wind burning my cheeks, I certainly feel you here. Please, what are the teachings of winter?"

I've worked with the elements of nature for many years as an artist, with energy medicines, and in ceremony, turning the wheel to meet each solstice and equinox. I was taught to journey into an energetic merge with different elements, asking what they might offer to teach me on that day through experience and observation. This is essential to all the ancient wisdom traditions. We can bring harmony to our world by finding it within ourselves and it is remembered in nature. This alignment was natural for us as children. Our society often does not encourage the cultivation of such relationships, yet our hearts know its value.

What emerges organically through the playful experiences with don Alberto is again that very personal relationship through which he lives his life as both a prayer and a party. "Simple!"

SB: Yes, well you have a lot more background in this than I do. I really don't have any, so for me it is trying to go in a direction that I have never been in. I'm sort of surprised I'm in the place I am, but psychological testing has told me that, having in the past been primarily an intuitive thinker, in this last stage of my life that I'm in now, my area of greatest development could be feeling and sensation. This is what don Alberto teaches.

SP: You were brave to follow your intuition. Modern society often tells us that the mind and its logic are what should be revered. They are indeed wonderful, yet we also are sensual beings full of soul. Our sensory perception reaches far beyond what we have collectively defined as our everyday reality.

We can give ourselves permission to accept who we are and how we are in relationship with Pacha Mama, the stars, and the unseen worlds—permission to fully discern which experiences we allow ourselves to embrace as reality. We can feel afraid and disoriented when our minds no longer recognize ourselves as who we've been told we are supposed to be. Yet from what I've experienced, the more deeply people connect with their sacred self within the web of life, the more their ego's grip can be dismantled. Then the authentic self can emerge naturally and with joy. Don Alberto is very skilled at such sacred play. He knows he is in connection to all that is. It is the vision of a mystic, and yet it can be our everyday reality.

SB: Yes, I think my sense of who I am is very much connected with mental processes, because that was the way I have always been trained. Thus I'm now exploring the other side of things. In my view, though, we need our ego; it's rather a case of keeping one's mind from overprogramming.

SP: You chose to listen to your knowing and to grow. I was taught that we each express the gift of our divinity through our uniqueness, and access the gifts that others bring through the sacred web. Thank goodness there are those who can expertly organize their technical abilities and logic! Those are certainly not my gifts, yet to access them through others is a great gift to me.

SB: Shari, what else might you like to talk about?

SP: I find it amusing that when I gathered a circle of dear friends to come work with don Alberto again, many of us got caught up in the maze of trying to understand the how-tos of his teachings. Our eagle minds wanted to fill our baskets with new techniques. Yet he was asking us to do nothing but to slow down and learn through our own expanded sensorial connection. We exercised those muscles that help us to show up, listen, let go, and be the hollow bone through which Spirit can work. Don Alberto talks about the ceremony of life so beautifully. Giving myself permission to walk through life as a sacred ritual was a profound gift from him—and of course that's what my heart really yearns to do. I am grateful.

I was so excited when don Alberto shared the prophecies of Eagle and Condor, which had been passed down to him by his grandparents. I first learned of these wisdom teachings from the Qero of Peru. Hearing them from don Alberto created a heartbeat beyond the borders between countries.

The legend speaks to this time as a portal of extraordinary potential for human transformation. As we with the Eagle's gifts, the mind and technology of North America, receive the intuitive heart of Condor from South America, and they, the Condor, receive ours, we can all learn to fly in harmonious relationship. It speaks to a marriage of the divine masculine and feminine energies within individuals and across cultures and calls for us to soar together in unity.

Don Alberto brings to us the essence of Condor. When we choose to listen from our hearts we open naturally into compassion for ourselves and others. His teaching of Condor's surrender is one that I source from frequently. It quiets my busy mind, allowing me to open to guidance. It helps me to remember that with awareness I always have a choice as to how I hold my experiences. When I find myself standing upon that rocky cliff of adversity, in fear of the pain of falling, I summon his words:

When the winds blow very strong against us, we can fly higher. That's what I learned from the Condor. The Condor waits until there's strong wind against him, because he is the largest bird in the world, and when there's a strong wind against him he throws himself into the void and flies higher. . . . And I remember what my grandparents told me, and I start giving gratitude with all of my heart and I throw myself and now I've flown high.[1]

23

Connecting with Animals

Julie Bloomer

Julie Bloomer is a writer, farmer, and recovering attorney, whose interests include animal communication, healing, meditation, photography, and the exploration of creativity. A graduate of Bucknell University in 1971 and Loyola Law School in 1980, she resides in Ojai, California, where she is studying and practicing animal communication and energy healing for animals. She has just finished writing a book entitled *Gracie's Tail: Conversations with DoG,* in which she describes how don Alberto introduced her to animal communication, which enabled her to confront a difficult past, come to believe in herself, and understand that we humans can communicate with nature to our mutual benefit. Gracie, her writing partner in the book, was a magnificent spiritual being who lived and worked side by side with Julie on their ranch in Ojai from 1998 until 2012, when Gracie made her transition. Gracie is still involved in writing from the other side, however. Walter, Gracie's grandson, also had a big role to play in helping finish the book. One hundred percent of the profits from *Gracie's Tail* will be donated to better the lives of animals.

◆◆◆

Following are excerpts from *Gracie's Tail,* which I wrote with my dog Gracie. It illustrates how don Alberto deepened my ability to communicate with animals, shifting it to a different plane.[1] I am a long-time student of Alberto's; he has been one of my most important teachers along the way. Don Alberto, without even knowing it, or perhaps he did (knowing him), was instrumental in me finishing my book and in transforming my life.

My book is about my spiritual journey from attorney to animal communicator and energy healer. It has been quite an odyssey, and don Alberto has played a big part in helping me to see and to fly in new ways. I met Alberto through what some would say were a series of misinterpreted emails. To me it was magic; suddenly Alberto was at my house in California giving a lecture called the Magic of Gratitude. I firmly believe there are no accidents. And if there are, this was one of the best. Alberto, his daughter, and the wonderful Helen Slomovits stayed with me at my home in Ojai several times, and I am grateful for every minute we spent together. I learned so much and have so much to learn going forward as the journey continues and we get to fly higher and higher.

I am so grateful to Alberto and for being asked to contribute to this book. He is a wonderful teacher, as he allows the student to discover the inner landscape while out walking in the field of infinite possibilities.

◆◆◆

I arrived in Quito, Ecuador, late at night and took a taxi from the airport to my hotel. When I got there the hotel was closed, and no one answered the door or the phone. The nice cab driver took me to a hotel he knew that was about ten minutes away. I had no idea how to contact Alberto to explain that I wasn't at the hotel where we'd agreed to meet the following day. The next morning I tried calling various phone numbers I had, but the one person I spoke to said Alberto was already in Quito, and she didn't know how to find him. As I sat having breakfast in the hotel, wondering how I was going to find Alberto, you can imagine my surprise when he appeared. I had no idea how he found me, but I was learning not to question things when Alberto was around.

We took a taxi back to the airport and rented a car. Although I'd listened to Spanish tapes for three months getting ready for the trip, my command of Spanish was still in its infancy. I could say hello and be polite, order food, and get to the bathroom, but that was about it. Somehow, however, I understood Alberto most of the time. As we drove around to a few sacred spots close to Quito, he started my lessons.

"What animals do you like? What animals speak to you?" he asked in Spanish as we drove along looking at the beautiful mountains in the distance.

"Dogs, whales, elephants, horses, dolphins, bears, maybe alpacas, and birds, hawks," I added. "I like all animals really."

"But which one calls to you the most right now?"

"I think dogs."

"The first step is to feel the animal, be the dog. *Soy el perro.*"

"How do you do that?" I wondered out loud in English.

"You and I have walked together before. I was a horse and you were a dog," Alberto said. "We were great friends roaming the plains together. Your connection has remained strong to animals. You are ready."

"Really?"

"My connection, my communication, is more with the elements: the plants and the rivers and the mountains—the cosmos," he said. "Animals are part of the whole. They're part of you. They're part of me. We're all connected."

Alberto explained that he wanted us to visit the ancient site at Rumicucho so that I could absorb the energy of this pre-Incan place. Once there, I wandered alone and meditated. I saw Alberto standing on a mountaintop in the distance, bowing in prayer, and then extending his arms to the sky, clearly offering himself to the elements. I made an offering to a plant, as instructed, out of some candy Alberto had given me from his pocket.

Later that night at the hotel, I started to feel like I was getting the flu, but we went out anyway and had a delightful Italian dinner in Quito. When I awoke the next morning, I didn't feel well, but I garnered my strength because I was at the beginning of my adventure in Ecuador. Alberto took me to bathe in some volcanic waters of Ecuador. It was delightful. Then we drove about four hours to Alberto's home in the Andes. By the time we got there, I was not well at all. Alberto told me to go to bed and rest, so I did.

For the next several days I lay in bed, shaking with chills and a fever. I would try to stand and then feel like I was going to pass out. So I stayed put. Food was brought to me, but I wasn't hungry. I rarely saw Alberto, although he was right next door. I learned from his wife that he was sick, too, that they were all sick with a strange illness. I guessed it was some type of spiritual cleansing, or at least that's what I told myself every time I felt bad and almost keeled over. I wondered why Alberto didn't just heal everyone. I knew he had the power to do so. When I remembered to ask him about that later, he said, "Sometimes you cannot interfere. Things happen for a reason."

The only thing I could really do was lie in bed, read, and meditate; so I decided to view this trip to Ecuador as a silent retreat, instead of being bummed that I was sick. I started to read Jack Kornfield's book *A Lamp in the Darkness* that a friend had recommended I bring. It was a series of meditations, just perfect for my bedridden state and my desire to forgive and let things go from my past. Although the book was filled with simple stories and advice, I particularly liked the part about forgiveness:

> Forgiveness is not primarily for others, but for ourselves. It is a release of our burdens, a relief to our hearts. A story I like to tell is about two ex-prisoners of war who met again years later. One said to the other, "Have you forgiven our captors yet?" And the second one answered through gritted teeth, "No, never." With this the first one looked at him kindly and said, "Well then, they still have you in prison, don't they?" Only by learning to forgive, can we let go of what is holding us back and move on with our lives. Forgiveness means giving up all hope for a better past.

Although I'd been analyzing the effect of the past on my behavior for years, through meditation, therapy, and any number of books, classes, and exercises, I realized I was still in prison. I still subconsciously wished or hoped for things to be different than they were. When I truly internalized that my past was never going to get better, that it just was what it was, I understood that it didn't have any power to hold me back. If my heart was full of forgiveness and love, I could just let the past go and move on. I could find my authentic self in the present moment. That one phrase—"giving up all hope for a better past"—helped me move forward that day in Ecuador.

The trip certainly was not turning out as I had expected. I started to feel better physically and emotionally, but Alberto was still sick. I was essentially stuck in the middle of nowhere, with no ability to go anywhere. I took walks and tried to feed and communicate with the two alpacas Alberto had, Chocolate and Crema, and I played with Alberto's daughter's little dog. There was very little formal study about animal communication.

Alberto told me to feed the alpacas and sit with them. He said to try to go inside them and see and feel what they were feeling. Then he said I should go somewhere and summon an animal to me.

I went to the top of the hill behind the house and mentally called Chocolate, the more shy and elusive of the two alpacas. I sat there quietly with my eyes closed and was surprised when I looked up and saw that Chocolate had climbed all the way up the hill and was standing about ten feet in front of me, acting as if she didn't know why she was there.

As instructed, I said, "Hi, Chocolate. Thank you for coming. What's going on with you?"

Chocolate said that she was fearful of people because she didn't know what would happen next and that she needed water. I looked at her, surprised at the message, and said with love and compassion for the scared little alpaca, "You can stay or go when you want. Thank you for coming."

The little alpaca turned and ran back down the hill as fast as she could. I followed her down the hill a little while later and noticed that the alpacas' water bowl was bone-dry. I filled the bowl and thanked Chocolate for letting me know. Alberto later told me Chocolate had come from a difficult situation and had been moved around a lot and was afraid of most people.

One evening Alberto stopped over at the house where I was staying. He was feeling a little better. I asked him if I could have some instruction about animal communication, since that was my reason for coming to Ecuador.

"Yes," Alberto said. "Now?"

"*Si, perfecto,*" I replied, anxious to learn.

"Go lie in your bed, get comfortable, meditate, and empty your mind," Alberto instructed. "I'll come and call the animals in. When they come, pay attention to who comes, thank them for coming, and ask if they have any gifts for you. Accept their gifts, thank them, and when you're ready, tell them they can go."

I took my shoes off, put on comfy pants, and lay down, snuggling under the covers of my bed. It was early evening, the sun had already gone down, and my room was dark. I felt a presence in the room but kept my eyes closed. I assumed it was Alberto who entered the room with representatives of fire, earth, air, and water. A drum beat gently in the background, sounds started to fill the room, and animals started arriving. I heard sounds I'd never heard before. They were animal sounds, not human sounds. The animals were there.

A giant white bird came swooping in gracefully; my dogs Gracie,* Lily, and Walter arrived together; a whale, a bear, and a large feline, not a lion exactly, but similar, all joined me very vividly in the room as it began to fill up. There were lots of other animals that weren't so distinct. Later I realized the lion-like thing was a jaguar. They all just

---

*Gracie had the appearance of illness at home but was perfectly fine to travel in the spirit world.

stood or sat quietly. At one point I thought an actual bear sat on the bed next to me, but I wasn't frightened. It felt wonderful, like someone was at my side to protect me and keep me safe. I felt calm and secure.

When the animals were all gathered, I remembered what Alberto had said. I asked them if they had any gifts for me or any wisdom they wanted to share with me. It was silent for a minute.

Then I heard, as clear as day, "If it's alright with you, we'll rest in your heart. We will not leave."

I was stunned and didn't know what to say, but then realized there was plenty of room in my heart for all the animals of the world.

"Please, yes, stay. There's plenty of room," I invited them silently. I sent love, welcomed them into my heart, and thanked them for coming. Then I fell into a restful sleep. I had no idea when Alberto left, but when I awoke, a candle was burning, and I had Noah's ark in my heart.

The next morning when Alberto came over, I explained what had happened and told him that the animals wanted to stay in my heart rather than leave. I'd participated in other indigenous ceremonies over the years, the effects of which usually subsided overnight, so I was quite surprised that the animals were still there in the morning.

Alberto just smiled and looked at me intensely, like he was peering through me and seeing the inside.

"I didn't know what to expect," he said. "I didn't know if the animals would come. Last night confirmed that you have been trained for many lifetimes. You have all the knowledge you need to communicate with animals or to help heal them. You just need to trust your gift and access the information from within."

I realized I had received a very powerful gift indeed.

Days later, the animals were still there. I told Alberto that the bear, in particular, felt very powerful and protective, but I really didn't know what to do with the bear or any of the other animals in my heart.

"You will know what to do," he said. "Trust in the cosmos.

Remember, you are a conduit. It has nothing to do with you. You might make an offering to the bears out in your orchard when you get home, though," he added.

"What do you mean?"

Alberto's seven-year-old daughter, a shaman in training, who had joined us around the table, chimed in, "Put out some food for them on a plate, offer it to them, make friends. They like berries and fish."

I told Alberto about Gracie being sick, and he suggested we do a remote healing ceremony together, so that I could learn the steps to conduct a ceremony and perhaps stop worrying about Gracie. Alberto and I climbed up the hillside to a little secluded place I had been using for meditation, the same place Chocolate had come to be with me when I called. Along the way, we gathered twigs for a fire. We brought a drum from the house and a feather for air, a candle for fire, and water to use as symbols. Alberto showed me how to use all of the elements in the ceremony.

"The power isn't in the symbols, but in the air, the water, the fire, the earth. It's our connection with the power of the elements, with all of the cosmos, but it isn't me or you." He explained that rituals were important, but there was no right or wrong way to do this one.

"Follow your heart," he said. "Let your feelings flow from the heart. Having symbols for all of the elements is a good place to start. Chant, dance, sing from the heart. Only a few words are necessary. There are no strict rules, just an expression from your heart of love and gratitude."

He started to beat the drum and chant and sing in his native language, and I tried to join in the best I could.

"Call to Gracie and ask her to come," he continued, after we stopped chanting. "See her as well and in good spirits. Explain to her where you are. The greatest healing occurs when you have love and gratitude in your heart, in yourself, and all around you. Do not see illness. See the perfection. See the balance."

I tried to feel that love and gratitude and got the sense that Gracie was there, but my mind was very wrapped up in my own sadness and worry. I tried to quiet my mind and go within, but it was difficult.

Alberto said, "Gracie is here. She likes to go play in the fields and run around. That's what she does sometimes when she looks like she is sleeping. She will be okay while you are gone."

I felt better after the ceremony, and I thought Gracie did, too.

24

A Journey with don Alberto

Shirley Blancke

Shirley Blancke grew up on a farm in England. As an undergraduate she studied at Cambridge University, specializing in archaeology and anthropology. Later she earned her doctorate from Boston University. As a scientific assistant at the American Museum of Natural History in New York, she created exhibits for the Hall of Man in Africa. For many years she has been an honorary curator at the Concord Museum in Concord, Massachusetts. Here she has identified and cataloged more than thirty thousand Native American artifacts and created new exhibits to showcase the Native American history of the area. Don Alberto recognized her as a mama yachak. She is a sacred dancer and an amateur violinist as well.

◆◆◆

I met don Alberto on a hot June evening at a talk he gave near my home in Massachusetts. As mentioned in the introduction, I almost didn't go but reluctantly got myself out of the house despite the heat. However, on the way there I felt strangely excited, which caught my attention. What transpired immediately appeared to me to be truly remarkable and inexplicable.

I tell that story here as well as an account of how my first two weeks in Ecuador provided me with experiences that have taken me years to process. What I experienced during that first stay expanded my recognition of how I could benefit from something that my rational mind did not comprehend. But it took trust to do so.

At the small gathering don Alberto spoke of his understandings and led the group in some shamanic journeying exercises, singing to the accompaniment of his drum, a seed rattle marking time as it hung from his drumming wrist. During an intermission for snacks I slowly sipped some water and became aware don Alberto was behind me, reading into me. He then took a poster off the wall that showed Mt. Cotopaxi, came up beside me, and said quietly in Spanish, "This is where I live." I was surprised I could understand him since my Spanish dated to classes in high school. I perused his literature set out on a table and saw he was a shaman of the elements, so it came to me that I should let him know my dance group would soon be dancing to purify water in the Global Water Initiative against pollution. It would be at the Old North Bridge in Concord.

At the end of his talk I asked the interpreter to convey this to him, and was shaken when, as mentioned earlier in this book, he projected a most extraordinary laser-like beam of light from his eyes to mine. The intensity of its light and energy felt as if I were looking at the sun. I was hooked, but did not at that moment have a chance to ask questions. I had to find out what this meant. Thus I spent the next several months asking advice from people I knew who'd had shamanic experiences, but no one could explain it.

Don Alberto's hostess for that momentous evening invited me to accompany her to Ecuador the following summer. I said yes, and knowing I wanted to be able to talk to him, I set about relearning Spanish. On that trip I eventually found myself alone with him and had a chance to ask about the laser beam from his eyes that I experienced when we'd first met in Massachusetts. He seemed diffident about answering me, shuffling his feet and looking down, but finally he said, "It was a signal."

"What kind of a signal?"

"We knew each other in previous lives."

I reeled backward.

"Knocks you back, doesn't it?"

Knowledge of previous lives was not a part of my consciousness and I had no inkling that such a thing could be a part of anyone's experience. I asked him in what way we had known each other, and he said that on one occasion we were both healers in an indigenous setting in Colombia. Then he cut me off with, "However, the present is more important than the past."

The astonishment this encounter produced in me was something that was to happen over and over again.

Don Alberto rented a car to take my friend and me on a tour to show us some of the sites in the Andes to the south of where he lives. At the start he indicated to us that we were going on a spiritual journey or pilgrimage. Outside his house he lit a small fire, saying prayers in Kichwa and blowing his conch shell four times to the directions. In the car he said he was inviting us to allow a connection to Pacha Mama to occur through what we would see, hear, and smell. We are all made of the same atoms and molecules—the elements are in our bodies—and so we can naturally fuse with the natural world around us. We just have to allow that to happen.

Occasionally he opened the car window to feel a shower or let the breeze blow in, and I would follow suit. At intervals he would stop by the roadside or at some ancient Incan site and ask me to accompany him to pray at that spot. He would often sing, and I occasionally prayed out loud or more often silently. On one occasion a beautiful valley inspired me to raise my arms and give thanks out loud to the Great Spirit of Life, expressing that although a stranger in a strange land, I had found deep friendship there. It felt liberating to be able to pray free-form without adhering to any formal prayer structure. At sacred places we would also leave plant offerings of gratitude in locations we felt drawn to.

Our first destination in the journey was to participate in sweat lodge ceremonies don Alberto was conducting. I have told the story in chapter 2 of how he introduced me to the assembled gathering as the Eagle of the North, stunning me because it reflected two shamanic journeys I'd had before coming, which I dared not believe could be true. I felt confronted because I did not know how to understand this or what it might mean. Don Alberto was, after all, generally known as the Condor of the South.

We traveled next to the great Incan astronomical site of Ingapirca in the south of Ecuador, not without some problems on the way with the car breaking down at night so we had to be towed. Ingapirca was connected to the Incan *seke* system, a series of invisible lines radiating from the sun temple at Cusco, along which sacred sites of many kinds were recognized that included rocks, springs, and buildings among other things. These lines are thought to have been created by the Incan priests of Peru who mapped them by means of their knowledge of the stars.[1]

Don Alberto tells it differently. He says that the pre-Inca people noted the mountains where the sun rose and set at the solstices, using that information to site their sacred places, and that the Inca learned how to do it from them.[2] These ancestral shrines are still honored today in Ecuador by leaving gifts. Don Alberto holds initiation ceremonies for yachaks at Ingapirca. Also important spiritually to don Alberto's people is the Llanganates mountain range on a seke line; its foothills are where he trains yachaks.

Ingapirca is impressive, with remnant walls of a small structure at the top of a hill, presumably an observatory. Below it are the foundations of encircling walls and structures, the remains of a once-extensive compound. The observatory has two walled-in doorways on either side of the little house, and its walls reflect sounds from one side of the building to the other. Don Alberto told us to lean against a doorway lintel with our backs, hands, and the backs of our heads against it while he went to the doorway on the other side of the structure. He made a low sound that we could hear perfectly and feel as a vibration. He gave us bread crusts and instructed us to go where we felt like going to leave an offering. I left a few pieces in the cracks of the walls.

While we were in the observatory I remembered that before my trip an archaeologist friend had given me a thick book on Incan astronomy, *The Secret of the Incas,* written by a friend of his, William Sullivan. Unsure why, I felt I should mention it to don Alberto in this place and his eyes flashed. When he visited me later in Massachusetts I showed him the book and he said he would like to meet the author, who lived locally, so we were able to arrange a meeting. Sullivan gave him a copy of the book in Spanish and subsequently visited Ecuador, where don Alberto arranged for him to give lectures on his interpretation of Incan astronomy. Sullivan decodes symbolism in Incan myth found in Peru in terms of astronomy, Incan history, and destiny. Don Alberto is interested in trying to recapture the Incan understanding of astronomy.

Leaving Ingapirca and returning north to don Alberto's house, we stopped on the way at sacred Lake Colta under the shadow of Mt. Chimborazo. The visionary experience I had there, where I saw him flicking water at my chest and face with a condor feather when in fact he was not present, is described in chapter 3. When we reached his home, I asked if he could tell me more about the meaning of the water vision. He said he was pleased with how open I was and thought I was a fast learner. He continued that although I was connected to all the elements, I was most connected to water and could use it in healing. He smiled broadly when I told him I was a healer at the church I attend as part of a group healing ministry that lays on hands.

My friend and I stayed a few days at don Alberto's home. The house don Alberto built himself near Salcedo is perched on a dry hillside where occasional violent rainstorms have scoured deep ditches in the dirt. The one-story structure has an overhanging roof that creates a veranda over a single entrance, and a laundry line hangs between two of the roof's supporting pillars. On a later visit I watched from the veranda as don Alberto advised an elderly indigenous couple on a health matter. He told the wife to make and drink an infusion of Taxo leaves to help her intestinal troubles, recommending a specific schedule. The couple gave bread rolls as payment, offering one to me, which I gratefully accepted.

The house is surrounded by bushes and the occasional small tree. Taxo vines with their pink blossoms climb the wall on one side. Further away are fields where sparse stalks of quinoa survive with little water. Don Alberto considers these quinoa plants especially sacred because they can grow in such conditions, dependent on scarce rain and no other water. He feels they provide a special opportunity for giving thanks to the Great Spirit of Life.

One day don Alberto took us into these fields to a sheltered corner of a ditch where he built a small fire. He blew his conch shell trumpet four times to the directions and offered a brief prayer in Kichwa that I assumed was to Mother Earth. Then he handed me a drum, asking me to sing a song. What came to mind was a Scottish lament, Robert Burns's *Ye Banks and Brays o' Bonnie Doon,* whose words I did not fully recall but I sang the tune a couple of times to a slow, accompanying beat. It became increasingly difficult to sing until my voice finally broke, and my friend gave a deep sigh. Later I realized this emotion was due to the song raising a memory of my last singing it as a lullaby to my baby grandson the night before he unexpectedly died. I wondered why that song came to me in that place but I believe I was intuiting the deep sorrow of the parched land. My friend received the drum and song request next.

Late one afternoon don Alberto and I stood on the dirt area outside the house and looked away from it in the direction of Mt. Cotopaxi, don Alberto's sacred mountain. During my time there the mountain had been almost entirely shrouded in cloud, and I had caught only brief glimpses of its flanks. The same was true now as don Alberto suddenly faced me and knelt in the dirt at my feet, asking me to pray for him. I was stunned by his humility and humbled and amazed to be placed in such a position. Not knowing what else to do, I resorted to the extemporaneous kind of praying I use in church while laying on hands. I put my hands on his shoulders and started to pray, while feeling tension at not knowing whether he would be bothered if he understood me when I invoked the name of Jesus.

As I touched don Alberto, the clouds suddenly cleared around the summit of Cotopaxi, the setting sun turning its snowy cone to gold. This golden dome shone and floated before my eyes throughout my prayers, dazzling and transporting me with its beauty so that I hardly knew what I said. When I finally stopped speaking he got up and said happily, "Well, I didn't understand a word of that, but it felt good!" I felt I had passed some kind of test, and I suspect he understood more than he would have me believe.

A day or two later he took my friend and me to Baños, on the flanks of Mt. Tungurahua, source of the thermal springs and baths that make the town a popular resort. He said we were going to give thanks to the water and take part in other actions. We checked into a hotel across from the most frequented baths at the bottom of the mountain.

That afternoon while my companion rested, don Alberto and I walked on a public footpath to the foot of a hundred-foot-tall but narrow waterfall adjacent to the path. At its base was a shallow pool with flat rocks that he stepped onto, going very close to the waterfall. He invited me to follow him. I stood a little unsteadily on two rocks and reached out for his left hand to feel more secure in his strong grip. Nothing was said. He had a flower with spiky leaves in his right hand that he dipped in the water, drawing it several times over my face and head, and then sprinkling the water on my chest. The whole ritual was very brief; there were other people around as we were close to the baths.

Later, I asked him what this would mean for me.

"Good question. The element you are closest to is water; you can relate to the power of water and can use it in healing." He had told me this before, but it was taking a while to sink in.

Don Alberto never used the word *initiation,* but I know that in the indigenous view of the Americas a visionary experience has to be enacted to actualize it in this world. I felt that what he was doing was making my visionary lake experience real for me. He was reinforcing my identity as a healer, adding another layer of understanding or perspective to the Christian one I already had. This was a process that continued the next day.

Don Alberto and Shirley at the waterfall
Photo by Dori Smith

Don Alberto asked me to be ready the next morning at 7:00 a.m. to go to a thermal pool that was up the flanks of Mt. Tungurahua that looms over Baños. He said there would be fewer people there than we had encountered the night before at the baths at the foot of the mountain in Baños itself, where the pools were so crowded one could hardly get into them. He drove up the mountain to a small resort. Here we entered a small hot pool first and then moved to a swimming pool with a pleasantly warm temperature, where one could float and relax. A few people, largely women and children, were mostly clinging to the edge. First we each swam a length; his an expert front crawl, and mine an adequate back crawl. He then floated; sometimes facedown in the water with his hands clasped behind his head. I floated on my back with my arms out to aid my flotation, and we stayed there about two hours. I did not notice the passage of time, but in watching the clouds pass overhead I achieved a dream-like state of relaxation and feeling of well-being.

The pool suddenly cleared of almost everyone, and he came over to me and started to teach: "What you are feeling now is ecstasy. It is very important that you maintain that feeling in every situation and give thanks. It is necessary to keep your heart and mind together too, keeping that feeling in your heart. I'm going to give you a thumbs-up sign from time to time so that you remember."

I quickly found that maintaining this feeling was anything but easy when in a difficult situation.

"How do I use this in healing?"

"Everything is energy. When you put your hands on someone, on their head or wherever, there is energy."

"I think I know that."

"Yes, you know it."

The next thing he said knocked me backward yet again.

"You are a priest." When he saw my reaction, he added, "It's *okay*. This is a great gift to you from the Spirit of Life, and it is for *you*."

We started to head north again and my friend stopped in Quito while don Alberto, an apprentice of his, the apprentice's wife, and I went to a town known as the "center of the world." This was Mitad del Mundo, a prime tourist spot, which we merely passed through. The real indigenous "center of the world" is a hill nearby, the Kata Killa in Kichwa, which we saw at a distance. We needed to find a place to spend the night. Don Alberto took us to a fancy hotel on the edge of a huge ancient crater where the president of Ecuador liked to stay. He didn't think I would want to stay there as it was expensive, but I was enchanted with the location. It was the end of my trip, and by American standards not that costly, so we stopped there. The others shared a very large room with superb views to each side, one toward the crater and the other over the valley, and I was in a similar, adjacent one. The crater was so large and old that the area within it was cultivated with fields and there were some houses in it too.

Don Alberto said he wanted to conduct a ceremony that evening, so we went to find a place before it got dark. We walked a short way down a dirt farm road past the end of the hotel's property where there was a small grassy area. Two llamas were tethered, grazing. Being on the rim of the crater the view was magnificent, revealing mountains in the South. During our trip don Alberto had told me how he saw me. "Many people study many years to become a yachak, but you walk in here and have everything needed: the inner tranquility. You only lack some technical knowledge that I can easily teach you, and you are a quick study. I have been thanking the Great Spirit of Life for giving me the opportunity to meet you. If you would like, I can teach you plant healing." Again stunned, of course I said yes, and then added, "But I know nothing about plants."

Later, after dark, when we came back to the place on the crater's edge, a boy had taken the llamas home, and no one was there. Don Alberto lit a small fire in the road, and then collected a few plants from the hedgerow. As we stood on the grass he cleansed me with the plants and then asked me to gather plants and do a cleansing for him. It was so dark I asked his help to find the plants, and he accompanied me to the hedgerow. I felt shy, but covered by the dark I cleansed him. We sat for a bit near the fire and he said that this ceremony was to give me the power of plants and asked if I had any questions. Then standing near the fire, he looked at the starlit sky to the south and pointed to four stars in a rhomboidal pattern between two barely visible mountain peaks. I absorbed the scene for a minute and then asked, "Is that the Southern Cross?"

In the firelight his face lit up. "It is the Southern Cross." (It was only later I learned that the Southern Cross is identified as the Chakana.)

Returning to Quito it was finally time to go home. I was staying at a small Spanish-style hotel in Quito waiting for don Alberto to return to be able to say goodbye, and my friend was on an excursion elsewhere. I waited on a garden seat in a charming, tiny patio with trees, shrubs, and flowers until he returned, accompanied by the same couple we had been traveling with. He joined me on the seat, and I had no idea how to take my leave. My heart was overwhelmed by all I had experienced in the previous two weeks, and I froze once more.

Don Alberto knocked his knee into mine, and with the jolt I began to see myself as an eagle rising. I got up slowly from the seat, raising my arms as wings, and as I turned toward him he rose also with raised wings; Eagle and Condor curving wings in a loose embrace. I immediately turned away, afraid that my British stiff upper lip would crack. As I moved to say goodbye to the other couple I saw the apprentice had tears in his eyes.

When I was five years old my mother taught me to recite a poem that had in it the names Chimborazo, Cotopaxi, and oddly, the Mexican mountain Popocatepetl. I remember the excitement and pride with which I said those names but recall nothing more of the poem; I was entranced by the sound of the names. In looking for the poem, I came across one that had all three names and a verse that seemed to sum up my experience in Ecuador:

I walked home with a gold dark boy
And never a word I'd say
Chimborazo, Cotopaxi
Had taken my speech away.[3]

During that first stay in Ecuador I began to absorb on a nonverbal level don Alberto's core message of the importance of feeling awareness in spirituality and the need to feel gratitude and give thanks for everything. I absorbed it in the indigenous way, not through his telling me, but rather by watching his example. It made me consciously aware that I needed to pay more attention to my intuition and liberate my feelings. Don Alberto has an unusual openness to the potentiality of all forms of religion, philosophy, and spirituality. These lead the individual beyond belief and faith to a relational experience with the great mystery of life. I was highly inspired by this, and it continues to enliven my life's journey today.

As mentioned earlier, one morning during don Alberto's first visit to me in Massachusetts but during a day when he happened not to be staying at my house, I was startled to see a foot-long ring snake by my chair at the breakfast table. When don Alberto returned I asked him what it meant and he kindly said, "Wisdom." I later learned that the *uku* serpent is a female symbol that can indicate a new beginning, and my meeting him was certainly a new beginning for me. What's more, I continue to see grass snakes when I walk that I never saw before.

Our friendship has developed over the years and recently I had another shamanic Condor and Eagle dream that led me to support don Alberto in his effort to try to bring irrigation to the arid hillside behind his home, to make that semidesert live into abundant life.

25

Becoming a Yachak

Lucas K.

Lucas K. grew up in upstate New York until attending college on the West Coast, where he graduated with honors. After completing his studies in anthrology, he moved to Salcedo, Ecuador. He lived and studied with Alberto Taxo for two years, until receiving the honor of yachak. He currently lives in Brooklyn, New York.

———————————————— ◆◆◆ ————————————————

Shirley Blancke: Lucas, you have a very varied background of living in different places although only twenty-five. What led you to spend time with don Alberto and get into the yachak training?

Lucas K.: I grew up on the border of a state park that was very rural and very beautiful, and I spent the first eight years of my life being outside. I feel I had a very sheltered upbringing, which allowed me to maintain, or never lose, a feeling of being deeply connected to the woods and "nature." I think that helped me to not ever feel separate from that, separate from nature. The divide of humans from nature never felt natural or made sense to me. I think it allowed me to maintain or maybe generate a deep love, this feeling of well-being while outside. I believe this is shared by many, many people, but I was never socialized out of that you could say; I never unlearned that.

But then when my parents moved to a much more suburban

place closer to the city when I was eight or nine, I really hated it. I didn't have the same woods to play in, the lawns were manicured, things were a lot more taken care of and domesticated. I think that was really unsettling for me. It felt like I had no relationship to that landscape and to the culture that was kind of nibbling at that landscape. So I didn't feel like I had a relationship to society in a way that many of my peers did in the sense that I just felt uncomfortable there. I wanted to be in the woods and I wanted to be in a much more rural area.

The way I was educated about indigenous peoples was deeply problematic. For instance, I grew up hearing stories of different indigenous peoples, who they were and what they did. But it was always presented without the truth of the genocide that occurred, and never was it taught that native peoples still face oppression. So I would grind acorns, and forage for plants, and do all these things based on what I had been told about them and the stories I had read. Then when I was probably about thirteen, I read a book by John G. Neihardt called *Black Elk Speaks* about the Lakota medicine man Black Elk. It includes a detailed account of the Massacre at Wounded Knee and the attempted Lakota genocide in the Dakotas. That was a pivotal moment for me because I guess people must have mentioned it, but I never really recognized the history. I was deeply angry when I realized that I was living on land that had been taken from people who had been ruthlessly murdered for it, in order to put "civility" on top of it.

On the one hand I felt that I had this deep relationship to nature and on the other I also had a phase of being miseducated about indigenous people and U.S. history. Then I learned more history about what had happened and that generated a deep cynicism toward suburbia. Now that I'm older I feel that way about this society, about colonization, about all these different things. So I developed this idea in my head that I was going to go live off the grid and not be a part of this society because I disagreed with it so fundamentally. That's where my head was at when I was in my early teens.

To build on this I started to spend as much time as I could in the woods, and I was reading a lot of books about foraging, hunting, and more political texts and more accurate things about the history of the United States and indigenous peoples. Then Alberto Taxo came to the school where my mother teaches. He came to give a talk there, and my parents mentioned that this was happening. So I went, and he was speaking to things that were very much on my mind at the time.

He talked a little bit about his role and activism in Ecuador and leading a huge indigenous uprising, the levantamiento of the '90s. He also had this quality of presence that was, well, just very, very *present,* you might say. He was the first person I met whom I felt that I would want to be like when I was older. I think that part of my distrust of society and suburban culture was a distrust of adults. I felt that I didn't want to be like them, that they were missing some kind of key in life, that we and our society were missing some important point. Alberto was the first person who I felt like, Wow, he's got something else going on, he's got something that I don't know, he knows something that none of us here knows. That's how I became interested in him and in studying with him.

SB: So you've always had this connection with nature, and some of the courses I've taken on shamanism say that it's possible to hear nature speak to you or you can feel it touch you, and so on and so forth. I don't think I've ever really had that kind of experience even though I also grew up in the countryside and was close to it. I am wondering, do you have some kind of direct conversation, or how do you listen to what is coming to you from nature?

LK: One of the first times I was at a talk of Alberto's, I had just read an account by an anthropologist. I can't remember who it was, but he was reporting on how this group of people could hear plants singing and that's how they devised their classification of species. It was based upon the song that the plants were singing, and I just found the idea that a plant could sing and that we could have the capacity to hear it so fascinating. So I asked Alberto if plants could sing and he said in this very Albertine way, "The joy that you feel when you hear the wind blowing through the leaves of the tree is the plant singing, so in other words, the joy that you feel is the song of the plant." At the time it was interesting to hear that, but it felt like a non-answer in some way because I wanted something clearer; that they maybe sing in this key or hit this note, for example.

There was a plant growing beside his house that is called a *chilka* in Kichwa. I don't know the Latin name. It wasn't until I was maybe a year into living with him, when one time I was going back to my room in the evening or at nighttime, when I noticed this plant. The wind came rustling through the leaves and it just made me so deeply happy to be with that plant. It was a kind of certain joy, and that joy maybe turned into a vibration. Or I sensed it as a vibration in my body, in my cells. It was just this very subtle underlying feeling that the plant was also very happy that I was next to it. There was this kind of exchange in a very subtle way. It was almost like a wavelength that you can't normally hear, which happens below day-to-day sound. It was very much in my body. It was kind of cellular, and beyond a shadow of a doubt this feeling indicated that I was having a relationship with this plant and communicating with it.

It wasn't that I was hearing an auditory thing in the same way that you and I are talking now, but I've heard of people having these experiences and I've heard Alberto speak of them. However, I haven't had an auditory experience in that way. But I've had these very, very strong, yet very subtle feelings of interconnection with plants that do seem like a conversation. But it is very much in my body. It has taken a while to figure out how to allow that to take place without doubting it or cutting it off, because it doesn't have much to do with the mind. So when my logical mind gets involved, it's harder to feel.

I have a plant in my room that I'm sitting next to right now and I feel the same thing happening. It's very natural and I don't think it's something extraordinary. It feels very fundamental, very natural. I think it is just through being born on this Earth with a body made out of what it is made out of, that these things take place. And I think Alberto's lesson was that paying attention to gratitude and joy puts you in your body in a way that allows you to be more present to these things. The joy becomes part of the medium through which these more subtle things are experienced. He says that joy and gratitude are the forces that make the Divine manifest; they are the pathways to lead you to more subtle things that we might call Divine.

SB: Now that you say this I realize I did have an experience at one of don Alberto's retreats when I sat close to a tree. It was a pine, and its needles were right up against my cheek and I felt like there was a connection there. I was very happy about it and it made me late to return to class. I was embarrassed that Alberto interrupted himself in the middle of teaching to say, "You're just shining." I was taken aback by his reaction and realized that sitting with a plant like that is not something I usually take the time to do.

But I want to ask you about your yachak training, having to get up early in the morning to greet the sun, and I am wondering if there were any other requirements like that?

LK: When I first went down there I had a very romanticized idea of what my training would be like, and I remember saying to Alberto, "If you ever want me to go up into the mountains and spend the night there, and if you want me to fast, if you want me to do these challenges, I really want to do it."

And he said, "Oh, the mountain has challenges but they are not that helpful." So I think I had this idea of what it would take to be a yachak, a very grandiose, Carlos Castaneda idea of what it would take. However, the majority of my apprenticeship and my time with him was spent being bored in a certain way. It was spent in a very day-to-day way in which I had to try to let go of my expectations. Thus I had to let go of what talking to a plant would look like or what being a yachak would look like. I think the majority of my relationship and time with him was spent in following him around every day, observing him and observing myself.

On the way to the market we would stop and he would sing a song, and I would sing a song, and we'd see how it felt. We'd continue on our way, talking about it or not talking about it. Then we'd be on the bus and I'd ask him a question about what happens after we die, Where do we come from? Can you see the aura of this person? Can you see the aura of that person? Can you see the aura of a plant? What are our past lives? What were your past lives? These were my questions, and he would either answer me in depth in a pleasant way, or he would brush off the question and be bored or tired and not interested in answering for whatever reason.

It really felt like I was repeating my infancy, like I was a child again and that he was rebirthing me into the world. I felt for a while there, for months, that I didn't want to leave his side. I felt very dependent on him, and it seemed like slowly I had to re-age until by the end of it I again felt like a twenty-five-year-old but this time with something deeper, and a different sort of maturity.

I had expectations of what training to be a yachak would be and largely it was a lot slower and a lot less "interesting" externally. A lot of really interesting things happened for me internally that are very hard to talk about. There were a few points where I felt like there was a kind of a death of expectation, or of ego, or a death of some part of me and a kind of rebirth. Then after the rebirth Alberto would recommend something.

After I had completed a two-week fast, he was interested in my regaining physical strength and so he had me wake up with the sunrise that was at about 5:00 a.m. and do—it was very short—fifteen minutes of very difficult exercise. And a fellow student of Alberto's would come to the house and we would do them together and then jog down to the spring and we would bathe in the spring. I did that for probably three months. But that sort of regimented practice of something only came after a year of uninterrupted study, and at a very specific time in my development.

SB: You fasted for two weeks?

LK: Yes, I ate four days of fruit and for eight days nothing, and then there were a few more days of fruit before I slowly returned to a regular diet. I had an experience of disassociating from my body, of leaving this world and attachments to this world. It was difficult, but beautiful.

SB: I've only ever fasted totally for twenty-four hours, and I can't imagine being able to go on for that long.

LK: There's one more thing I'd like to say about this. When you tell people about the fasting and exercises they say, "Oh wow," and become interested or impressed; and yes, these are impressive things, but they were the exceptions. I want to be clear that the majority of his time was spent working against "impressive" things; against the Western impression that shamanism only involves things that are spectacular and out of the ordinary. It was actually harder for me *not* to fast and *not* to do the exercises, and instead simply do something ordinary like go to the market or be present. But from some very simple thing, something very different, something more subtle than I was used to emerged. Fasting is a story that is fun to tell people, but in some way it is more egotistical than the idea of just following Alberto as he ran his errands for six months. Also it's important to say that he had me fasting and doing these exercises at very specific moments in my training with him. I think a lot of times we might read things about somebody, like they were fasting, and we might think, *Oh now I want to fast,* which might be fine, but it was in a very specific context, a specific moment on my path in relation to him. It may not be a good idea to take that out of context.

SB: Yes, that's a good point. You mentioned his singing. He took me around and would get out of the car and say, let's pray, and I would come up with whatever. Usually I was speaking, but then I began to think about what songs I might know. He has his own songs. How did you learn those; just by listening?

LK: He never really sings the same song twice although they are very similar. When I was very young, I read a white anthropologist's account of Apache healing traditions. In some groups there was this idea that each person has their own song that was given to them, a specific song. So very early on I asked Alberto about that and he laughed and said, "No, no, no, we don't have specific songs. You sing what you feel in the moment, and each time it will be different. The important thing is that you feel it, that it comes from a place of joy and a place of gratitude that we were talking about earlier."

He usually sings in Kichwa. It's often just naming the elements, naming the place where he's singing, thanking the people who are there, thanking Pacha Mama, thanking Allpa Mama. They're very simple songs. There's a naming, an addressing of all the things that are involved in the creation of that moment, and giving thanks to them; and there may be a specific request, such as "help us with this thing" or "help us let go of that feeling" or "I would really like this to happen, but I understand if it doesn't happen." He is always very careful of what he asks for. And he usually asks to be guided, and not for a specific want. I should also just clarify I'm not fluent in Kichwa, but learned some through listening to his songs over and over again.

SB: Do you sing in English?

LK: I usually sing in Kichwa and Spanish because those are the languages I speak with Alberto. Those are the languages that feel more directly related to the part of myself that's praying. English, on the other hand, feels like three steps away from the actual feeling of the thing, if that makes sense.

SB: You conducted some cleansings at don Alberto's Vermont retreat. Did you do this at all in Ecuador, and did he teach you how to do this? For example, what kind of remedies to apply and what to collect if they are plant-based?

LK: Probably six months into living with him in Ecuador might have been the first time I did cleansings with other people. I went to Ecuador a few times before going there for a year and a half. But right after we got back to Ecuador from the trip to Vermont, I started doing lots of cleansings and he would have me do it most of the time. For a while whenever someone visited him for a cleansing I was the one to do it, often to the chagrin of the patient who was more interested in Alberto doing the cleansing than me. I think with Alberto it wasn't that there were specific steps for listening to a patient and making a diagnosis. It was more living within a certain space, of receiving information from the natural world, or receiving a song, or receiving a feeling of gratitude from the plant. It was being present enough to receive all of these subtle messages that are being offered up by the natural world to us all the time.

For Alberto, when you live in that space you are able to see someone's illness or someone's dysfunction a lot more clearly. And I have had moments where I would look at somebody and feel, you know what, such and such is happening in their life. Or they are being mistreated by their husband, or that person's liver is not healthy.

That being said, I do not think I am at a point where I can look at someone and actually scientifically diagnose them. I did a cleansing for someone in November of this past year. It went pretty well, although I didn't feel that I really entered into a state of deep, deep connection that is necessary for a deep cleansing. A month later they were diagnosed with breast cancer, but I didn't see that during the cleansing.

I have seen Alberto do some diagnostic work, and I myself have done and seen Alberto do very therapeutic, transformative cleansings. But diagnosing someone just by sight and just from that sense perception, with very serious illnesses, is something that I have yet to really prove to myself can happen. So until then I remain open, maintaining a balance between believing and disbelieving. I am waiting to see how true that is, which is something Alberto has told me throughout my whole apprenticeship: don't believe anything that he tells me until I prove it to myself. So that is one of the things he has told me, and I have some experience in it, but I am also skeptical of it as well.

SB: I want to comment here that the church healing group I am in has discussed the difference between curing and healing, which I believe is relevant in this instance. *Curing* is applied to healing that leads to physical wholeness, but *healing* is used for spiritual or mental healing that provides strength and support and brings tranquility to the person but does not necessarily lead to a physical cure. However, there are some cures that appear "miraculous" after prayer. So I would say that the cleansing you did for the person with breast cancer provided spiritual healing while leaving open the question of whether don Alberto's style of cleansings can also achieve curing.

Don Alberto had me do several cleansings with one person, a pregnant lady, after only two weeks there and I felt good about it on one level—that he thought I had the ability to do that. But I also had a basic insecurity about the whole thing even though he indicated to me that she was fine with it. I guess it's a question of growing into it.

LK: Well with Alberto, the time frame of two weeks is a very logical time frame because for him there are many levels of reality that exist simultaneously. So the maturity of someone's spirit and therefore their ability to perform a cleansing is not so dependent upon physical time or the day-to-day context. What seems logical to us, that logic doesn't really hold up when we get into things of this sort, into cleansings and subtle spiritual things. I think he also likes to put people, his students, into situations that are very difficult for them. These situations require them to respond and react and to develop and to shift. Whether he believes it or not, or would agree, in my experience he is operating within a different sense of truth and time. So the information he has access to we might not have access to. When he was having you do the cleansings, it may have been for a reason that you and I don't understand.

SB: I would like to shift gears at this point if you have said everything you would like to say on this and ask about ceremonies. Don Alberto told me he initiated you in a ceremony at Ingapirca, the ancient Incan astronomical site at Cañar in southern Ecuador. I also visited this place with him; it started an important chain of events that led to our meeting with the author William Sullivan, who has written on Incan astronomy. Could you give a description of that?

LK: Yes, but I need to give a bit of background to answer this question. The first time I went to Ecuador I was nineteen. I remember that in the beginning when Alberto introduced me to his friends he'd say, "This is my friend Lucas, he's coming to stay with me." Then, by the middle of the stay he'd say, "This is my student Lucas, he is studying with me." And then by the end of it he introduced me as his son. Later on he broke it down for me that in his tradition, in order to become a yachak or to study with a person, you must first become the "child" of your teacher. This was something that didn't depend upon age but on the idea that you have to become very, very close to him or her. These are only things that can be learned through deep observation and living alongside someone. So you become a child of your teacher, and that facilitates a dynamic of learning that this kind of method requires.

So I became his *wiñachiska,* "the one I am bringing up," and that is how you enter into the medium through which this kind of knowledge can be passed on. At a certain point he initiated me as a *hambik,* which means somebody who cures. That's somebody who can start to perform the limpia that you, Shirley, are a part of and which you have done. Generally I understand it to mean somebody who is at a point where they can receive the energy from the natural world sufficiently that they can then transfer into the patient. They are able to receive certain forces from plants and rocks and rivers and mountains, and they can transfer that, through ceremony, into the body of the patient, and they can cure. So that's *hambik.*

Then after that, one becomes a yachak, which is "somebody who knows." So not only are they someone who cures but they know what they are doing and how they are doing that. And so maybe a few months after he told me that I was a *hambik,* he told me I was also ready to take on the responsibility of a yachak. This was not so much an initiation as being told that I was ready to receive the responsibility of becoming someone who knows. Now you and your responsibility are deeply related, so it is taking on this title in the understanding that in taking it on I was now responsible for living out the example of this tradition. So my life from this point forward is going to be an example of what a yachak is, because it is a living tradition. The healers must live it in order for it to be passed along. A yachak is someone who has taken on that responsibility to know, to heal, and more importantly to live, so that others may learn it and pass it on.

I believe he did the first initiation, the ceremony, in March or April 2018. I can't remember the dates exactly but two other students and I did about five ceremonies. One of them had already been a yachak and was reaching another level of responsibility, and another one had been studying with him for many years but hadn't previously taken on the responsibility or reached that level of connection or willingness to publicly take on the responsibility.

We had one ceremony at the house where Alberto lives and we did a ceremony in Llanganates, which is a mountain range close to where he lives that is very sacred in his tradition. We did one in Quito on the equator at zero latitude. We did another at the beach, and we did one in the beautiful ruins at Ingapirca.

Each time the ceremony was basically the same. We'd make a little offering of flowers and fruit, incense and food, and light a fire if we were able, and burn incense. Alberto would sing and give a little speech about what we were doing there. The idea was that at each of these places we would be absorbing the kind of unique energetic footprint that each place holds, a certain power. We were absorbing that power into our bodies and into our current path.

The thing with Alberto is that the ceremonies themselves are extremely simple. The songs he sings are very simple; the path to becoming a yachak is in many ways very simple. He is not one who would say first you enter with your left foot into the circle and you place rocks here or sixty rocks there, and so forth. He is very improvisational, because for him what is important is the underlying energetic process of what's happening and not so much the physical structure of the ceremony that takes place. I think that has a lot to do with his Eagle and Condor sensibility; mind and heart together. Thus he is much less interested in having a step-by-step formula than in having the process be alive.

Ingapirca was our most public ceremony. One of the other people who was being initiated is from there, so his family and community came. Ingapirca is a tourist site, so there were a lot of tourists there as well. Basically it was just Alberto stating that the three of us were taking on this responsibility. He told us that we now had the capacity to act as healers, to charge for healing, and to be sought out for healing and advice. He did the ritual, sang, we spoke, and then we performed cleansings for the people there. It was very beautiful.

SB: Yes, I can really appreciate that. Don Alberto also told me that each yachak has his or her specialty or specialties that may eventually be added to, and he gave me the technical names for two of you. You are a yachak purik, someone who is starting to walk the path and who has visionary potentiality. One of the others is a yachak rimak, whose specialty is public speaking.

Now I want to ask you about the cultural ceremonies, things like the Day of the Dead, or the solstices and equinoxes. How much of that did you experience or was that more in the public sphere?

LK: Listening to Alberto's stories of when he was a kid, he really was born in a very, very different time when his community was much more separate from the rest of Ecuadorian society. Kichwa was the principal language spoken there. His pre-Inca Atik people who have their own pueblo near Salcedo became Kichwa speakers, the language of the Inca. Kichwa-speaking people comprise many different traditions, lineages, and tribes in addition to his.

Alberto would tell me that the Day of the Dead meant a lot to his family, and they would go to the gravesite and share food on that day. There would be a sharing of this and a partaking of that, a kind of celebration of the idea of death and reincarnation and the journey of life and that sort of thing.

But now the Day of the Dead is much more of a commercial holiday in which we drink *colada morada,* a sweet purple corn beverage, and eat *panes de wawas,* breads shaped in the form of little dolls (which I like). It does not feel like the larger culture has much of a relationship to what Alberto has to say about that, and the same is true with the equinoxes, but I think it really varies where in Ecuador you are talking about. There are parades and festivals that happen with people celebrating *Inti Watana,* the idea of the sun getting closer or farther away. However, I didn't observe whether there are the same, more subtle and spiritual rituals that Alberto talks about.

I don't know if that answers your question, but my take on this is that there are a lot of beautiful rituals and customs that happen. Yet the more subtle spiritual purpose behind them, as Alberto describes them, does not seem to be in practice as much outside of his household. But that is my limited perspective, and I'm sure many people would disagree with it.

SB: I have a somewhat different take on this, for don Alberto took me to Otavalo, an indigenous town north of Quito. As you know, we attended a Day of the Dead ceremony one November where spirituality was certainly in the forefront. I also sensed it in an equinox ceremony he took me to. He told me the equinoxes were more important to them than the solstices, so I'd like to take the opportunity here to describe my experience of those two ceremonies.

To start with the fall equinox ceremony, it was led by a senior yachak, an associate of don Alberto's, on the top of a high hill that is on the equator north of Quito. About a dozen people were there, mostly non-indigenous. At what has been determined to have been the position of an Incan calendrical marker, an obelisk had been erected that serves as a sundial, with calendrical positions marked on the ground. We were able to observe that at noon on the equinox the obelisk is without a shadow.

The ceremony started with a young Amazonian yachak offering a

ritual drink of tobacco juice. This had the effect of knocking me off my
feet so that I lay a long time, hat over my face, overcome by a very bright
light (the brilliance of the sun?). From my position on the ground when
I was finally able to look, the ceremony seemed to consist of physical
exercises culminating in a circle dance. After I struggled to my feet, don
Alberto took my hand and led me into the dance, but I missed the rest
of the ceremony and anything that might have been said. The yachaks
were surprised and concerned at my reaction, and don Alberto thought
the drink must have come from a *datura* plant, a powerful hallucinogen, but no. They arrived at no conclusion, and I didn't suffer any ill
effects afterward. I have since learned that tobacco has been found to
contain harmala alkaloids, hallucinogens used in Amazonian shamanism, but no one else reacted to the juice as I did.

As you mentioned, ceremonies differ very much according to location, and in indigenous Otavalo I would say the Day of the Dead has
retained its meaning successfully. Don Alberto and I arrived the previous evening to participate in bread roll baking. The rolls were to be
taken to the cemetery the next day. I found myself in the middle of
a joking, laughing group of indigenous women on an open patio with
tables, working dough into whatever shapes we might imagine: twists of
all kinds, animals including an elephant, birds, and people. Then we put
them on tin trays to be baked in a beehive oven. Having arrived there
about 10:00 p.m., by midnight I was growing weary and wondering
where I was going to stay the night, I looked around for don Alberto. I
felt quite discomfited when he was nowhere to be found. I knew he was
exhausted and figured he had left, but assumed my hostess had to be
there. I finally spoke to a lady who started laughing and would tell me
nothing so I thought it must be she. Sure enough, around 1:30 a.m. she
drove me, loaded down with rolls, to her home—a very large apartment
over a pharmacy that she owned and ran. Speaking fluent English, she
informed me that I needed to be at the cemetery by 6:00 a.m.

Don Alberto was at the cemetery with another hostess, an older
lady visiting the grave of her son. She had brought fruit and corn and a

drink, and I offered my rolls. We ate in silence in the hot early morning while waiting for the official celebrant to come to offer prayers for the dead, a woman in indigenous dress. Some of the food was given to her, I would guess as payment. The hostess's daughter was there too, and unlike her mother who kept silence, she wanted to chat. She explained to me that her brother had died at twenty-one. At this I felt I could talk about my brother who had also died at twenty-one. This was a very touching moment for me, because it seemed I could feel the spirits were there enjoying the aromas of the food with us, something I understand is an important aspect of this ceremony.

The alleyway up to the cemetery at the top of the hill was broad and had many stalls selling food, the crowds growing bigger as the hour grew later. As we left I was startled to see another alleyway with similar stalls and crowds leading to a cemetery next door to the one we were at. It was the nonindigenous cemetery. My initial reaction was that this separation was discriminatory, and perhaps originally it was. Today, however, it has the value of allowing the indigenous people to maintain their customs without disruption from the dominant society.

LK: Yes, I think it is really presumptuous of me to try to judge how spiritual these indigenous experiences are as obviously I am a white American who comes from a very different culture. Thus I don't think I can be a judge about how spiritual these things are in general. I think that's for people practicing these things to decide. What I do know is what Alberto would tell me. And that is that during the spring equinox, for example, there is a potential for boosting one's capacity to absorb energetic vibrations and connect deeply with the sun in a very literal sense. He described the potential capacity that moment has to further one along the path. There are certain rituals one can do in that moment that allow you to receive more energy from the sun that can help you on your way.

26

Every Moment Is Sacred and Full of Possibility

Caty Laignel

Caty Laignel was born in Caracas, Venezuela, and has lived in Latin America, Europe, and the United States. She is the director of Blue Rock School, a progressive nature-and-art-infused K–8 school in New York where she also runs the theater program. Caty is an actress and director and has been on a spiritual search since a young age.

◆◆◆

In assessing what the teachings of don Alberto Taxo have brought to my life, let me begin by saying that I do not feel that I have achieved a static level of understanding of his teachings. For me, this spiritual work is not akin to learning a skill that, once mastered, is complete. Through don Alberto's teachings, my experience and knowledge are evolving and I benefit from and am grateful for reminders to keep diving deeper and more consistently into this practice. For this reason, for the past several years, I have been one of the people to host don Alberto when he travels to the Northeast to hold workshops. I am very grateful to be of service to his teachings by translating. Being in his presence continues to be an important part of my life.

As a longtime student of don Alberto, some things feel easier now.

The shift is mainly in my attitude toward my own ability to incorporate all that he offers us. I have softened toward myself. During the exercises he gives I have come to accept myself more and question myself less. I seem to judge myself less harshly—in terms of my ability to "practice" his teachings—than when I first met him. Perhaps at the beginning, I felt that it was possible to "advance" if only I tried hard enough. My expectation of a kind of neon-light signage around enlightenment was also higher. With this lessening of expectation and greater acceptance of my ability to just be, I have begun to feel more open to what is around me.

That is not to say that I am not disappointed when the stressors of daily life sweep me away and I forget to connect to the present. However, don Alberto's invitations to flow, to come back to the moment if the mind wanders, to be patient and loving with oneself, are wonderful touchstones. He offers a path that's less full of self-importance and a wish to arrive at a certain level of spiritual awakening, and instead gives us one that encourages a genuine curiosity and attention to what is.

An intellectual wish or drive to be more conscious in and of itself can bring about judgment, a sense of "you must" and frustration when invariably one falls short of the goal. Or when a teaching is only approached with the mind it can put the emphasis on acquiring more and more theoretical knowledge, followed by posturing to avoid facing one's practical difficulties in being present. Don Alberto's use of the word *invitation* removes this sense of obligation. With don Alberto, one's attitude about effort shifts from discipline to openness, from a goal-oriented work, to a sinking into reality with all one's senses and the possibility of having a playful, gentle, relationship with everything. His way provides a lighter touch all around than spiritual schools that encourage a practice with exact rules and repetitive exercises. Naturally, I am not speaking about don Alberto's teaching for the apprentice to become a yachak, which I understand has many different layers of instruction. I am speaking of his teaching to groups of interested men and women who wish to learn from him, starting just where they are spiritually.

Since I organize workshops and talks for don Alberto I am often approached by prospective participants or even some who have done a workshop or two with him before, and they've asked the following questions. What will he be speaking about? Will we go up a level if we do the next workshop? In trying to answer these sorts of questions I believe I can address a fundamental difference between don Alberto and other shamans or teachers who hold teaching workshops.

First, don Alberto is completely unattached to a "topic" or series of topics to lecture about. He is perfectly capable of speaking profoundly on any number of subjects: death, love, dreams, anger, awakening, and consciousness, for instance. However, when he gives a talk he encourages participants to come to some simple ways of connecting to the present moment through one's senses and the elements in nature surrounding us at all times. His talks are always different and yet may have some similar aspects. What I have found fascinating is his ability to connect to the energy in the room and then to respond with the direction he takes. I have seen him address people and children who have just lost a loved one or gone through a divorce, with uncanny precision despite having just met them and not "knowing" their circumstances. Don Alberto would say that this type of intuitive knowing or sensing comes from connecting to the moment, and those present with all one's senses.

In terms of levels and the importance of objects or exercises, don Alberto does not advocate having this object or that object, this book or that prayer, for instance. Nor does he advocate repeating certain steps in a precise order, although I am sure that if that is someone's way to connect he would not be against it. I have seen him create a very focused and powerful circle with different objects at different times: a candle, a large fire, a feather, a stone, a glass of water, a plant. This can happen at dawn, at dusk, or midday, and never be the same and yet always be special. Anything readily available from nature can represent and transmit the power of the elements. Nothing needs to be purchased or held on to tightly. All that we need surrounds us all the time. In our consumer and school-based society this is quite shocking. We don't need to "have" anything or climb a specific ladder to be present to the great powers of life.

At once respectful of both sacred objects and simple pebbles, don Alberto is also singularly unattached to them. In one gathering, a young child took the large condor feather he had been using and experimentally stuck it into the flame of a candle. One of the participants was shocked and voiced her concern for don Alberto's "feelings" since the feather was so rare and slightly singed. Don Alberto was unaffected and articulated that everything is a part of everything else: the curious child, the flame, the feather, were all just manifestations. He said that of course as an adult one does not intentionally mistreat things, but none of these symbols are permanent. They are just vehicles for a more sublime energy. In the same way our bodies are simply packaging for life's energy. We will let them go, having thanked them and cared for them but without getting too attached since they are only the trappings for that same force that is within everything. That force is interconnected simultaneously to everything in the cosmos. Our sense of being separate is as much an illusion as it seems a reality.

In terms of achieving a "certain level," to me his invitation is rather NOW. Not if I do this, I will get to a special state later. The moment is now. I do not need to wait for a special cushion or a special time or surroundings to be present. In the beautiful and the challenging moments, and both beauty and challenge are always present, all I need is to accompany myself and notice what is. For example, our inhalation and exhalation, our breathing, is always here. If I bring my awareness to it, I experience the exchange of energy in my breathing, the breath coming in and then the breath going out. It is so clearly the vital force of life accompanying and working through me every moment.

Don Alberto has faith in the great power of Pacha Mama and believes that what needs to happen will. As well, it will be full of inherent learning. All of this is quite impressive to watch. I have never seen him shaken by ill temper, impatient with circumstances of delay, fearful even when others are, or fazed by contretemps that can be frustrating to most of us. His general equanimity in the face of these disturbances is a teaching in itself, as is his solid belief in the subtle energies at work around and through us.

At one talk, I was very taken by his response to a mother who was having a very hard time with her adult son (who still lived at home) and some of the choices he was making in his life. Their relationship had become quite tense and strained. Don Alberto asked her not to talk to him about her wishes, fears, or demands, but rather to do things for him, to express all her love and wishes through actions like cooking some food for him or washing and folding his clothing with love. Importantly, she was not to tell him what she had done nor recriminate against him by using her gestures to request that he change, "I did your laundry so you should . . . " Rather she might allow her energy and positive wishes to come to him through other than verbal and intellectual means.

Whether or not this practice "made" her son change, I do not know. But what I felt was so powerful was that it was an invitation for *her* to be in a different state, putting her energy into positive actions without worrying or having angry and judgmental thoughts. So in essence, it was an opportunity for her to be with herself differently and to emanate more harmony. Don Alberto often speaks of our energy impacting those around us and ourselves. That is why releasing negativity and taking in positive energy from the air, fire, water, and plants (earth element) is so important. We can be carriers of light.

He teaches that one can communicate through subtle vibrations and physical manifestations. In fact, we are always communicating that way consciously or unconsciously, but to do so with awareness can make us beings of light capable of bringing love and healing to ourselves and those around us. Although invisible and less tangible, these forces are around us and when more alert or conscious, we do perceive them. So starting to improve a relationship in that realm when harm has been done is a recognition of these energies. On a certain level we are all picking up our unwitting manifestations from each other and affecting each other as well as impacting our surroundings. By tuning in and choosing to emanate and express love, care, and gratitude, we can be agents of positive energy in the world.

And this is perhaps the most important aspect of his teachings for me—the realization that we have a choice in how we wish to live and what we wish to bring to the world and those around us. He will often say we need to smile and catch ourselves in the mirror, to laugh at our serious faces. We need to recognize that we choose whether we remember positive experiences or negative ones, talk of positive things, or bring up pain and resentment: in our choices we are determining what we bring into the world and our lives.

One of his most powerful teachings is about gratitude. He speaks often about how expressing gratitude is a way to be connected to the cosmos: that by enjoying the simple gifts of the moment we are expressing gratitude. Through our pleasure, not just our words and intellect, we can truly share our appreciation for life's gifts. Gratitude is felt by the flower we admire. The Pacha Mama senses our gratitude when we slowly savor the food that we eat, and in turn we are able to receive not only the nutrients but the more subtle healing energies in the food.

Don Alberto encourages us to be like children and play gratefully with the gifts of Pacha Mama, not waiting to pray or create a ruray only on Saturdays or Sundays or before eating, or in a church or temple. Instead, he recommends we create our own rurays regularly, with intention. These personal practices bring us into the moment. They can range from more elaborate expressions to simple gestures such as lighting a candle, singing, or appreciating the water we are drinking. When we are awake to the subtle vibrations—the breath, the light, the air, the plants and animals around us, our own bodies, feelings and thoughts—then we are connected. By allowing our intuition to flow in this way, we can live more fully, less governed by the mind and abstractions. We can be present and alive, conscious of being a part of a much larger and powerful universe. *Es fácil,* "it's easy," he often says. Only our thoughts separate us from what is right here, right now. His invitation is to open to life through our senses and to experience that every moment is sacred and full of possibility.

My studying with don Alberto has given me an opportunity to connect my love of nature to this quest for presence in alignment with the wisdom of ancient teachings. For this, I am forever grateful to don Alberto Taxo.

A Christmas Story

At Christmastime in 2018, don Alberto came with his teenage daughter to spend Christmas with me. He wanted to experience my family's celebration of Christmas through gift giving, holiday food, and general good cheer. I am blessed in having family members who get along well and who enjoy one another. He also wanted a rest from the constant demands on him in Ecuador. I arranged to be on healing duty at my church while he was here, thinking he might be interested to see our approach, which seemed so very different from his own. People who want prayers come during Communion. The two healers lay on hands, extemporize prayers according to what is requested, and offer anointing.

The space for healing in my church is in a transept near a small altar and kneeler. On the altar are a copy of the icon of Jesus from St. Catherine's Monastery in the Sinai, two candles and fresh flowers, and oil for anointing. When it occurred to me that these represented three of the five Andean elements (fire, earth, and oil, which is a symbol of ushay), I started, when on duty, to add two small woodpecker feathers and a shell for air and water. This was something that was quickly adopted by others on the healing team.

Don Alberto came with me the Sunday I was on healing duty. I invited him to receive Communion given that my Episcopal Church belongs to a liberal Christianity that offers Communion to all who "seek God." He accepted. On an earlier occasion when he took Communion at my church the priest took a step backward in astonishment at the look of intense devotion on his face. Our current priest is a woman, and when she was at the altar, don Alberto took a photo of her with his iPhone, explaining to me that such a thing was unknown in Ecuador. I like to think that he would have shown this picture to his indigenous elders, as we are now entering their era of the rise of female energy and women's power.

The healers are given Communion first so that they can go quickly to the transept. I had not invited don Alberto in advance to be part of the healing team as I did not know how my partner, who was the leader of the team, might feel about it. However, when we arrived in the transept she immediately asked me if don Alberto would like to join us. When I relayed the message he jumped at it and seamlessly folded himself into our hands-on approach while maintaining silence, not understanding the language. I was struck by the beatific smile that lit up his face during that time; he looked happier than at any other time during his stay. One of the people who came for prayers was a member of the healing team himself. He told me later that it felt very special to have don Alberto there. I was happy to be able to offer him hospitality in a church where he was able to practice his healing vocation along with the rest of us.

The title of this book is based on the name of one of don Alberto's workshops, "Abundant Life: An Introduction to the Rituals of Andean Spirituality." The principle of Sumak Kausay, "Abundant Life," is basic to the spirituality of the Andes. As I understand it, don Alberto's aim is to teach gratitude for life while doing everything possible to enjoy it, the thankfulness coming from the heart, not just delivered in rote prayers. If one practices being aware through the heart and the intuition sufficiently, it can lead to a consciousness that is elevated to a higher level of energy, a greater connection to the wonder of this world. I am well aware that I am very much a beginner, and he has told me that I need to practice more. For me he is an inspiring practitioner of the claim made by Jesus of Nazareth, "I came that they may have life, and have it in abundance."[1]

Don Alberto considers Jesus to have been a very powerful shaman, a view I can relate to, a view that gives me a new perspective on the gospel descriptions of Jesus in his own time. My encounter with don Alberto Taxo has been a Chakana for me, a bridge to an indigenous view of the universe that builds on my previous understanding to offer a deeper appreciation and experience of the world. For that I give my heartfelt thanks to him and to the Great Spirit of Life.

Notes

CHAPTER 1. A WALK IN QUITO

1. Don Alberto's text from here to end of chapter translated and reordered from Noriega Rivera, *El vuelo del águila y el cóndor,* 28–30, 32, 33, 67–68, 116.

CHAPTER 2. GRANDPARENT WISDOM

1. Don Alberto's text in this section translated and reordered from Noriega Rivera, *El vuelo del águila y el cóndor,* 87, 89, 92, 100, 138, 143, 164.

CHAPTER 3. THE POWER OF WATER

1. Don Alberto's text in this section translated from Noriega Rivera, *El vuelo del águila y el cóndor,* 30–31.

CHAPTER 4. INITIATION

1. Don Alberto's text in this section translated from Noriega Rivera, *El vuelo del águila y el cóndor,* 33–35.
2. Blancke interview, June 15, 2016.

CHAPTER 5. AN ENCOUNTER WITH FRANCIS

1. Personal communication to Blancke, 2016.
2. Don Alberto's text in this section translated from Noriega Rivera, *El vuelo del águila y el cóndor,* 43–46.
3. Personal communication to Blancke, 2016.

CHAPTER 6. THE FORMATION
OF A PUBLIC YACHAK

1. Don Alberto's text in this chapter translated from Noriega Rivera, *El vuelo del águila y el cóndor*, 40–42, 136–38.

CHAPTER 7. A COLOMBIAN YACHAK

1. This introduction is based on Noriega Rivera, *El vuelo del águila y el cóndor*, 48–54; *Quién es Kelium Zeus? La Biografía de Luis Gustavo Morales Sierra*, www.keliumzeus.net, accessed 2/1/2018.
2. Don Alberto's text in this chapter translated from Noriega Rivera, *El vuelo del águila y el cóndor*, 48–54.

CHAPTER 8. CONTRARY WINDS
AND THE VALUE OF SPIRITUALITY

1. Mijeski and Beck, *Pachakutik and the Rise and Decline of the Ecuadorian Indigenous Movement*, 2.
2. Don Alberto Taxo talk at Itzhak Beery's Zoom Andes Summit, June 17, 2020.
3. A general description is found in John Perkins's *Touching the Jaguar*, 117–19.
4. Don Alberto's text from here to end of chapter translated from Noriega Rivera, *El vuelo del águila y el cóndor*, 140–42.

CHAPTER 9. THE EAGLE AND
CONDOR DREAM

1. Don Alberto's text from here to end of chapter translated from Noriega Rivera, *El vuelo del águila y el cóndor*, 139–40, 166–67.

CHAPTER 10. SUMAK KAUSAY,
"ABUNDANT LIFE"

1. Don Alberto's text in this chapter translated and reordered from Noriega Rivera, *El vuelo del águila y el cóndor*, 58, 74, 96, 148, 159–64.

CHAPTER 11.
BUILDING HABITS OF CONNECTION

1. Don Alberto's text in this chapter translated from Noriega Rivera, *El vuelo del águila y el cóndor,* 144–47, 149–59.

CHAPTER 12. A YACHAK APPRENTICES' RETREAT

1. Translated from Noriega Rivera, *El vuelo del águila y el cóndor,* 60.
2. Abbreviated account of the retreat translated from Noriega Rivera, *El vuelo del águila y el cóndor,* 59, 67.
3. Don Alberto's text from here to end of chapter translated and reordered from Noriega Rivera, *El vuelo del águila y el cóndor,* 69, 77, 81–82, 97, 104, 111–12, 114–18.

CHAPTER 13. LEARNING PLANT HEALING

1. Translated from Noriega Rivera, *El vuelo del águila y el cóndor,* 120.
2. Don Alberto's text from here to end of chapter translated and reordered from Noriega Rivera, *El vuelo del águila y el cóndor,* 33, 36, 38–40, 67, 71–72, 74, 80, 88, 118, 120, 122.

CHAPTER 14. RESOLVING CONFLICT:
THE NATURE OF GOOD AND EVIL

1. Translated from Noriega Rivera, *El vuelo del águila y el cóndor,* 101.
2. Translated from Noriega Rivera, *El vuelo del águila y el cóndor,* 102.
3. Don Alberto's text from here to the end of the section from Blancke interview, June 15, 2016.
4. Don Alberto's text from here to end of chapter translated from Noriega Rivera, *El vuelo del águila y el cóndor,* 82–83, 133–35.

CHAPTER 15. MEDICINE WHEEL OF THE FOUR WINDS:
LIFE LESSONS DRAWN FROM NATURE

1. Text from here to end of chapter translated and abridged from Guerrero Arias, *La chakana del corazonar,* 548–56, 561–85.

CHAPTER 16. THE CHAKANA AND
THE STAFF OF GOLD

1. Don Alberto Taxo, personal communication with Blancke, July 16, 2014.
2. De la Vega, *Comentarios Reales de los Incas,* 64–65.
3. Acosta, *Natural and Moral History of the Indies,* 259.
4. Urton, *At the Crossroads of the Earth and the Sky,* star constellation table accessed on Pomona College astronomy page, 2/25/2020. The villages are Misminay and Sonqo.
5. Jaffé, *From the Life and Work of C. G. Jung,* 68.
6. Isaacson, *Leonardo Da Vinci,* 148–59.
7. Lajo, *Qhapaq Ñan,* 42.
8. Lajo, *Qhapaq Ñan,* 112.
9. From don Oscar Miro Quesada's Internet course, The Path of the Universal Shaman, 2017. His Pachakuti Mesa tradition, derived from two Peruvian shamanic traditions from the Andes and the coast, has created this path for modern initiates.
10. De la Vega, *Comentarios Reales de los Incas,* 35–41. The author estimated this story happened about 1200 CE.
11. José Pichizaca, in Spanish, December 21, 2017.
12. Don Alberto Taxo, personal communication with Blancke, 2018.
13. Don Alberto text from here to end of chapter translated from Noriega Rivera, *El vuelo del águila y el cóndor,* 135–36.

CHAPTER 18.
CONNECTING WITH AWARENESS

1. Martha Travers first published this in *The Healing Garden Journal,* October 2002, as "The Way of the Condor: Spiritual Lessons from the Andes," by Martha Stoner. Reprinted with permission of the author.

CHAPTER 19. FURTHERING DREAM CHANGE

1. Perkins, *Confessions of an Economic Hit Man,* 216.
2. Blancke telephone interview, June 20, 2018.
3. This section from John Perkins E-Newsletter 5/8/2018, "Plants: Our Teachers in the Consciousness Revolution."

4. This section from John Perkins E-Newsletter 6/5/2018, "Why Do I Shapeshift and Use Sacred Plants?"

5. This section from John Perkins E-Newsletter 7/10/2018, "Message from Immigrants and Plants."

6. Blancke summary of John Perkins text from E-Newsletter 7/10/2018, "Message from Immigrants and Plants."

CHAPTER 21. INITIAL IMPRESSIONS

1. Gottwald submission translated from Spanish by Blancke.

CHAPTER 22. CONNECTING WITH SPRINGS

1. Taxo and Slomovits, *Friendship with the Elements,* 119.

CHAPTER 23. CONNECTING WITH ANIMALS

1. Excerpts from chapter 45 of *Gracie's Tail: Conversations with DoG* by Julie Bloomer and Gracie © 2014 by Julie Bloomer.

CHAPTER 24. A JOURNEY WITH DON ALBERTO

1. Christie, *Rock Shrines,* Ceque *Lines, and Pilgrimage in the Inca Provinces;* Laurencich-Minelli and Magli, "A Calendar Quipu of the Early 17th Century."

2. Don Alberto Taxo talk at Itzhak Beery's Zoom Andes Summit, June 17, 2020.

3. From "Romance" by W. J. Turner in Methuen, *An Anthology of Modern Verse.*

EPILOGUE. A CHRISTMAS STORY

1. John 10:10 (New Revised Standard Version).

Bibliography

Acosta, José de. *Natural and Moral History of the Indies.* Edited by Jane E. Mangan. Durham, N.C.: Duke University Press, 2002. Originally published in 1590.

Bach, Richard. *Jonathan Livingston Seagull.* New York: Scribner, 1970.

Bloomer, Julie. *Gracie's Tail: Conversations with DoG.* Ojai, Calif.: DoG Books, 2014.

Burns, Robert. "Ye Banks and Braes o' Bonnie Doon." Edinburgh: James Johnson's Scots Musical Museum, 1792.

Cañar, Enrique T. *Kichwa Unificado: Sistema de escritura de fácil aprendizaje.* Salcedo, Ecuador, 2016.

Castaneda, Carlos. *The Teachings of Don Juan: A Yaqui Way of Knowledge.* New York: Penguin, 1990.

Christie, Jessica Joyce. *Rock Shrines,* Ceque *Lines, and Pilgrimage in the Inca Provinces.* Oxford Handbook of the Incas, Oxford Handbooks Online, 2018.

Crowley, Jonette. *The Eagle and the Condor: A True Story of an Unexpected Mystical Journey.* Greenwood Village, Colo.: Stone Tree Publishing, 2007.

de la Vega, Inca Garcilaso. *Comentarios Reales de los Incas.* Mexico City: Editorial Porrúa, 2006. Originally published in 1609.

Freidel, David, Linda Schele, and Joy Parker. *Maya Cosmos: Three Thousand Years on the Shaman's Path.* New York: Perennial/Harper Collins, 2001.

Guerrero Arias, Patricio. *La chakana del corazonar: Desde las espirituales y las sabidurías insurgentes de Abya Yala.* Cuenca, Ecuador: Universidad Politécnica Salesiana, 2018.

Isaacson, Walter. *Leonardo Da Vinci.* New York: Simon & Schuster, 2017.

Jaffé, Aniela. *From the Life and Work of C. G. Jung.* New York: Harper Colophon, 1971.

Kornfield, Jack. *A Lamp in the Darkness: Illuminating the Path through Difficult Times.* Louisville, Colo.: Sounds True, Reprint edition, 2014.

Lajo, Javier. *Qhapaq Ñan,* CENES, Center for New Economic and Societal Studies, 2007, Peru.

Laurencich-Minelli, Laura, and Giulio Magli. "A Calendar Quipu of the Early 17th Century and Its Relationship with the Inca Astronomy," Cornell University online (2008), accessed 6/2/21.

Methuen, A. *An Anthology of Modern Verse.* London: Methuen, 1921.

Mijeski, Kenneth J., and Scott H. Beck. *Pachakutik and the Rise and Decline of the Ecuadorian Indigenous Movement.* Athens: Ohio University Press, 2011.

Neihardt, John G. *Black Elk Speaks.* Alcoa, Tenn.: FINE Communications, 1996.

Noriega Rivera, Patricia. *El vuelo del águila y el cóndor: Historia de vida del tayta yachak Alberto Taxo.* Quito, Ecuador: Casa de la Cultura Benjamin Carrión, 2015.

Perkins, John. *Confessions of an Economic Hit Man.* Oakland, Calif.: Berrett-Koehler, 2004.

———. *New Confessions of an Economic Hit Man.* Oakland, Calif.: Berrett-Koehler, 2018.

———. *Touching the Jaguar: Transforming Fear into Action to Change Your Life and the World.* Oakland, Calif.: Berrett-Koehler, 2020.

Pollan, Michael. *How to Change Your Mind: What the New Science of Psychedelics Teaches Us About Consciousness, Dying, Addiction, Depression, and Transcendence.* New York: Penguin, 2018.

René, Lucia. *Unplugging the Patriarchy.* Williamsburg, Va.: Crown Chakra Publishing, 2009.

Sairy, Lligalo. *Kuntur Jaka: la Sabiduría de mi Abuelo el Cóndor.* Quito, Ecuador: Ayuda Directa, 2010.

Stoner, Martha. "The Way of the Condor: Spiritual Lessons from the Andes." *The Healing Garden Journal* (2002).

Sullivan, William. *The Secret of the Incas. Myth, Astronomy, and the War Against Time.* New York: Three Rivers Press, 1996.

Taxo, Alverto, and Helen Slomovits. *An Invitation from the Andes: Entering the Wisdom of the Condor.* Ann Arbor, Mich.: LittleLight Publications, 2002.

———. *Friendship with the Elements.* Ann Arbor, Mich.: LittleLight Publications, 2010.

————. *Reconnecting with Our Indigenous Heart.* Ann Arbor, Mich.: LittleLight Publications, 2008.

Urton, Gary. *At the Crossroads of the Earth and the Sky: An Andean Cosmology.* Austin: University of Texas Press, 1981.

Wesselman, Hank. *Spiritwalker: Messages from the Future.* New York: Bantam Books, 1996.

Index

BOOKS OF RELATED INTEREST

Shapeshifting
Techniques for Global and Personal Transformation
by John Perkins

The World Is As You Dream It
Teachings from the Amazon and Andes
by John Perkins

Original Wisdom
Stories of an Ancient Way of Knowing
by Robert Wolff

Shamanic Healing
Traditional Medicine for the Modern World
by Itzhak Beery
Foreword by Alberto Villoldo

Cleansing Rites of Curanderismo
Limpias Espirituales of Ancient Mesoamerican Shamans
by Erika Buenaflor, M.A., J.D.

Bird Medicine
The Sacred Power of Bird Shamanism
by Evan T. Pritchard

Medicine and Miracles in the High Desert
My Life among the Navajo People
by Erica M. Elliott, M.D.
Foreword by Joan Borysenko, Ph.D.

Speaking with Nature
Awakening to the Deep Wisdom of the Earth
by Sandra Ingerman and Llyn Roberts

INNER TRADITIONS • BEAR & COMPANY
P.O. Box 388
Rochester, VT 05767
1-800-246-8648
www.InnerTraditions.com

Or contact your local bookseller